ROBIN
HOOD

About the Author

Jim Bradbury taught history at Borough Road College and the West London Institute of Higher Education for twenty-five years. He lives in Selsey, West Sussex.

Praise for Jim Bradbury

The Medieval Archer

'A delight to read' *Sunday Telegraph*

Medieval Siege

'An antidote to the popular and prevalent idea of war as Great Battles' *Times Literary Supplement*

Stephen and Matilda

'Carefully researched' *Times Educational Supplement*

The Battle of Hastings

'A stimulating and radical re-appraisal' Ian Dawson, author of *Medicine in the Middle Ages*

Philip Augustus

'The first major study in English this century' Professor David Bates, author of *William the Conqueror*

ROBIN HOOD

JIM BRADBURY

AMBERLEY

This edition first published 2012

Amberley Publishing
The Hill, Stroud
Gloucestershire, GL5 4EP

www.amberley-books.com

British Library Cataloguing in Publication Data.
A catalogue record for this book is available from the British Library.

ISBN 978-1-4456-0860-0

Typesetting and Origination by Amberley Publishing.
Printed in Great Britain.

Contents

Preface

Unlike all the other books I have had published, I finished writing this book before making any agreement with a publisher. The reason was that I did not want a contract with a date to meet; I wanted to take my time over this book because I could not forecast how long it would take or indeed quite how it would go. I also wanted to do it even if no one wanted to publish it.

The other unusual point about this book for me, is that it is a subject I have treasured for some time and saved until the point where I felt time, in the sense of my age and how much more I would do, was beginning to run out. There were two subjects dear to my heart that I wanted to write books about. They were topics that I knew would be an absolute pleasure to work on. I will keep quiet on the second of these, as it is my intention to tackle it next.

The subject of Robin Hood had appealed to me long ago. When I wrote my second published book, *The Medieval Archer*, I naturally developed an interest in our famed English outlaw. I did add a chapter on him to that book, but it was no more than an outline. That book was published in 1985, so there has been quite a delay before I returned to the subject. My last book, on the Capetians, was finished in 2006 and published in 2007. Since then I have concentrated on *Robin Hood*.

A fascination with Robin Hood hardly needs to be explained. Like many others, my interest was sparked from quite a young age by film and TV. For me, the quintessential film remains the old Errol Flynn classic. In my mind, Robin still really looks like Errol Flynn. But I also have enjoyed all the subsequent films and TV series, including the recent efforts — though somehow they do not quite measure up to the Errol Flynn version for me. I suspect that is true for many people — early impressions are hard to erase.

Probably for me, like most people, Robin Hood was the Robin Hood of the media. It was only with the book on archers that I began to think about his historical background and the puzzles that surround it. I thought, in the 1980s, that there might be a solution in Robert the Bruce as the origin of the real Robin Hood. A more thorough research has destroyed that concept, though I still think that Robert the Bruce has had a more important impact on the development of the image of Robin Hood in popular imagination than is generally believed.

Like hundreds of historians and literary critics, I hoped I would find evidence of the real Robin Hood. I still believe in my heart that he existed but must admit that I have failed to find him. I cannot persuade myself that the evidence for any of the candidates put up by other historians quite fit the bill. The mystery remains. Perhaps it will be solved one day. Perhaps someone reading this book will be inspired to search and find the vital and still missing evidence. I suspect that one day it will turn up by accident from someone searching for something entirely different.

As I write the first draft of this introduction, I have still not visited Nottingham or, indeed, Sherwood or Barnsdale. I plan to do this shortly, both in order to experience the places and to take some photos for the book. I have had connections with Nottingham. My long-term friend Malcolm Thomis taught in Nottingham and wrote an excellent book on its history. We were together in the history department of King's College, London, as students, though he was a year above me and rather brighter. Malcolm has been settled for many years in Australia. Together with our wives and another couple of mutual friends we had a recent get-together and holiday in the New Forest.

Another link with Nottingham is that my wife had her fortune told long ago. I do not place much trust in such things, but I think she is a little more inclined to believe in it. The fortune-teller forecast that Nottingham would play an important part in her life. This was an odd forecast, as we had no connection with the place at all. Since then, I have rather avoided Nottingham in order that the forecast should not come true! Now it looks like happening.

Anyway, I must say I have thoroughly enjoyed the past years of investigating Robin Hood in fact and fiction. My interest has not waned and I think it never will. I hope that readers will perhaps set off on a similar trek and experience similar rewards. I note that my two grandsons, Matthew and Will, watch Robin Hood now in the current TV series. This book roughly follows my trek back through time to try and see how the Robin Hood legend has developed over the ages and try to work out the historical origin of the hero as far as possible.

Selsey 2009

Robin Hood in Modern Times

I would ask you before you read this book to try jotting down the answers to the following few questions. The point of the questions is to outline, in a general way, how you think Robin Hood is seen by most people at the present time. It might then be interesting to compare your answers with what you think by the end of the book. Most readers are unlikely to be practising historians or literary experts, who might have a view that differs from the normal, but even so I think we all have an idea of Robin Hood that is based to some extent on how he is treated in the modern media. The question to ask for the time being is not about what has been shown by modern historical or literary research, but simply what the general public believes to be true. The form of the questions you should ask is along the lines of: 'what do you think would be the common answer to this question about Robin Hood nowadays?' Anyway these are the questions to answer.

Questions about Robin Hood

1. In what historical period is it thought Robin Hood lived?
2. What link was there between Robin Hood and the Crusades?
3. How is Robin Hood seen in relation to Saxons and Normans?
4. Who were Robin Hood's chief enemies?
5. What was Robin Hood's attitude to the church?
6. Who were the original members of Robin Hood's band?
7. Who does Robin Hood love?
8. Whereabouts, geographically, did Robin Hood chiefly operate?
9. What was Robin Hood's intervention between rich and poor?
10. What was Robin Hood's place in society?

There are not necessarily 'correct' answers to these questions. The point is not to score ten out of ten, but simply to check on how Robin Hood is usually seen at the present time. We shall return to the questions and answers in the final chapter.

In effect, everyone knows about Robin Hood. There must be very few of us who did not see him in films and comics or on TV. This, of course, is how we know what we know. That is the source of information that will answer our questions.

There are, however, some aspects that we may not know. Not everyone will realise that Robin Hood as we know him stems from a series of late medieval poems. There is nothing earlier — nothing in historical records or in chronicles. He is, therefore, not in the same league as Hereward the Wake or William Wallace. The medieval poems are the starting point of our knowledge, but it soon becomes clear that the Robin Hood of the poems has some significant differences from the Robin Hood in his modern personification. One aim of this book is to see how the changes occurred. Another aim is to see what could be found from chronicles and records. We shall not find an original historical figure but we shall look for how he might be found. We shall consider what historical records might be relevant and what historians and critics have made of the records.

This book plans to go backwards in time, so we shall begin by seeing what is made of Robin Hood by the modern world, that is, since about 1900. We shall then move backwards in fairly large steps towards the origins of the Robin Hood story. The stages will be 1900 to the present, the period from 1700 to 1900, the Tudor and Stuart period and the later Middle Ages. The reason for this approach is the difficulty of finding the original historical Robin Hood. No one truly knows whether or not he existed. The historical evidence is slight, though the literary material is considerable. By probing backwards, we may be able to trace a line that will lead to the original. We shall not find a final answer but it may help to put the legend of Robin Hood into its proper context.

The chief reason for this approach is that so much has been added to the Robin Hood story since its beginning. If there was an original man who was Robin Hood then we need to shed all that later material until we find whatever was there to start with. This approach will help us to appreciate how much of the modern story is myth and invention. It also provides a means of displaying the perennial popularity of Robin Hood through the ages. The story has had many accretions, but the kernel of the original remains and has retained its appeal to a wide audience throughout the centuries.

In modern times, Robin Hood has appeared in various media, including books, comics and the radio. The appearances of Robin Hood nowadays are widespread and often peculiar, from theme parks to computer games.[1] Thus we find a sort of theme park in Nottingham called Tales from Nottingham.

We shall concentrate our attention on what seem to have been the two most influential forms in modern times: the cinema and television. It seems beyond argument that the modern view of Robin is based chiefly on what we have seen in films and on television. Of necessity, with such visual media, an added degree of realism has entered the legend. Whatever Robin's actions, they now have to be seen moment by moment. Since the cinema began with silent movies, it was essential to concentrate on action rather than dialogue. Robin Hood visual products have never altogether lost the emphasis on action that appeared in the early silent films.

Television

In modern times, it is probably television that has done most to project a view of Robin Hood upon the British public. The tendency has been to produce the stories in series. This means that the TV Robin Hood stories are more detailed than those in film. In addition, each new series needs to project some new and original material to keep viewers interested. As a result, more invention is required and hence the increasing embroidery of the old stories in various ways. But for all the invention, the story of Robin Hood retains a common basis that most of us recognise and accept.

There have been a number of TV series about the great outlaw, starring, among others, Richard Greene, Jason Connery and, most recently, Jonas Armstrong. Richard Greene had appeared as Robin Hood in a film but is probably better remembered as Robin in the black and white Associated Television series starting in 1955, *Adventures of Robin Hood*. It was a British series but some American writers were concerned in the scripting. It was a popular programme and ran for 143 episodes to 1960.[2] In this series, Bernadette O'Farell was Marian and Paul Eddington, Alan a Dale. Alan is a member of the band who comes to greater prominence in modern versions, and is partly a deliberate harking back to the ballad element in the original tales. In this series, there was a distinct hint of left-wing politics — the need to help the poor having a clear modern parallel. Here Robin returns from the crusades. The Normans oppress the Saxons, and Robin is the Saxon champion Robin of Locksley. King Richard is the good king who returns from the crusades to save Robin from the clutches of his younger brother, Prince John. It is from this series that we derive the popular verse from the song that accompanied it, which I for one can still recite from memory:

Robin Hood, Robin Hood
Riding through the glen
Robin Hood, Robin Hood
With his band of men.
Feared by the bad
Loved by the good
Robin Hood, Robin Hood, Robin Hood

This song was written by Dick James. Presumably 'glen' was chosen to rhyme with 'men' rather than for any theory about Robin being in Scotland. Its popularity at the time is better expressed by Madelon Dimont, daughter of Penelope Mortimer and a member of the famous John Mortimer family. She recalled a family trip in the car when her sister suggested a song, 'and a mighty shout broke forth such as I've never heard, of six children screaming Robin Hood at the tops of their voices, out of tune and out of time'.[3]

Television has been responsible for an evolution in the Robin Hood story. A longish series of programmes, such as that starring Richard Greene, in contrast to a single hour or two of film, necessitated more detailed plots. It led the programme writers into greater investigation of the early Robin Hood characters, to expand the members of the band and so on. It has also, of course, led to an increase in invention and new material.

The Legend of Robin Hood appeared on BBC TV in 1975, but little has been heard of it since. It seems to be a version that few recall, though it was a reasonably worthy effort. It had Diane Keen as Maid Marian with Martin Potter as an acceptable Robin in the Errol Flynn mode. It provided a biography for Robin from childhood, as unaware heir to the earldom of Huntingdon who had been brought up in secret. His adoptive father was a king's forester who taught him to shoot with the bow. The goodies were, of course, all Anglo-Saxons. Sir Guy is the Norman villain who rivalled Robin for the hand of Marian. There seemed little to choose between the brothers Richard the Lionheart and John in the series, both presented as somewhat effeminate characters. Marian was the niece of the rather unlikely-named Sir Kenneth. The narrative of the plot was, at least, generally well done.

A new series, *Robin of Sherwood*, was made by Goldcrest for Harlech Television from 1984, starring Michael Praed and with music by Clannad. It gave some stress to the forest as fairy territory, with magic and the supernatural, which has become a fairly common element in modern versions. The music, appropriately, has a sort of mystical and Celtic touch. Herne the Hunter (a giant with antlers) chose Robin to oppose the corrupt and powerful in society. This series also contained elements of the Saxon against Norman conflict — with the Normans as villains. There was, however, some move away from the noble Robin, who here, at first, became a peasant. Interestingly, two of the main villains, Gisborne (Gisburne here) and the sheriff of Nottingham, were presented as homosexual. Marian here moved away from the traditional lady and became virtually a member of the band, able to shoot a bow with the best of them. As in several modern versions, an Arab character was introduced in the person of Nazir, who had returned with the villainous Simon de Bellême from the crusades, but who then joined the outlaws. Will Scarlet was played by Ray Winstone, as somewhat more masculine than his counterpart in Errol Flynn's film. Unusually, Richard as well as John was shown as untrustworthy. When Praed chose to leave the series he was replaced by Jason Connery (Sean's son). Praed's character, Robin of Sherwood, had been born as a serf. He was killed off and Connery was then introduced as Robert, the heir to the earl of Huntingdon — two Robins for the price of one. This was an odd way to resolve the question of Robin's social position — have him as two characters, one a serf and the other noble. Robin then collected together the old band and continued with the adventures. The twist in this series was the emphasis on mysteries and pagan spirits — Herne the Hunter in particular — which gave it a surreal touch. There were odd introductions, such as Irish settlers, devil worship with the sacrifice of children, and peculiar time shifts. This seemed rather overdone and spoiled the simplicity of the usual Robin Hood plots. As Friar Tuck says to Much, 'you'd never believe it'.

A somewhat irreverent version of Robin Hood was produced for the BBC as *Maid Marian and her Merrie Men*. The script was by Tony Robinson, who also played the sheriff. The leading part in the series was that of the heroine, Marian, played by Kate Lonergan. One of her band was Little Ron — a dwarf! Instead of Alan a Dale, with lute, we have Barrington, a rapper. Robin here was a figure of fun rather than a hero, who goes to an archery competition disguised as a chicken.

In 2006, yet another TV version of the outlaw tales appeared. It was simply called *Robin Hood* and starred Jonas Armstrong. It has, again, had popular appeal, with its lively plots and perky humour. Despite many attempts to ennoble Robin or make high-brow literature, he has remained chiefly a hero who appeals to an ordinary popular public. As this new series has progressed, it seems to have moved further away from any usual presentation and from much attempt at historical reality. It has become a sort of *Doctor Who* version of Robin with odd magical and scientific elements, chemical poisons and antidotes. The costumes have been less and less suitable for the twelfth-century or even the medieval period at all. The German Count of Schleswig-Holstein seemed to belong to perhaps the eighteenth century. One wonders why Robin uses a shortbow and why Marian appears in combat jeans or what the twentieth-century commandos in berets are doing. If some viewers found Alan Rickman's sheriff too over-the-top they should watch Keith Allen!

As mentioned above, we have had the oddities. BBC TV presented *Maid Marian and Her Merrie Men* in 1988. The point seemed to be not so much pro-feminism as humour. It was written by Tony Robinson of *Blackadder* and *Time Team* fame. In this series, Robin was Robin of Kensington, a tailor and Little John became Little Ron.

The appeal to children seems constant, as noted by those who made the cartoon of *Rabbit Hood* with Bugs Bunny. For adults, the Robin Hood stories remain common knowledge, fully understood by all, as witness even-double entendre jokes on the radio — 'So that's why John is called Little?'[4] It will be a rare generation that does not possess its own versions of Robin Hood.

The Cinema

In the twentieth-century, Robin gained wider acquaintance with the public through the new art form of the cinema. The major influence of film preceded that of TV. In the case of films, we are dealing with individual productions that last a few hours at most. This means, in general, a single main plot and a fairly compact gathering of events. This makes the films rather closer to earlier stage plays and to the original brief poems about Robin than TV is. There is less room for more exotic inventions.

There have, in fact, been so many Robin Hood films that we shall only consider a selection of the more significant ones. From the beginning, Robin was a screen favourite. He figured in silent films. The first of all Robin Hood films was the British *Robin Hood and His Merry Men* released in 1909.[5] The setting of the film is Sherwood Forest; Robin is a noble, and Maid Marian a central character. *Robin Hood — Outlawed* appeared in 1912. In this film, Robin rescued Marian from an evil knight. A third English silent film, out in 1913, was *In the Days of Robin Hood*. In this movie, Robin took on the disguise of a monk to rescue one of the outlaws from the sheriff.[6] A fourth early British film was *In the Days of Robin Hood,* also from 1913. It was actually filmed in Sherwood Forest.

Two American films appeared in 1912-13, both called Robin Hood.[7] So our hero became 'Robin Hood of Hollywood'.[8] This may sound catchy but it is also significant. The film industry has been the medium most influenced in modern times by American views. When European traditions, like the Robin Hood tales, have been taken up by Hollywood, they have been much altered. It was the first time that Robin Hood received a strong non-English twist. Here we have medieval England, perhaps merry England, as seen through American eyes. Also, like all such developments, Hollywood Robin became a medium for modern American political ideas. The cinema altered the scale of Robin Hood stories. Traditional tales had been mainly confined to the greenwood. Now the tales were placed in a grander setting with kings and princes, castles, tournaments, and distant crusades.

In the first of these longer American films (from Eclair), we have Guy of Gisborne, who has since become a common figure in modern versions. Gisborne is frequently spelled as Gisbourne in American films, but we shall keep to the former spelling. The second of the films (from Thanhouser) concentrated on an archery competition — another popular subject for visual versions. It featured Richard the Lionheart appearing in disguise in the closing part. The love theme with Marian was used and has also become an essential part of modern visual tales.

Robin came to greater prominence and a far wider audience with Douglas Fairbanks playing the main role in the silent, black and white *Robin Hood* of 1922, setting the tone for Robin as an acrobatic hero. This was one of the great early Hollywood films. Its success ensured a wide public for Robin Hood in the modern media. Fairbanks had already made his mark as an active and handsome hero, arguably the first great male film star — though a little plump to modern eyes. The story had to be restyled to suit the star before he agreed to do it. Apparently, Fairbanks feared he would look like 'a heavy-footed Englishman' and the merry men as 'flat-footed outlaws in Lincoln green'.[9] Part of the change demanded led to the production of a set that allowed Fairbanks' athleticism to be shown to best effect — seen by one critic as a 'cinematic jungle gym'.[10] Robin Hood became more clearly 'an action hero'.[11] He was not, however, presented as the macho male. One caption has him claiming 'I am afeard of women'.[12] As Stephen Knight puts it, 'Robin Hood, like Shane, like Philip Marlowe, cannot cope with women'.[13] At one point, to escape a mob of admiring ladies he jumped into the moat! In fact, the acrobatics often seem amusing rather than daring, and the constant skipping motion and arm-waving of the outlaws is quite hilarious.

The chasing around the castle seems at times rather pointless. The cast included Wallace Beery as Richard, Sam de Grasse as Prince John, Alan Hale as Little John, and Enid Bennett as Marian. Robin opposed Guy of Gisborne (here Gisbourne) who rivalled him for the hand of 'Lady' Marian Fitzwalter. Also added in, was practically every visual effect one could imagine that had a medieval slant, which included bringing in the crusades and tournaments and all sorts of goings on in Nottingham castle and town, as well as Locksley town and a very crowded outlaw lair in Sherwood Forest. Thus Robin became second in command to King Richard the Lionheart on crusade before 'deserting' in response to a message from Marian about John's misdeeds in England. When Prince John discovered that Marian had sent a message about his deeds to Richard, he angrily declared (via the dialogue screen) 'I'll put an end to tattling'. In similarly odd pseudo-medieval language, Robin Hood tells Marian he will send a message to 're-speak' his love. Occasionally, the ballads are raided for words put into different mouths, as 'I'll knop your scop' — here by Friar Tuck to Richard.

Robin's fame blossomed further with talkies when he was played by various great stars of the screen. Probably the most important example, and arguably the greatest Robin Hood film of all, was the 1938 film *The Adventures of Robin Hood* starring Errol Flynn. There was an excellent score by Erich Wolfgang Korngold — sometimes referred to as 'Robin Hood in the Vienna Woods'![14] Korngold's score was actually written against the background of having his own home in Vienna seized by the Nazis. It is probably no accident that the forces of John and Robin's enemies marched in precise Nazi-like order, while Robin's men were casual. As to the scene, what we in fact see is not an English forest but a park in the Californian woods where the film was shot — no doubt always being summer in the forest was more guaranteed than it would have been in England! Amusingly, some of the film was shot in what had been re-named 'Sherwood Forest' after its use in the Fairbanks film. Originally, the part of Robin was marked for James Cagney, until he walked out on the studio. One can only believe that it was a fortunate change for the resulting film. Michael Curtiz, who replaced William Keighley, played the major part in the shaping of the final film. The strong cast included Basil Rathbone as Guy of Gisborne and Claude Rains as 'treacherous' Prince John, pointing to the emphasis on villains in the plot. The final screenplay only emerged after a long period of new contributions and alterations.[15]

In *The Adventures of Robin Hood*, Prince John was played as somewhat effeminate, while Richard the Lionheart is manly. Historically there is no evidence for John being homosexual while Richard may well have been.[16] This film also starred Olivia de Havilland as Marian. Will was rather oddly dressed in scarlet and is also somewhat effeminate. Like Douglas Fairbanks, Errol Flynn was already seen as a hero figure in the cinema, and a star, before he took the part. Interestingly, this film marked one of the major changes in modern versions, a move back towards the original literature or at least to earlier Robin Hood tales. The move was deliberate and partly the result of taking advice from someone who knew the sixteenth-century literature.[17] This film has little on the Crusades, and although it was originally planned to include a tournament, this idea was abandoned. The film featured traditional members of the band, including Little John, Will Scarlet and Much the Miller. It did, however, retain the Saxon/Norman slant with Robin called 'a Saxon noble' and a 'Saxon hedge robber', and speaking of 'we Saxons'. Robin was Saxon and Guy of Gisborne, Norman. The Angevin period background of Richard and John is retained though seen as 'Norman'. Richard the Angevin's capture on crusade was seen as 'a luckless day for the Saxons'! And Marian admits 'I am ashamed I am a Norman'.

The Flynn film has its share of unhistorical material. Quite why the historical Richard (only in England for six months as king) is seen as protector of Saxons is never clear. Nor is it any clearer why outlaws should steal treasure and use it to pay the ransom to gain Richard's release. Richard, like John, was, of course, an Angevin and not a Norman. The Angevins, not the Normans, ruled England in this period. This historical placing of Robin Hood commonly ignores the fact that Richard was killed in 1189 and the dreadful Prince John became King John — what hope was there for Robin Hood and his men then? Friar Tuck is called a curtail (curtal) friar of Fountains Abbey. Fountains Abbey was not a priory for friars (either Franciscan or Dominican) but an abbey for Cistercian monks. There were no friars in England until after Richard's death. Robin in the film is seen as the defender of the poor and oppressed against corrupt and vicious powers, but he is presented rather as the leader of organised popular rebellion than of an outlaw band. He is seen as being really Sir Robin of Locksley who finally gains his inheritance. The emphases in this particular film are particularly significant because it has made such a strong impact on practically every popular visual version since. One should say that it does bring in several stories based on the ballads, such as the episode with Friar Tuck and the stream, the archery contest and the meeting with the king in the forest. Robin follows tradition as the protector of the poor: 'It's injustice I hate, not the Normans'.

In films, we have also been given sons of Robin Hood, including Cornel Wilde as Robert of Huntingdon in *The Bandit of Sherwood Forest* in 1946, and John Derek as the son of the earl of Huntingdon in *Rogues of Sherwood Forest* in 1950. In the latter, Alan Hale played Little John for the third time. In *Son of Robin Hood*, from 1958, we even had a 'son' of Robin who turns out to be a daughter! She was called Deering and played by June Laverick. The other unusual feature of this film was that it was set late in the time of King John and into the beginning of the reign of his son, Henry III.

Later players of Robin Hood have included the English actor Richard Todd. In 1952, he appeared in a Disney version directed by Ken Annakin, *The Story of Robin Hood and his Merrie Men*. Todd was a rather more stolid hero than Fairbanks or Flynn but was genuinely English. This film left out some of the most unhistorical material — no Normans against Saxons — but it added other dubious material, such as the outlaws raising Richard's ransom. The sheriff returned as the major villain rather than the now absent Guy of Gisborne. Robin here was not of Locksley but still of noble descent as Robert Fitzooth. This was clearly based on knowledge of an invented pedigree, which all modern historians dismiss as nonsense.

One important film for our purposes, though not specifically about Robin Hood, was the 1952 production of *Ivanhoe* directed by Richard Thorpe. This is partly because the film was a lavish Technicolor production and popular. It was based on the Walter Scott novel *Ivanhoe*, which we shall look at in the next chapter. Suffice to say for now, the film starred several screen favourites, including Robert Taylor as Wilfred of Ivanhoe and Elizabeth Taylor as Rebecca, as well as Joan Fontaine and George Sanders. It returned to and expanded on the idea of a Saxon-Norman conflict, with Ivanhoe as a Saxon, supported by the Saxon outlaws under Robin Hood. In this film, Robin was 'Loxley' and carried out a rescue from the castle. The film showed plenty of evidence of Hollywood production, including Elizabeth Taylor wearing an anachronistically short skirt, Cedric the Saxon pronounced as Cee-dric, and arrows that looked rather like matchsticks, apparently harming no one.

Hammer Films produced three versions of Robin Hood, the first being *Men of Sherwood Forest* in 1954 with Don Taylor as Robin Hood. In 1960 came *Sword of Sherwood Forest* or *Sword of Honour*. It was not a horror film but it did have Peter Cushing as the sheriff of Nottingham. Richard Greene, who also co-produced, was Robin and Sarah Branch appeared as Marian with a scene of her swimming naked in a pool.

Another Hammer version followed in 1962, *A Challenge for Robin Hood,* with Barrie Ingham as the hero. It wandered from the traditional plot but makes a reasonable film. Rather confusingly, Maid Marian (Gay Hamilton) was maid to the impostor Lady Marian. The cast included James Hayter as Friar Tuck, Peter Blythe as Robin's villainous cousin Sir Roger, Lockwood West as the steward and Alfie Bass as a carter who sells pies. Here, Robin was actually presented as a Norman but managed to maintain the historical inaccuracy by making him leader of a Saxon band! The outlaws render in a tunefully orchestrated chorus: 'O let us sing of days gone by when Saxon men were good and true'. Equally oddly, Fitz Warin is the Norman name given to a Saxon. We virtually expect by now that the Angevin King Richard I will be called a Norman. The film does retain the light-hearted tone of most Robin Hood adventures. The sheriff's bailiff rides in a sort of travelling telephone box and, when caught, is debagged. Sir Roger is killed, but at the end of the film, after marrying Marian, Robin promises to continue his outlaw efforts against the sheriff and Prince John.

Richard Lester made *Robin and Marian* in 1976, with Robin, played by Sean Connery, as a returning crusader after twenty years on crusade — no doubt to allow for Sean Connery's age. The connection with the early ballads is very slight. The only reference in the ballads to Robin in old age was his return from the royal court to the forest for his last years and the story of his death at the hands of a prioress. Audrey Hepburn plays Marian, who in Robin's absence had become a nun! The good British cast included Robert Shaw as the sheriff, Nicol Williamson as Little John, and Ronnie Barker as Friar Tuck. The aged Robin also witnessed the death of King Richard, with whom he had quarrelled. The carelessness over any attempt at realistic history is demonstrated by the method of Richard's death, which unlike Robin Hood's life, is well documented in historical records. In the film, Richard is killed by an arrow thrown by hand! Robin's death at the hands of an abbess (not a prioress) harks back uncertainly to early ballads, but not very exactly, since she turns out to be Marian who then chooses to poison them both! The tone of the final stages of the film is mournful and the whole production rather lacks the light, adventurous style of most modern Robin films.

A popular modern film version is Kevin Reynolds' 1991 *Robin Hood: Prince of Thieves*, with Kevin Costner as Robin and Alan Rickman as the villainous sheriff. This had a lively and generally traditional approach, with lots of action and fighting. The soundtrack features Bryan Adams' hit pop song, *I Do It For You*, as a tune through the movie and sung during the final credits. The film begins with Robin on crusade in Jerusalem in 1194. Robin has returned from crusade. He is the noble Robin of Locksley. Azeem, a Black Muslim played by Morgan Freeman, helped Robin to escape and introduced another common modern novelty with the appearance of black and Asian members of the outlaw band. The crusades are the obvious excuse for this interjection. There is less historical excuse for a battle with Celts employed on behalf of the sheriff! Much the same must be said of the appearance of gunpowder in the rescue of captured outlaws in Nottingham at the film's conclusion — gunpowder did not appear in the West until well after the reign of Richard I. In this movie it is Robin rather than Marian who appears naked in a pool. The film was further enlivened by the performance of Alan Rickman as a particularly devious and lustful sheriff, though most oddly named as George. Sean Connery pops up again in this Robin Hood film during the final sequence where he is King Richard who attends the marriage between Robin and Marian and insists on giving away the bride.

Another film, less successful with the public, starred Patrick Bergin as Robin and Uma Thurman as Marian. This was *Robin Hood* directed by John Irvin in 1991. In opposition to the old ballads, when it was always summer in the forest, this was filmed in a misty Cheshire where the sun only came out near the end of the picture. Again, we have Saxons against Normans. New fictional characters are included with Sir Miles de Falconet in pursuit of Marian, and the oddly named Harry as an outlaw leader. Robin and Marian actually marry in this version.

There have also been humorous versions including *The Zany Adventures of Robin Hood*, 1984, with George Segal in baggy tights as Robin. Better known is *Robin Hood: Men in Tights* from 1993 directed by Mel Brooks. This film fitted Maid Marian with a chastity belt. Stephen Knight saw her as 'a bedroom barbie'.[16] The black member of the band is Achoo son of Asneeze. The villain is the sheriff of Rottingham. It was hardly the most successful of Mel Brooks' comedies. On the whole, the comedy versions of our hero have not worked very well and not been very successful.

There have been several cartoon versions of Robin Hood made for the cinema. *Rabbit Hood* was a vehicle for Bugs Bunny in 1949. Porky Pig played Friar Tuck in 1959's *Robin Hood Daffy*. Disney also made a cartoon version in 1973, in which Robin was represented by a fox, with Peter Ustinov as the voice of Prince John. In the Muppet effort Robin turned into a green frog (Kermit) opposed by Sheriff Gonzo. One can surely suggest that all of these comic, satirical and gender-changing efforts are not taken too seriously by their viewers — they simply confirm in the mind the traditional modern Robin Hood story — and we smile, laugh or groan at the deliberate distortions.

The Stage

Robin Hood has figured on the modern stage but to a lesser extent and with less significance than his film and TV appearances. The stage versions of the late nineteenth and early twentieth centuries, however, clearly influenced the early black and white film versions from 1909 onwards.

Comic Robin Hoods have turned up in the cinema and on TV but are especially to be found on the stage. A hat with a feather, tights and perhaps a bow, and who could it be but Robin Hood? The folksinger Danny Spooner performed a sketch called *The Death of Robin Hood*. He retold the famous story of the prioress and the hero on his deathbed. Robin concluded: 'Where the arrow lands...bury me'. The performer ended: 'So they buried him on top of the wardrobe'.[19]

Musical Efforts and Pantomimes

Although it would seem a natural subject for opera, Robin Hood has barely figured in recent works by major composers. There have been a few lighter musicals. Lionel Bart wrote *Twang!*, which appeared in 1965 but within a week nosedived into obscurity; its stars included James Booth as Robin, Bernard Bresslaw as Little John and Barbara Windsor as Delphina (another name for a character that replaced Marian). The attempted cockney humour somehow did not match the subject and it simply did not work. In 1993, appeared *Robin, Prince of Sherwood* in an attempt at a pop music version, but that also gained scant attention.

Robin Hood has featured in several pantomimes and again seems a natural subject but usually he has figured only in a minor role, as in some versions of *Babes in the Wood*. The Bristol Old Vic did produce a panto called *Robin Hood: the Truth Behind the Green Tights* in 1985, the title itself enough to put off most potential audience. It attempted to relate Robin to modern social protest and, for example, Will Scarlet was transformed into Will Scargill.

Modern Literature

Literature has been less influential in developing the Robin Hood story in modern times than at any time since its origins. This is clearly because of the increasing influence of visual media in the cinema and television. We could perhaps include illustrated comics as another visual medium and we shall briefly consider them.

As for literature, it may have been less influential since the onset of cinema but it has not been absent or entirely uninteresting. If nothing else, modern literature as well as older literature has often provided the stimulus for visual versions.

Probably most modern literature on Robin Hood has been aimed at children rather than adults. We have taken the year 1900 as our starting point for the current chapter, and this emphasis on children's stories is a continuation from the nineteenth century in both England and America. Henry Gilbert's *Robin Hood* was published in 1912. His Robin wore a velvet hat with a feather in it. He used semi-spirit characters such as Ket the Trow and Hob o' the Hill, and the villains' stronghold is Evil Hold.

In 1921, *Robin Hood and his Merry Outlaws* by J. Walker McSpadden and Charles Wilson was published. It was not specifically aimed at children but that was probably the main readership — though it is a lengthy work of 290 pages. It had illustrations by N. A. Wyeth, which were in colour, dramatic and at times amusing. One, for example, is of Little John chasing the cook in the sheriff's house: 'The twain fought with anything that came to hand – plates, dishes, pots, pans – even spoons'.[20] The book claimed to be 'retold from the old ballads'. In an introduction that attempted to give an historical background we were told that Robin Hood is 'first of all, a Saxon'. It is accepted here that he was Robert Fitzooth. It was set in the Planatagenet age as if this is the correct historical period. To fit with this the appearance of 'King Harry' is taken to be Henry II. The various ballads are all given equal importance and used to construct a kind of biography of the hero. It showed that even when the intention was to return to the ballads and make the work genuinely historical, modern versions have kept to the mythical and mostly unhistorical view of Robin Hood common to our age.

Enid Blyton, better known for *Noddy* or the *Famous Five*, produced *Tales of Robin Hood* in 1930. Geoffrey Trease, who wrote many children's historical novels, began in 1934 with one involving Robin Hood called *Bows Against the Barons*. Its hero was the boy Dickon rather than Robin. Carola Oman was the daughter of the respected historian, Charles Oman. Her work aimed at children, *Robin Hood: the Prince of Outlaws*, was published in 1939 and has been one of the most influential of the juvenile literary publications. Its plot was based largely on the old ballads and especially on the *Gest*. It did, however, like most modern versions, incorporate such material as the marriage of Robin and Marian. Roger Lancelyn Green's *The Adventures of Robin Hood* was published in 1956. Green returned to the ballads but also has further inventions and improbable historical reconstructions, besides keeping to the period of Richard and John. Antonia Fraser, chiefly noted for her popular historical works for adults, had the children's novel *Robin Hood* published in 1957 with illustrations by Victor Ambrus. Surprisingly perhaps, as a genuine historian's work, it kept the Norman against Saxon element and introduced odd new characters such as Black Barbara!

Although there is a clear emphasis in modern literature to using Robin Hood as a subject aimed at children, there have been some more adult efforts. One such was Jay Williams' *The Good Yeoman* of 1956. Like other modern versions, its structure was based mainly on the *Gest*. Unlike most modern versions, this latter work took in some modern historical argument and was placed not in the reign of Richard the Lionheart but in that of Edward II. Robin Hood is introduced as a nobleman who allied with the serf John Nailer, otherwise Little John. Nailer, rather than Robin Hood, was the hero.

There have been several attempts simply to retell the old ballads in modern terms for young people. Parke Godwin wrote two Robin Hood novels in 1991 and 1993, *Sherwood* and *Robin and the King*. Even here, though, Robin is given an historical background that is without any historical justification. He is placed in the period of the Norman Conquest and called Edward Aelredson. This may give some apparent rationale for the Saxon versus Norman conflict found in much modern Robin Hood material but in general seems rather absurd.

Equally ignoring the content of the earliest ballads, a good deal of modern literature has increased the significance of the part played by Maid Marian. The love interest, virtually essential for popular visual versions, has its parallel in literature. *The Outlaws of Sherwood* was published in 1988 is by Robin McKinley (a female author). She later wrote *Lady of Sherwood*. There are even feminist literary versions, such as the 1992 *Lady of the Forest* and *Lady of Sherwood*.[21] In the former, Marian played a prominent part, winning an archery competition. The king (historical evidence please?) asked her to be sheriff! Marian is the clear heroine in Jennifer Roberson's *Lady of the Forest* from 1992. For once, Marian was not the rather prim lady of most modern material, at one point calling herself 'Robin Hood's whore'. Again, we meet odd additional characters, including a nymphomaniac sheriff's daughter

There have been several efforts in literature that are basically follow-ups to the film and TV versions. There have also been efforts to translate Robin into science fiction and into space. Others have turned back to the origins and re-invented Robin. One such is *The Death of Robin Hood* by Peter Vansittart in 1981. This returned to making a connection between Robin Hood and woodland spirits and also took him through time. A reinterpretation more in the normal modern tradition of historical background was made by Nicholas Chase in his novel *Locksley,* 1983. This keeps Robin in the age of Richard the Lionheart, and on crusade with the king. In the fictional additions here were included Robin personally killing Arthur of Brittany, Prince John's rival to inherit the throne. These modern adult novels have not been very influential, except possibly in giving inspiration for the content of film and TV scripts. The Robin Hood tales simply do not seem to work so well in modern novels as in visual works.

Comics

Robin Hood has frequently appeared in children's illustrated comics. As long ago as 1941, National Comics introduced a modern version of Robin Hood as

Green Arrow in *More Fun Comics*.[22] One of the most notable comic versions was *Robin Hood's Schooldays* in the *Beano*. This ran during the 1970s. The humorous TV programme *Maid Marian and Her Merry Men* was also produced in comic book form. Both these efforts were basically in the form of the knockabout gang humour of the comics of the period. By and large, Robin in the comics has been a tongue-in-cheek caricature of the usual depictions of our hero.

Robin Hood the Tourist Attraction

At the present time, certain locations can attract custom through their supposed connection with Robin Hood. The most obvious place for this is Nottingham. There is a forest park, Tales of Robin Hood — basically a theme park — which was opened in Nottingham. It has a museum, though real finds attached to Robin are virtually non-existent. The museum depends largely on the history of Nottingham. Its setting, rather oddly, is in an old kitchen and bathroom showroom! Perhaps soon the Barnsdale and Yorkshire connection will inspire a different kind of tourist attraction.

Selected Themes

In order to make useful comparisons later, we need to examine a number of selected themes that appear in Robin Hood presentations in the modern period. You will note that our opening questions relate quite closely to these themes.

The Historical Period

There is no great variation in modern times for the historical background to the life of Robin Hood. He is made active during the reign of King Richard the Lionheart, that is, Richard I (1187-99). One of the villains is usually now Prince John, while Robin supports King Richard, who finally returns from his Third Crusade. Since Robin is an adult by the time of the stories, one must assume he had been born during the reign of Henry II (1154-87). Robin Hood is, therefore, nowadays firmly placed in the period of the Angevin dynasty. Sometimes, the stories run on into the reign of King John, hardly ever a pleasant character in any form of literature (or indeed of history).

The Significance of the Crusades

The crusading career of Richard the Lionheart affects Robin and his men through his absence, allowing Prince John to pursue various threatening activities. A number of modern productions have Robin going on the crusade with Richard and returning, usually before him. However, the crusading episode rarely features Robin to any great extent. The crusading element has allowed some versions to introduce an Arabic character brought back from the East. In the original works, there is no reference at all connecting Robin to either King Richard or the crusades.

Saxon and Norman

Although the idea of Saxon against Norman is anachronistic, even in the reign of Richard I, the clash between them has remained a common factor in modern versions of Robin Hood. Robin stands for the poor and downtrodden Saxons against the vicious Norman conquerors and lords. Somehow, in this misrepresentation of history, Richard I — in reality more French than practically anyone else who ever appeared in England at the time (and he appeared less than most) — has remained a goodie, the just king. Of course, Richard was French but he was one of the Plantagenet kings of England who were Angevins from Anjou and not Norman at all — but that is generally ignored. The Angevin dynasty consisted of Henry II, Richard I and King John and reigned from 1154-1216. It is true that the Angevin counts had conquered Normandy and made it part of their Angevin Empire but they were not Normans. They were seen by the Normans as conquerors in much the same way that in 1066 the Normans were seen by the Saxons. However, in modern Robin Hood stories, the nasty lords are Norman and the nice peasants are Anglo-Saxon. The Saxon-Norman confrontation, though basically unhistorical, has survived into modern versions, including Bergin's *Robin Hood*. It has become so ingrained that even a historian of the Robin Hood movies can state that 'The most potent of all Anglo-Saxon folk heroes is Robin Hood' — though surely Robin was not really an Anglo-Saxon, was not known in the pre-Norman or pre-Angevin period and was not a hero in any way to Anglo-Saxons of that age.[23]

The Sheriff of Nottingham and other Enemies

In modern versions, apart from Prince John, the main enemy of Robin Hood and his men is now always the sheriff of Nottingham. The third major enemy of Robin Hood is commonly Sir Guy of Gisborne. There is more reason in making Guy an enemy. One of the earliest ballads is indeed about him. In it he is a bounty hunter who attempts to capture Robin. Robin foils the attempt and kills him brutally, beheading him and gouging out his eyes. The modern versions rarely follow this original story very closely.

Attitude to the Church

Modern tales of Robin Hood are not really hostile to the medieval church. On the whole, they ignore Christianity and religion. They do include occasional unpleasant prelates, but the only cleric who features to any great extent is Friar Tuck. He is partly a figure of fun and, in a sense, could be the object of attacks on the Church, but in general, he is seen as a jolly, friendly person and not as a renegade friar. The story of the abbot is sometimes retailed but rarely in order to voice any sort of attack on the Church. Robin and his men may pay lip service to the Church and to the Virgin Mary but religion barely enters the modern story. In the original poems too, only individual unworthy clerics are criticised, never the Church itself. There is no mention of archbishops or the pope. What is now missing is the clear acceptance of Christianity by the outlaws who frequently swear by Christ, the Virgin Mary or a saint, including, on one occasion, St Richard of Chichester. It is clear that their oaths were not mere crude swearing but reflected a genuine respect for those named. Basically, of course, this merely reflects the age of the poems as against the age of film and TV.

The Outlaw Band

Robin Hood is the leader of an outlaw band. He generally makes the decision to allow a new member to join and is responsible for most of the decisions over their activities. The outlaw band usually now contains the same men, though most modern versions tend to add a new figure or so — such as a Muslim. The common figures, though, are the familiar Little John, Much the Miller and Friar Tuck — though their characters can vary quite a bit. Little John is, of course, very large. Like most of the main figures, he enters the band after a match with Robin Hood. In modern versions, Alan a Dale and Will Scarlet are also nearly always present. The core of the modern band is generally also to be found in the old poems.

Maid Marian

Modern versions of Robin Hood must have a female lead. Robin is never without his love, Maid Marian. Occasionally, some other romantic interest is introduced, but Marian is the always present partner with whom he ends up. Added interest is often provided by having one of the villains pursuing the lovely maid — Guy of Gisborne, the sheriff or Prince John being the likeliest candidates. In modern versions, Marian, like Robin, is quite often ennobled. In the early poems, there is no love and no Marian. Her entry to the story is something we shall need to investigate.

Robin as a Noble

Almost always when Robin is given background, he is now presented as really a noble who has fallen from grace. Generally, he is the real earl of Huntingdon, who has been unjustly disinherited or possibly claimed as illegitimate but really the true heir. Prince John in particular is the obstacle to Robin gaining his true inheritance. Richard the Lionheart finally allows it, along with a pardon for outlawry. In the earliest poems, Robin is a yeoman and never a noble.

The Location

The modern versions virtually all take place in Sherwood Forest, with its proximity to Nottingham. When a town enters the plot then it is Nottingham. The outlaws have a permanent home in the forest, where only they are safe. There is justification for this in the early poems — both Sherwood and Nottingham do feature largely. The main point to note here are the locations mentioned in the early works, which are usually now ignored — when do we find Robin in Yorkshire, in Barnsdale, or other neighbouring places?

Archery

Robin Hood and his men are all archers, and all excellent archers; Robin is always the best of all. Robin wins archery competitions and deals with threats by absolutely accurate shooting. His men are also all archers and many are excellent. This element is one from the early works that has survived. It is true that nobles could shoot bows but, basically, it was always a skill of lesser men. In military terms, the medieval archers were lowly infantry as against the noble cavalry. Robin Hood and his men did also use the sword in the early works and that was more a recognised noble weapon, but there are no fights on horseback. The outlaws are not knights. They do not take part in tournaments. Robin, in modern versions, is often ennobled but oddly retains his old skill as an archer rather than as a horsed knight.

Robbing the Rich

Inevitably nowadays, Robin Hood is a goodie. He is not a thief or a violent criminal. He is only outside the law because he has been forced there by injustice. He never acts unjustly, even when robbing the rich. They always deserve it by lying or cheating. Robin is commonly shown to be righting wrongs committed by his victims. He then aids the poor to keep their land, regain the goods and so on. Robin robs the rich to give to the poor and acts in a charitable manner.

There is some justification for this attitude in the early works. However, the main example of Robin's charity in the early works was to assist the knight who had got into debt through the grasping abbot of St Mary's. In other words, Robin was not giving to those we should consider poor. The giving of this attribute did allow Robin to be presented as a popular hero for all, despite his social position as an outlaw. Undoubtedly, there was some sympathy among the lower classes in the medieval period for outlaws. They were sometimes forced into outlawry for activities that we should not see as criminal, such as debt. On the other hand, to survive as outlaws they generally had to commit criminal offences.

Conclusions

The modern age has confirmed several of the developments in the Robin Hood myth from the previous centuries and has added to them. The developments of the nineteenth century have probably had a greater impact than anything that came before — apart from the very origin of the story. Thus, virtually everyone now sees Robin as opposed chiefly by the sheriff of Nottingham, Guy of Gisborne, and Prince John. King Richard is the good king to whom Robin is loyal. Robin represents the Saxons oppressed by the Normans and fights on their behalf. His band includes Little John, Will Scarlet, Much the Miller, and Alan a Dale. Friar Tuck is another ever-present colleague. Robin's true love is Maid Marian. Both Robin and Marian are of noble birth. Robin's home as an outlaw is Sherwood Forest, but he is generally known also as Robin of Locksley by birth. He often goes to Nottingham. He is a superb archer. He robs the rich to pay the poor and helps the oppressed against unjust representatives of authority. This is the picture we have to examine — and question — as we move backwards in time.

It is clearly true, as Stephen Knight has argued, that the modern view of Robin Hood is largely an idealistic one.[24] The forest is the welcoming greenwood; the general atmosphere is one of a sort of rustic content. In present times, the occasional representation of Robin as a rebel, or a left-wing activist, has been generally mellowed. His aid to the poor has become rather softened to equal a kind of harmless liberalism. To a degree, this matches the ballad versions. Robin Hood stories have become suitable for children, rather fun and harmless. Robin is no Russian revolutionary or Che Guevara. He is no criminal, murderer, thief, poacher or highwayman, but rather a wronged noble who seeks to right the injustices of the time. The time, being medieval, is safely distanced from any modern connotations. His continued popularity is largely in comics and rather bland adventure series.

There is a present clash between academic views based on the original Robin Hood ballads or historical study of the early evidence about Robin Hood as against the modern presentation of the Robin Hood story for popular consumption, especially in the visual media. The work of historians and scholars on texts of the early ballads and historical records we shall need to examine in later chapters. It must be said now, though, that there is little agreement between the views. With historical discussion, the major problem for experts is over what is relevant to study. There is no real agreement over when Robin lived or even if he lived. The investigation of any particular medieval period is, therefore, not altogether a satisfactory approach as it may be missing the truth entirely. The students of the early ballads also have serious problems to resolve, such as which were earliest and to what degree do the surviving ballads give the full picture. Clearly, much that once did exist has been lost. What is now the earliest surviving literary evidence was clearly not the earliest ever, since we have reference to it before anything actually survives.

Even so-called modern historical works can miss the mark. The author of a recent book on Robin Hood, Mike Dixon-Kennedy, claims that his work is based on an historical approach and the use of six recognised early ballads.[25] The author claims to 'have been systematically weeding out the fact from the fiction'.[26] Yet the book's content seems derived almost entirely from somewhere other than the named ballads and contains a great deal of material that does not appear at all in these early works. It assumes that the answers are that Robin was Robert of Locksley and he lived in the twelfth and thirteenth centuries. It mysteriously introduces, as if from these early works, characters such as Ket the Trow, Alan de Tranmire, Hob of the Hill, Alfred of Gamwell, Sir Ector of the Harelip, Nether o' the Meering, Richard Malbête, Sir Niger le Grym, Sir Bernard of the Brake, Reuben of Stamford, Captain Bush, Cog the Earless, Sir Gosbert de Lanmbly, Rafe of the Bilhook, Old Bart the Bandry, Sir Scriwel of Catsty, Grame Gaptooth, Sir Baldwin the Killer, Sibbie, Fenella, Sir Drogo of Dallas Tower, Damon the Monk, Beat the Bush, Denvil of Toomlands, Dudda Dodd and so on. I should be interested to learn in which of those six named early works these characters appear! In other words, we have to beware of modern pseudo-historical approaches, which only serve to confuse an already confused picture.

If there ever was a real Robin Hood then perhaps the people of Nottingham are nearer to the reality than most. According to a recent analysis by Endsleigh Insurance, the town in England that is riskiest for burglary is Nottingham! [27]

Further Conclusions

In modern times, there has been some interest in the old ballads that first introduced Robin Hood to the literary world. These have now been worked over by intellectuals and specialists, literary and historical. Such studies sometimes move away from popular understanding. One recent writer has commented on 'Why transgression of deconstructionist doctrines about the absolute "impossibility of history" and about "literary intentionality" are called "totalitarianism" can be explained by the doctrines of *difference, dissemination* and active interpretation'.[1] Quite! Our interest, however, is in the popular view of our hero as demonstrated in the popular media. We shall, indeed, come to examine the views of scholars later on, but for the time being we shall stick with Robin as he is commonly perceived.

There is no question but that the main media interest in Robin Hood in modern times has been visual. To a small extent, this includes printed works, such as drawings in comics and book illustrations, but primarily it has been in the form of the moving picture — whether through the cinema or TV. From early black and white films we have moved to major colour films and TV series.

The importance of the media concerned is that it has dictated the nature of the modern view of Robin Hood. What has particularly attracted film makers has been the action element. We may add to this the possibilities of medieval action in such things as tournaments, crusades, sieges, fights between individuals and archery competitions. Inevitably, a romance interest has been sought and Maid Marian has been the usual answer. The hero of such action movies must also be young, virile and handsome – hence Robin has been played by such as Douglas Fairbanks and Errol Flynn.

On the whole, it is the visual excitement that has dictated the form of the Robin Hood films. Political and social comment has not been altogether absent but it has taken a secondary role. Robin is opposed to corruption but is virtually always a noble, who recovers his rightful inheritance. He is in no sense a revolutionary or a criminal. Robin has attracted film makers because he can leap about and fight rather than because he is an outlaw and a rebel against authority. It is true that the occasional version does not keep to these rules, but there is no doubt as to the accuracy of the commonly accepted ideas.

TV influence has been a little later in time than movie influence. On TV, Robin has nearly always appeared in a series of programmes, therefore covering a longer period of time than a single film. This has led to more involved and ingenious plots and has taken Robin rather further away from the original stories. The most recent series have delved into such unlikely areas as science fiction and fantasy. Even so, the basis of virtually all plots is still a recognisable handful of ideas: the outlaw and his band, the love of Marian, the matches, the dining, the defeat of a few leading villains.

Over the next few chapters, we shall move backwards in time to see how this modern vision has been reached and gradually discover what the original really was.

Endnotes

[1] See various essays in Hahn.

[2] Knight, *Mythic*, p. 161.

[3] Grove, p. 121.

[4] Radio 4, 19/11/06.

[5] Knight, *Complete Study*, p. 219.

[6] See Jeffrey Richard, 'Robin Hood on the Screen', pp. 429-40 in Knight, *Anthology*.

[7] Jeffrey Richards, p. 429. (From ed. K. Carpenter, *Robin Hood: the Many Faces of that Celebrated Outlaw*, Oldenburg, 1995). See also Knight, *Complete Study*, chapter 6, pp. 218-61.

[8] Knight, *Mythic,* p. 150.

[9] Knight, *Complete Study,* p. 221.

[10] Kevin J. Harty, 'Robin Hood on Film', pp. 87-100, in Hahn, p. 89.

[11] Knight, *Mythic,* p. 151.

[12] Knight, *Mythic,* p. 154.

[13] Knight, *Complete Study,* p. 225.

[14] Richard in Knight, *Anthology,* p. 431.

[15] See Rudy Behlmer, 'Robin Hood on the Screen: from Legend to Film', pp. 441-60 in Knight, *Anthology.*

[16] John Gillingham, in various works, has argued that the evidence of Richard's homosexuality is not convincing; it does however remain possible.

[17] Knight, *Complete,* p. 231; the expert was F. M. Padelford.

[18] Knight, 'Robin Hood in Tights', pp.461-67 in Knight, *Anthology,* p. 463.

[19] Knight, *Mythic,* p. 205.

[20] McSpadden & Wilson, opp. p. 64. My friend Ian Morton found this interesting book for me.

[21] Knight, *Mythic,* p. 189.

[22] Sarah Beach, 'Robin Hood and Green Arrow, pp. 21-8, in Hahn, p. 22.

[23] Jeffrey Richards, 'Robin Hood on the Screen', pp. 429-40 in Knight, *Anthology,* p. 429.

[24] Knight, *Complete Study,* p. 8-9.

[25] Mike Dixon-Kennedy, *The Robin Hood Handbook, the Outlaw in History, Myth and Legend,* Stroud, 2006

[26] Dixon-Kennedy, p. 408.

[27] March 2008 as reported in the *Independent.*

[28] David Aers, 'Medievalists and Deconstruction: *An Exemplum*', pp. 24-40, in Simons; p. 29.

2

Robin Hood from 1700 to 1900

This chapter will take us back to the period of the early ballads. We have seen the modern (post 1900) impact on the ancient myth. The period we are about to examine is the period of transition that linked the early works, including the earliest poems and a play text, to modern visual versions. 1700 to 1900 was the age that shaped our modern Robin Hood by extending the legend. The forms that dominated in the nineteenth century, notably novels and plays, required further elaboration of known stories. Robin today has become a figure largely seen through the visual media. In this chapter, we strip off that most recent layer of the legend and move back to the age before cinema and television. In this period, the main medium of significance was probably the novel, which was then a new literary form. Its very length demanded that the old tales be refashioned and elaborated. Tudor and Stuart plays had begun this process but further elaboration was necessary. The longest ancient work was the medieval poem called the *Gest of Robyn Hode* but even that had insufficient content for a novel. Authors, therefore, had to expand and invent and so a new Robin Hood emerged — the basis for our modern concepts.

By 1700, the early ballad works had been published and, to a large extent, then forgotten. There had always been an oral element to the Robin Hood material and that did continue but always at a fairly low level. Sayings about Robin Hood were not forgotten and an outline of his career was still in the popular mind but, again, not to a great extent. The story of these two centuries, from 1700 to 1900, is one of the revival of Robin Hood's popularity plus a new injection of ideas and material.

Medievalism

In the eighteenth century, Englishmen discovered a new interest in the Middle Ages beginning in about the 1760s.[1] The Renaissance view of the Middle Ages was to see it as the unproductive middle or medieval period between ancient and modern times. That was now brought into question — though the term medieval survived. An early convert to the new view was Robert Walpole, son of the great politician Horace. Robert Walpole built and wrote his own creations with medieval models in mind. The concept of medievalism became a movement that matured in the mid-nineteenth century. Through the period following 1760, Britons produced a romantic, idealised and inaccurate picture of the medieval past. This inspired many creative people and affected their poetry, prose, drama, art, architecture and religion. Figures in most artistic and intellectual fields took a new interest in the medieval past, from architects like Pugin to writers such as Ruskin.

One of the effects of this new interest was the collection of old medieval works, thus often saving them from permanent loss. There followed some attempt to emulate these works. Even more significant was the use of the old material to produce new original works, both in prose and poetry. Robin Hood remained a relatively minor player in this, but was certainly part of the movement. More important at the time were the tales around King Arthur. Early works, such as that of Malory, were reprinted and many writers used the tales for their own purposes. *Morte D'Arthur* was reprinted in 1816 and soon inspired writers from the Romantic poets to Scott and Tennyson. One aspect of the movement was its nationalism, hence interest in British figures. The very English background of Robin Hood — Nottingham, Sherwood — helped to make him an attractive figure, along with the fact that he was one of the earliest heroes to be celebrated in the English tongue.

In the nineteenth-century, medieval architecture influenced modern buildings. In 1835, the new Houses of Parliament were built in a pseudo-medieval style. For the Great Exhibition of 1851, Pugin designed a Medieval Court. The Victorians restored medieval churches and built various buildings anew in the Gothic style. Families sought to establish heraldic arms for themselves. Tournaments and archery contests became popular entertainment for the wealthier in society. In 1839, the Eglinton Tournament was staged. Its first day was ruined by rain when the Marquis of Londonderry, wearing steel armour from head to foot, protected himself with an umbrella![2] A similar interest was felt by artists and inspired the pre-Raphaelite movement, which might well be called the pre-Reformation movement in art. Leading figures included Dante Gabriel Rossetti and John Everett Millais. They were followed by such as William Morris and Edward Burne-Jones. Arthurian romance became a popular subject for paintings — white knights and so on.

Historians were among those inspired by the new interest in the Middle Ages. It has been said that it was now that academic history became a profession.[3] Arguably, the greatest English historians of the age turned to medieval history, from Bishop Stubbs to John Horace Round and Edward A. Freeman. Gradually, it became clear that the Romantic ideas of the medieval past were not historically accurate. It was one reason for an eventual decline in the popularity of Sir Walter Scott's novels. Changes in historical thinking frequently prevent an enduring life for historical novels. Oddly enough, one of the 'romantic' themes that did survive historical criticism and remained popular despite being historically inaccurate was the eighteenth-century version of the tales of Robin Hood. Hence we retain still, for example, the Angevin Plantagenet background period (for which there is no proof) and the Saxon-Norman conflict, which is anachronistic.

The new medievalism also had an impact on society, notably as a spur to those who sought social reform in aid of the weak and the poor. Among those in whom interest was inspired were antiquaries and then historians, who gradually produced a more accurate view of the medieval age. Both groups, the romantics and the historians, took some interest in Robin Hood. The social reformers were horrified by what they saw as the failings of modern life, especially the effect of the industrial revolution on the workers and of urbanisation on the poor. Their view of the past might have been romantic but it nevertheless provoked sympathy. They sought to take the world back to its former, and supposedly better, state. A natural hero in this development was Robin Hood, who was presented as seeking to use the wealth of the great and powerful in order to aid the poor and needy. Medievalism, along with Robin Hood, was, therefore, an inspiration to radicals rather than to conservatives. In this sense, medievalism can be seen as a forerunner of socialism, with Robin Hood as one of its spurs.[4]

Indeed, Robin Hood became a direct spur to actual revolutionaries. It was no accident that the Luddites emerged in the town of Nottingham from 1811. They have been seen as 'nineteenth-century Robin Hoods, emerging from the fringes of Sherwood Forest and redressing society's wrongs'.[5] It might seem odd that this group, generally seen as conservative opponents to machinery in industry, should be inspired by Robin Hood. However, the Luddites have been unjustly maligned and their real objectives were to defend the rights of workers. They were protesting against poor pay in the hosiery and lace industries, the employment of poorly trained workers and bad practice in producing sub-standard goods. They were attacking those who seemed guilty of such practices rather than the machinery itself. Their bad reputation rests on distortions placed upon them by contemporary manufacturers and politicians.[6] One notes that, like Robin Hood in the tales, the Luddites had a good deal of support from ordinary folk.

The Collecting of Robin Hood literature

One aspect of the new medievalism, the renewed antiquarian interest in the Middle Ages, had great significance for us. This was the emergence of antiquarians who devoted themselves to making collections of medieval works, many of which were published. In the Stuart period, there had been some effort to collect old ballads in order to preserve them. The diarist Samuel Pepys was one interested party, who took an interest in broadsides. In the eighteenth and nineteenth centuries, these collections were examined and newly discovered items added where possible.

Thomas Percy

The collection made by Bishop Thomas Percy has been called 'the most important single document relative to the history of balladry'.[7] His manuscript collection included eight Robin Hood ballads, but when his *Reliques of Ancient English Poetry* was published in three volumes, in 1765, it contained only one Robin Hood ballad and that was *Robin Hood and Guy of Gisborne*.[8]

Thomas Percy was actually born Thomas Piercy in Bridgnorth, Shropshire, in 1729. He chose to alter his name to that of the noble family of the earls of Northumberland, from which he claimed (almost certainly wrongly) to be descended.[9] He was actually the son of a grocer but rose in the world.[10] He became chaplain to the noble Percy family and dedicated his work the *Reliques* to the countess of Northumberland. He was educated at Christchurch Oxford and became vicar at Easton Mauduit in Northamptonshire where he lived for twenty-five years. He then became chaplain to the duke of Northumberland and then to King George III. He was made dean of Carlisle and then bishop of Dromore in Ireland, which is where he moved to take up his appointment. Percy married and had six children, though four died young. He found a number of works held in the British Museum library. He collaborated with other contemporary collectors and chose what he considered the best of his finds for publication. Other newly discovered works were added to later editions. Then, at end of his life, Percy lost his sight. He died in Ireland in 1811.

It was Bishop Percy who put the Robin Hood works on the literary map and ensured the survival of the legend in an age when works in print multiplied enormously. The literate world was now aware of the basic evidence about Robin Hood. Bishop Percy was the first to note the reference to the Robin Hood works in *Piers Plowman*.[11] He also shared the attitude of the eighteenth century that saw Robin as a sort of social revolutionary with his 'levelling principle of taking from the rich and giving to the poor'.[12]

Some of Percy's published works came from a very important manuscript now known as the Percy Folio — though Percy himself only came to possess it, selected poems from it to use and never published it as a whole. Percy told the tale of how when visiting the home of his friend Sir Humphrey Pitt of Priors Lee in Shropshire he saw the manuscript 'unbound and sadly torn'. He went on 'I saw it lying dirty on the floor under a Bureau in ye Parlour: being used by the Maids to light the fire'.[13] Percy rescued the remains and some of its contents became part of his collected *Reliques*. That manuscript, since known as the Percy Folio, was compiled about a century before it came into his hands. It contained ballads and other works that were probably written between the fourteenth and seventeenth centuries. He described it as 'a long, narrow folio volume, containing 195 sonnets, ballads, Historical Songs, and Metrical Romances'. He noted that many of the pages were 'mutilated and imperfect'.[14]

Only eight of the works in the Percy Folio were Robin Hood ballads. It is not known how these works were collected. Half of every leaf of fifty-four pages had been cut off. It was left 15½ inches long by 5½ inches wide and was 2 inches thick.[15] There are pages missing at the beginning and the end, and the person who bound it for Percy cut off some lines at the top and bottom of pages. Percy himself did not treat the Folio with respect. He scribbled in the margins and removed leaves in order to transcribe them.[16] He saw the work as a 'parcel of Old Ballads', which were simple and artless, possessing 'rudeness' and lacking any 'higher beauties'. He chose to cross out some parts that he considered 'indelicate'!

Three volumes sounds like a pretty hefty amount but, in fact, there were about six times more works in the original manuscript than those Percy published. Percy was upset when Ritson suggested that, since he would not let anyone see the Folio, it really did not exist. Percy then had himself painted with the Folio in his hand. He ridiculed the 'personal abuse of poor made Ritson' but still refused access to the Folio.[17] The works not published by Percy would not see the light of day for many years. Percy's descendants, who inherited the Folio, allowed a few scholars to see parts of it but prevented publication or even complete transcription or listing of the contents. It was finally published in full, from 1867 to 1868, in an edition by Hales and Furnivall. According to Furnivall this edition was now 'without Percy's tawdry touches'.[18] It is widely believed that many of the works in the Folio were much older than the date of their collection but there is no easy way to prove this. Throughout in this book, we shall rely on the first dated manuscript version of any poem or the first dated publication version if not known in manuscript form. This is not to forbid speculation but does avoid certain unwarranted assumptions. The Percy Folio itself was written out in the seventeenth century when the person responsible for copying it out was at work. Percy claimed that it had been copied by one Thomas Blount (1618-79) but this has been disputed and remains uncertain.[19] It is thought that the Folio was part of the library of old books owned by Blount. We do not know if the penman was also the collector or if either of them was actually Blount. It seems more likely that Blount had simply acquired the Folio.

Percy's collection inspired various poets and writers, including Walter Scott and the Romantic poets, and played a great part in the blossoming interest in medieval literature and history. The old manuscript was finally published in full in 1867-68. It included romances, metrical histories, ballads and songs. It had been compiled originally in about 1650, probably from both written and oral sources.[20] One of the most acclaimed works in the manuscript is *Child Waters*. It also included works on Arthurian legends and Gawain, as well as those on Robin Hood.

Percy's contribution was of great importance. Many students of literature and poets appreciated the works they could now read, including Dryden and Addison. Percy's published work has its faults for modern scholars but remained invaluable. Perhaps the greatest effect of the *Reliques* was its grip on the imagination of the young Walter Scott, who confessed to the great delight he found in reading the poems in his garden at the age of thirteen and being so engrossed that he forgot his dinner. It was felt necessary in Percy's day to 'improve' works for readers. In a sense, this is still the case — abbreviations are enlarged, errors corrected and so on. In the eighteenth century, it probably was necessary in order to reach the reading public of the day to make these changes. Percy altered some words, added others, as well as providing his own poetic inventions — in his view to make the works acceptable to his reading public. Modern scholars, however, wish to return, where possible, to the original manuscripts and re-edit. Fortunately for us, a whole series of careful and hard-working editors have carried through this task, from Ritson to Child, and, more recently, Dobson and Taylor.

David Herd and Mrs Brown

Scottish collectors played a major role, including David Herd and Mrs Brown of Falkland. David Herd was an accountant's clerk who lived in Edinburgh and died in 1810. He was also a singer and composer.[21] His collection, called *Scottish Songs,* was published in 1769, a later and larger edition having two volumes. Anna Gordon Brown collected both English and Scottish ballads.[22] She died in the same year as Herd. She came from Aberdeen and married a Reverend Brown. Her collection consisted of different versions of thirty-three old ballads, including two about Robin Hood. She tended to 'improve' the works she found and invented one ballad about Robin's birth, so one needs to be wary about her work.

Thomas Evans

In 1777, Thomas Evans published a collection of ballads, including twenty-seven about Robin Hood, in *Old Ballads, Historical and Narrative.* This was a more or less complete collection of the Robin Hood works as known to him, twenty-seven in total — though he missed some.[23] The basis of his collection was the broadsides, and in total it resembled the garland collections. The attempted comprehensive nature of this work, and its concentration on Robin Hood ballads, gives it a significant place in our catalogue.

Joseph Ritson

The next great collector who is important in the story of Robin Hood works was Joseph Ritson. In 1795, he published *Robin Hood: A Collection of all the Ancient Poems, Songs and Ballads.* John Bellamy considers 1795 to be 'the most important year in the entire history of the study of the famous outlaw'.[24] Ritson might seem an unlikely candidate until you recognise the connection between Robin Hood, medievalism and the inspiration for social reform. Ritson saw Robin Hood as 'patriotic' because 'all opposition to tyranny is the cause of the people'.[25] Ritson was a pro-Jacobin lawyer, anti-clerical and a vegetarian — pretty rare then.[26] He was a brusque northerner, born in Stockton-on-Tees. He was wont to address anyone he encountered as 'Citizen'.[27] He was also a friend of Sir Walter Scott. Ritson was primarily a historian. Joseph Ritson committed suicide in 1803. Ritson's collection included all the main known texts apart from *Robin Hood and the Monk.*

Thomas Percy had been selective in his choice of material for the *Reliques* and less than a quarter of the poems in the Percy Folio were published in that work. Ritson now published these missing works. In 1795, he was responsible for *Robin Hood: A Collection of all the Ancient Poems, Songs and Ballads Now Extant Relative to the Celebrated English Outlaw.* This included the best texts then available for all except the ballad *Robin Hood and the Monk.*[28] The *Reliques* emphasised the major importance to all Robin Hood poems of the *Gest,* an opinion that has endured to the present time. Ritson's collection included no less than thirty-three of the thirty-eight ballads later printed in Child's definitive collection.

Ritson also added a 'Life of Robin Hood' as part of the preface to his publication. It was hardly constructed on what today we should see as historical methods. He used the work of Grafton, chiefly taken from John Maior and 'an olde and auncient Pamphlet', which was probably produced in the Tudor period.[29] Ritson also used the Sloane Manuscript for the *Gest* and other ballads. Ritson did, however, accept more questionable sources such as Stukeley's virtually invented genealogy, equating Robin Hood to one Robert Fitzooth, earl of Huntingdon. According to Ritson there was a clear historical pattern for this life. Robin was thus born in 1160 at Locksley. He was earl of Huntington. However debatable the results, this was the first serious attempt to present an historical account of Robin Hood. Ritson's method was in some ways akin to modern ideas, retaining more of the original spellings and form than had been the practice until then. His work also had great influence and was frequently reprinted.

William Motherwell and Sabine Baring-Gould

A collector whose contribution was not recognised for some time after his death was the Scot, William Motherwell (1797-1835).[30] He was a legal clerk and newspaper editor as well as a poet and historian. He edited a work on minstrelsy that was published in 1827. His collection of ballads was used by Francis Child with whom he collaborated, though his contribution was not given due recognition. No less than 108 of the ballads published by Child came to him from Motherwell. Child accused Motherwell of retouching and improving the works, which was probably true. Another collector who was in contact with Child was Sabine Baring-Gould. In this case, some of the collector's work was not passed on to Child and his collection in manuscript was only rediscovered in 1992. It has altered the knowledge of ballad origins in terms of location since his works came particularly from the West Country, from Devon and Cornwall.

John Gutch

After Ritson there was a publication by John Matthew Gutch in 1847 in two volumes, including *A Lytell Geste of Robin Hode, with other Ancient and Modern*

Ballads and Songs. Although it mainly consisted of Ritson's work, it did bring to new prominence the version of *Robin Hood and the Monk* not known to Ritson. Gutch also stressed the yeoman rank of Robin.

Francis Child

More important was the work of the American Francis James Child (1825-96) published in various editions of several volumes. Child was nicknamed 'Stubby' because of his short and stocky build. He was the son of a Boston sailmaker who received aid for his education. His intelligence won him a place at Harvard. His interests drew him to wide travel through Europe. Child was able to correspond in six languages and collected ballads in several languages.

Child's collection, *English and Scottish Popular Ballads,* first appeared in five volumes from 1882 to 1898 — though probably the most popular version appeared in 1904. Child's collection has received broad appreciation, called 'the general source of information concerning the ballad lore of England and Scotland'.[31] This edition is arguably the most influential and most used of all Robin Hood collections and, rather oddly, it is the work of an American. There has been some criticism from scholars, and some additions have since been made, but this remains the chief starting point of any modern Robin Hood collection — as well as any collection of historical ballads.

Modern Collections

A useful single-volume work, containing all the main Child ballads, though not all of their variants, was edited by Helen Child Sargent and George Lyman Kittredge. It came out in 1906 with the same title as Child's original work. In modern times, of course, we are grateful for the *Rymes of Robyn Hood* collection made by R. B. Dobson and J. Taylor.

Robin in New Literature

The novel was virtually a new art form of this period (1700-1900), certainly in popular literature. One of the earliest of the new novelists to mention Robin Hood was Elizabeth Villa-Real Gooch. In 1804, her work *Sherwood Forest; or Northern Adventures* was published. However, she gave little space to our hero and added nothing to the legend, apart from suggesting that Robin once took shelter in Sherwood House. Much the same is true of an anonymous novel called *Robin Hood* that was published in Edinburgh in 1819 — possibly also by a woman.[32] Although minor works, they were indicative of the trend towards the Robin Hood who was a hero in modern fiction.

Sir Walter Scott

At the beginning of the nineteenth century, a Scot emerged who transformed the popular view of the Middle Ages and of Robin Hood. This is Sir Walter Scott who was much influenced by the new collections of medieval literature. He also collected works from his own area of the Scottish border. He saw himself first as a poet but is remembered now chiefly as a novelist, indeed as 'the acknowledged inventor of the historical novel'. He knew Joseph Ritson personally and was influenced by his work. Scott, in his novel *Ivanhoe,* told his readers that they could discover more about the outlaw Robin Hood in 'black-lettered garlands', once sold for a halfpenny but now bought 'at their weight in gold'.[33]

Ivanhoe, a Romance was Sir Walter Scott's first novel to be based on English history and it introduced Robin Hood as a character — albeit only identified late in the novel. Friar Tuck was also a character along with other members of the outlaw band. *Ivanhoe* was published in 1819-20.[34] Scott chose the reign of Richard the Lionheart because it was a period 'abounding with characters'.[35] Scott was also in large part responsible for the connection between Robin Hood and the Saxon-Norman conflict. According to Scott, in his own comment on the book, at this time the Normans 'still reigned in it [England] as conquerors', while Normans and Saxons had 'hostile blood'.[36]

Scott perhaps rather overdid some of the fictional ploys. Several characters appear under pseudonyms: Robin Hood as Locksley the yeoman, Friar Tuck as the Hermit, Ivanhoe as the Disinherited Knight, Richard the Lionheart as the Black Knight. Richard's behaviour on his secret return to England, and his virtually lone exploits as the Black Knight, do not seem very likely. The reappearance of the apparently dead Athelstane is hardly credible, nor is the conduct of the witch-like Ulrica. All the same, the novel has a strong plot that carries the reader along. Modern readers will find some of the nineteenth-century attitudes reflected by Scott distasteful, not least his racist view of Jews or of Negroes with 'blubber lips'.[37]

The hero of the story, Wilfrid of Ivanhoe, is Saxon — as are virtually all the goodies with the exception of Richard the Lionheart. Scott clearly explains that many of his characters are fictional, including Ivanhoe (a name taken from one of the three places that had once been declared forfeit in a punishment for striking the Black Prince: 'Tring, Wing, and Ivanhoe') and Front-de-Boeuf, a name that he claimed to have found in an old manuscript.[38] Robin Hood appears at first as Locksley, only later revealed to be the great outlaw 'Robin Hood of Sherwood Forest' who claims 'in these glades I am monarch'.[39] He is a secondary character in the novel. The main plot revolves around the clash between Richard the Lionheart and his brother, Prince John, together with the effects of this relationship. The main story line concerns the problems for the Jew Isaac of York and his beautiful daughter, Rebecca. Although Ivanhoe's heart is given to 'the Saxon beauty' Rowena, he comes into contact with Rebecca, who has a soft spot for him.[40] She becomes of prisoner of the villainous Normans of the story, one of whom, Sir

Brian de Bois-Guilbert, falls in love with her. He tries to force himself upon her. In the end, the religious order to which he belongs, that of the Knights Templar, decides that she has bewitched him and deserves to die for it. She then claims the right to call on a champion to defend her and prove her innocence in the lists. The Templars, much criticised by Scott, make Sir Brian the unwilling defender of their position. Ivanhoe had been wounded and tended by Rebecca earlier and, in gratitude, despite his physical weakness, turns up to be her champion. They clash. Ivanhoe is felled but Sir Brian falls dead. Rebecca is then declared innocent. King Richard the Lionheart, fast on Ivanhoe's trail, arrives to provide the mostly-happy ending — the outlaws are pardoned, the Saxons welcomed at court, and Ivanhoe marries Rowena at York in the Lionheart's presence. The less fortunate Jewess Rebecca goes abroad to Grenada with her father for their greater safety, and so that she can devote her life to caring for the sick.

The fictional career of Ivanhoe provided much of the material later used by others for Robin Hood stories — the disinherited noble opposed to Prince John, who escapes to the forest and is later restored by Richard the Lionheart. It was part of Scott's story that in the archery competition, Hubert, the forester, hits the centre of the target, and then Robin (as Locksley) wins by splitting his opponent's arrow.[41] That now happens in virtually every Robin Hood film. Similarly, Friar Tuck is the jolly character invariably used in modern versions. One omission in Scott is Little John.

Within a year of the publication of *Ivanhoe*, its popularity was demonstrated by transference to the stage in no less than five versions.[42] In effect, Scott's *Ivanhoe* set the scene for nearly all subsequent fictional work on Robin Hood, notably in film and TV. The two main points being first making Robin a champion of Saxons against Normans, and secondly (if oddly) that the historical period chosen was that of the Angevin Plantagenets, specifically the reign of Richard the Lionheart.

Scott's work also had influence on such as Lord Tennyson and Thomas Hardy. Tennyson made use of Arthurian material to write *The Lady of the Lake* and *The Lay of the Last Minstrel*. The fact that *The Lady of the Lake* made him £10,000 — an enormous sum in that period — shows both his popularity and his influence.[43] Thomas Hardy probably partly based his own decision to stop writing novels and concentrate on poetry on his assessment of Scott's work — his poems against his novels. Scott was very popular in his day and for some time afterwards, but his reputation has waned in modern times, partly because the history of his historical novels no longer seems accurate enough. It has been suggested that he wrote too much and that his fame is now 'a large black hole'.[44] It may revive. The cinema has, for example, revived the story of Ivanhoe. Scott's effect on modern views of Robin Hood has been considerable. His novels have been used on films and television. Many followed his ideas on Robin as a supporter of Saxons against Normans, his idea of 'Merry England' and his nostalgia for the old forests.

Thomas Love Peacock

Thomas Love Peacock claimed to have written his short novel *Maid Marian* in the same year as *Ivanhoe,* though it was not published until four years later in 1822 and seems to borrow from Scott as if written after *Ivanhoe.*[45] Like Walter Scott, Peacock was inspired by the work of Joseph Ritson and influenced by Anthony Munday's sixteenth-century plays. Peacock was an educated man who worked for the East India Company. *Maid Marian* is again set in Plantagenet England and one can suggest that it was the choice of period at this time, by Peacock as well as Scott, that had an enduring effect on the modern period setting now used for the Robin Hood tales. *Maid Marian* was a more humorous and nostalgic effort than Scott's *Ivanhoe,* perhaps more in tune with the later ballads. Peacock himself called it 'a comic Romance' and claimed the political intention to make 'satire of all the oppressions that are done under the sun'.[46] He said of William the Conqueror that he 'took from the poor and gave to the rich', while 'Robin takes from the rich and gives to the poor'.[47] *Maid Marian* was probably influenced by the French format of the *conte morale.*[48] The work is now forgotten and has had far less influence than *Ivanhoe* — though it had some popularity in its time and did introduce the idea of a love rivalry between Robin and Prince John for the hand (or in John's case perhaps the body) of Marian. It also used the title that would survive for her as 'Maid' Marian.

Other now unknown works including Robin as a character soon appeared, by such as Thomas Miller. Less famed novelists took up the pen to contribute to Robin Hood fiction. These included G. P. R. James who wrote *Forest Days,* published in 1843. Interestingly, as some modern historians do, he set his Robin Hood in the period of Simon de Montfort and Henry III. This was because James had read an article by 'G.F.' in the *London and Westminster Quarterly* of 1840.[49] The article's point was itself based on a reading of the historian Walter Bower. In the novel, the outlaw leader is called Robert of the Lees by Ely and he fights for Simon de Montfort at Evesham. By and large, though, this period placing of the Robin Hood stories has rarely won devotees.

Poetry

Robin Hood also became a subject for poetry of a new kind. The Romantic poets were clearly aware of our hero. Wordsworth claimed: 'A famous man is Robin Hood'.[50] Keats was an early writer to use the Robin Hood story in verse in response to a poem on the same subject by his friend, J. H. Reynolds. Keats wrote his poem in the very same year that Scott wrote *Ivanhoe* and Peacock wrote *Maid Marian.* The poem was published in 1820. Keats imagined Robin 'cast/Sudden from his turfed grave' and nostalgically wished 'Honour to bold Robin Hood'.[51]

James Henry Leigh Hunt was a nineteenth-century poet with anti-authority views. He was imprisoned for two years as a result of writing a seditious libel against the Prince Regent.[52] In 1820, he published four ballads of Robin Hood in his magazine, *The Indicator*. He also composed a further series of ballads about Robin Hood, virtually a new garland. Among his inventions was a young Robin who shot a deer.

Popular Fiction

One of the most important early popular literary works was *Robin Hood and Little John; or, The Merry Men of Sherwood Forest* by Pierce Egan the Younger, published in 1840 as a book after its first appearance in serial form in forty-one parts from 1838. Egan illustrated his own work. His drawing of the dying outlaw makes Robin look rather like a collapsed Disraeli. Stephen Knight has recently argued that this is not a book for children.[53] Its very length suggests that — half a million words — as does the inclusion of romantic kissing. It is perhaps better seen as a popular adult novel that also had appeal to children. As with all novels, these 'popular' novels required additional material, and Egan invented new characters and plots. Thus, the author provided a new fate, a new and fuller career for the young Robin. Egan also introduced villains with the unlikely names of Caspar Steinkopft and Sir Tristram Uggeleretsch. He also, presumably as a joke, invented a character called Ritson, who died in agony. There has been criticism of Egan's work, as slipshod for example, but its popularity helped imprint the outlaw story widely in America as well as in Britain.

It is perhaps true that Robin was moving downwards in terms of the literary quality of the authors taking him as their subject, but he was crystallising into the figure recognisable today. Another novel was *Maid Marian or the Forest Queen* by Joachim H. Stocqueler in 1849. It is, again, set in the world of Prince John. Also, as was typical of the novel form, there are further inventions, including characters such as Hugo Malair, William of Goldsborough, Leila, Minnie Eftskin, the jester Gurtha (no doubt influenced by Scott's Wamba) and the villain Baron de Berkem. Thoughts of pantomime characters are impossible to ignore.

Robin in fiction also transferred into foreign languages. Possibly the most notable of these were the two works by Alexandre Dumas, translated into English in 1903 (first published in the 1870s), *Robin Hood: Prince of Thieves* and *Robin Hood: The Outlaw*. Knight considers these two as mere 'pot-boilers' but Dumas, with Scott and Tennyson, are among the few great writers to feature Robin.[54] One cannot ignore the use of the title of the first of these in a popular modern film.

Children's Fiction

Another significant development of this period was the deliberate angling of Robin Hood stories for children's consumption. This recognition of youthful interest was reflected partly by appearances of Robin Hood characters in toys and cut-outs but depended chiefly on literary effort in serials and novels. The popularisation of Robin in the adult novels spread to efforts aimed deliberately at children. These efforts were generally illustrated, which clearly aided the appeal. In 1840, Stephen Percy's *Robin Hood and His Merry Foresters* was published.[55] Juvenile works appeared, especially from the later nineteenth century. They included *Robin Hood and the Outlaws of Sherwood Forest* by George Emmett in 1869. This first appeared in parts in the *Young Englishman's Edition* and has more of the Saxon against Norman approach — Robin being Saxon. The author hoped his work would inspire boys to 'manly worth and gallant deeds'.[56] A series appeared under the pseudonym of Forest Ranger in the 1870s. *Boys' Own Tales* also serialized Robin Hood in the same decade.

In America, an influential juvenile work was *The Merry Adventures of Robin Hood of Great Renown in Nottinghamshire* by Howard Pyle, published in 1883 in the USA and England. One of the main reasons for its success was the addition of excellent illustrations by the author. Pyle was an artist who added text to his pictures rather than an author illustrating his work. The emphasis on the pictures helps explain its success with children and pointed the way to later visual works in the cinema and on television. Pyle's drawings are also interesting in showing how the idea of Robin Hood has changed over the years since. For Pyle, in the pre-cinema age, Robin was no youthful, athletic hero but rather a hefty, solid individual with beard and moustache and thick, muscled legs. The book, from a modern point of view, is a mish-mash of dubious historical material and stories from the ballads. His story is set in the reigns of Henry II and Richard I along with yeomen and longbow competitions that did not belong to that period. Friar Tuck appears in England before the orders of friars had even been formed. Robin is made earl of Huntingdon, Richard I dies on the battlefield and not wounded fatally at a siege as in recorded fact — and so on. The language is also pretty odd in its false medieval tone: 'Hark ye'... stand back thine own self, for the better man, I wot, am I' — and so on. Even so, Pyle's popular version still carried influence and has been updated (to a degree) and reprinted in modern times.

Robin on Stage

Plays about Robin Hood had been popular in the Tudor and Stuart period but then, for some time, interest in him as a subject declined sharply. The popularity of Scott's novel on Ivanhoe and other such works inspired renewed interest and led to presentations on stage. These included theatrical versions of *Ivanhoe*. Late in his life, Lord Tennyson was drawn to write a play about the outlaw. His work *The Foresters* was published in 1892, the year when Tennyson died.[57]

Lord Tennyson's plan for a production featuring Henry Irving and Ellen Terry was not to be, but the play was later put on in the United States in 1892 as a musical with a score by Arthur Sullivan.[58] In this work, our hero is the disinherited Robin Hood, earl of Huntingdon, though, rather oddly, he claims 'no Earl am

I. I am an English yeoman'.[59] His love is Maid Marian, daughter of Sir Richard Lea. There are also fairies in the cast, including Titania, referred to as Tit![60] The play is set in the usual Plantagenet period, with Prince John and the sheriff of Nottingham as villainous rivals for Marian's favours. John 'can pluck the flower of maidenhood/ From off the stalk and trample it'.[61] It was written partly in prose and partly in blank verse. Again, we find the — by now expected — Saxon against Norman clash, Marian declaring to her father 'I am none of your delicate Norman maidens'. She declares that she loves Robin as much as she would have loved Harold Godwinson or Hereward the Wake, 'who both fought against the tyranny of kings, the Normans'. Robin fights not for himself 'but for the people of England.[62] He robs the rich but is the 'friend of the poor' and 'never wrong'd a woman'.[63]

Tennyson's original play *The Foresters* was not a success but it has moments of poetic power — 'Not while the swallow skims along the ground,/ and while the lark flies up and touches heaven'.[64] As Marian claims: these oaks 'will whisper evermore of Robin Hood'.[65] The play also has, perhaps, more merit than is generally acknowledged, with comic scenes reminiscent of pantomime and of Shakespeare, much good humour and a fast moving plot.

Musicals and Opera

An interesting new medium for our hero appeared in the eighteenth century in the form of musical drama. The originator of this genre was John Gay (1685-1732), who used ballads as an inspiration for his musical works and of whom it has been said that he invented ballad opera.[66] In 1730, a work called *Robin Hood: An Opera* was performed in the Great Theatrical Booth at Bartholomew Fair in London.[67] It was the first known of many musical versions of the Robin Hood story. It was probably based chiefly on the ballads, particularly that of the pinner of Wakefield, and has more than a touch of pantomime about it. The cast included a comic band of outlaws and the show ended with a dance. Darnel, the equivalent of Little John, at one point has an affair with the Pinder's wife and has to hide under her bed pretending to be the dog.[68] Robin is the disinherited earl, but the rebel side is shown by an outlaw chorus proclaiming that liberty 'shall smile and crown our arms'.[69]

In the mid-eighteenth century, Drury Lane featured several musical works about Robin Hood. One such was *Robin Hood: a New Musical Entertainment* by Moses Mendez, performed in 1751 at Drury Lane, with music by Charles Burney.[70] It was written as a short afterpiece to follow a main work in performance. Its first outing came after a production of Ben Jonson's *The Alchemist*. Names such as Sir Humphrey Wealthy, Graspall, and Glitter reflect an approach close to pantomime. The main source this time was the ballad on Alan a Dale. It promised to do well but the run was cut short when the principal tenor, John Beard, became ill and lost his voice.

The comic opera *Robin Hood, or Sherwood Forest*, with libretto by Leonard MacNally and music by William Shield, was produced at Covent Garden's *Theatre Royal* in 1784. Shield was a friend of the historian and expert on Robin Hood, Joseph Ritson. The opera was performed regularly for some years, sometimes as an afterpiece, and proved a successful money-spinner. It invoked the pleasures of life in the forest, where 'we are free from care, my boys'.[71] It has been seen as Robin's 'greatest moment on the British stage' — though this seems a trifle exaggerated if one remembers the work of the Tudor and Stuart playwrights.[72]

Another comic opera was Frances Brooke's *Marian*, performed in 1788. In 1795, another work in this genre, used again as an afterpiece, appeared at Covent Garden as the Christmas entertainment, *Merry Sherwood, or Harlequin Forester*, by John O'Keefe, with music by William Reeve; it was described as 'an operatical pantomime' and included dance and mime.[73] It drew on the ballads of the tanner, Alan a Dale, and the Prince of Aragon — thus returning to older traditions. It did well, being performed on thirty-two occasions. Its music was published and proved popular. In 1822, Thomas Peacock's *Maid Marian* was also turned into a comic opera, with music by George Bishop. It was performed as a Christmas entertainment. The musical proved more popular than the book on which it was based.

A popular musical appeared in 1890 called simply *Robin Hood*, with music by Reginald de Koven and libretto by Harry Bache Smith.[74] It was put on in America and in London as *Maid Marian*. Robin was, again, the dispossessed earl of Huntington, and the villains were Guy of Gisborne and the sheriff of Nottingham. Marian first entered the story as a 'boy' who wished to join the outlaws. The sheriff and Guy disguised themselves as tinkers in order to find Robin, but the tinker's wife claims the sheriff to be her husband because he is wearing her husband's clothes. There was a plan to film this version in the 1930s, though it was never fulfilled.[75] In many ways, the comedy musicals and operas of the nineteenth century may indeed be seen as aiding the transition of Robin Hood from novels to the twentieth-century cinema and television since they had to present a prolonged visual version.

Pantomimes

An actual early pantomime was *Robin Hood and Richard Coeur de Lion* from 1846, co-written by the author of one of the novels we have noted, Joachim Stocqueler. Scene two opened with the outlaws Nuthook, Scut and Kestrel lying about and stringing bows. The curfew bell tolled and Nuthook remarked: 'The curfew tolls the knell of parting day!', to which Scut responds, 'The curfew may be toll'd, we shan't obey!'.[76] Will Scarlet brought the news that Sherwood Forest has been sold by Prince John to the New Nottingham Building Society. Robin Hood, Little John and all the outlaws, in pantomime tradition, were played by women. One interesting innovation was the introduction of a Muslim character as the Algerian Abd-el-Kadir, the Old Man of the Mountains — a pointer to later film characters.[77]

Other pantos followed, including one at the Theatre Royal, Manchester, in 1858, *Robin Hood, or the Forester's Fate*, which was performed in 1862 with a female 'she-riff'. In 1868, came *Once Upon a Time, or A Midsummer Night's Dream in Merrie Sherwood*. A woman played Robin and there was the traditional pantomime dame in Widow Hardcash.[78] A further nineteenth-century pantomime was *Robin Hood, or The Maid that was Arch and the Youth that was Archer* in 1891.

The Appearance of Robin Hood

Another by-product of the literary change that Robin Hood underwent between 1700 and 1900 was the way in which he was viewed. There are no medieval illustrations of our hero. The woodcut illustration for Chaucer's yeoman in the 1491 printed-edition of *The Canterbury Tales* was also used to depict Robin in the early printed version of the *Gest* and has been often used since. The earliest illustrations that are meant to be Robin belong to the Tudor-Stuart period and clothe him (anachronistically) in the dress of that period.

The new medievalism of the eighteenth century and the increased interest in historical accuracy had its effect on how Robin was portrayed visually. The literature of the eighteenth century was the basis for the art of the nineteenth century. The idea was to make Robin properly medieval in appearance. The result, like much else in Victorian medievalism, was more an invention than a genuine historical representation. But the way Robin was then drawn has had much the same impact as Scott's novel — it has had an enduring effect. The period chosen, as in the literature, was usually the reign of Richard the Lionheart in the late-twelfth century — though the costumes chosen were rarely accurate for that period. Robin was generally drawn with a beard, in Lincoln green, and wearing what we now think of as a Robin Hood hat, complete with feather. The early cinematic portrayals of Robin borrowed closely from the Victorian drawings. In the 1850 Pierce Egan book Robin is shown in a short belted tunic and tights. He wears a baldric. The Howard Pyle illustrations of the late nineteenth century bring Robin very close to our modern vision, with the plumed cap.

Robin Hood and the Historians

The renewed interest in the Middle Ages was not confined to artistic imagination and romantic reconstruction. Historians also searched for and studied records about the period and formed a more considered view of what might actually have happened.

The French historian Augustin Thierry accepted Robin Hood as an historical figure in his work on the Norman Conquest, which was published in 1825.[79]

Thierry claimed to be following the continuation of Fordun by Walter Bower, which placed Robin in the period of Simon de Montfort, though, oddly, Thierry then put Robin in the Plantagenet period — the one, around Richard the Lionheart and Prince John, that has stuck in modern times. Thierry's historical 'logic' seems to modern thinking more that of a novelist than an historian.

Other nineteenth-century historians followed Bower and chose to place Robin in the thirteenth century. One such was the author of an article in the *London and Westminster Review* who signed himself as 'G. F.' This may have been George Finlay, who was Scottish. He based his views on those Scottish historians of the earlier period who first mentioned Robin as an historical figure.[80] Thomas Wright pointed out the same references to a thirteenth-century Robin in an essay published in 1846 commenting on the ballads.[81] Wright, however, concluded that the period of Edward II was the most likely background period for the Robin Hood ballads, a decision followed by several modern historians. Wright's concentration on the *Gest* as the best ballad evidence is another approach that has since become common. As Robin Hood became a popular subject of fiction and literature so some began to search for a real figure behind the tales. Interestingly, the gap between the fictional picture of Robin Hood and the historical one has remained pretty much the same ever since.

An early researcher, and an important one, was Joseph Hunter, who came from southern Yorkshire. He worked at the new Public Record Office in London for almost thirty years.[82] In an 1852 article, he pointed out that the king in the early ballads is clearly called Edward, which must refer to one of the first three kings of that name.[83] Hunter then argued for placing Robin in the reign of Edward II, who travelled to the Midlands and the North in 1323. Hunter found a reference to one Perot who played 'Hobbe Fool' at court.[84] He discovered an actual Robin Hood (Robyn Hode/Hod) too, recorded as one of the 'vadlets, (or valets) porteurs de la chambre' of Edward II in the *Jornal de la Chambre* for 1324.[85] It was noted at York for 22 November that 'Robyn Hod jadys un des porteurs poar cas qil n poait pluis travailler', in other words, Robin Hood left royal service 'because he could no longer work'.[86]

Hunter thought he had found further evidence of the man as a property holder in Wakefield, but there is nothing to prove that the man at court and the landholder were one and the same man, and nothing to prove either of them was *the* Robin Hood. In modern times, as we shall see in a later chapter, several further examples of men called Robert or Robin Hood (or variants of it) have been discovered. It becomes clear that Hood was then a fairly common name and makes the association between any two of them very conjectural if there is no further evidence. Some of these other examples have possible interest, for example one called a 'fugitive', but none are certainly our man. From a current view, therefore, one might say that Hunter failed in his intention but his method was nonetheless significant — to search in actual historical records.

In the eighteenth and nineteenth centuries, the idea of Robin Hood was formed that has come to dominate modern times, both in fiction and in history. In fiction, the chief emphasis turned to a Plantagenet Robin connected with Prince John. In historical works, the three main periods for Robin were all put forward: the Plantagenet period of Richard I, the time of Simon de Montfort and his supporters, and the reign of Edward II — with the argument for Edward II and the fourteenth century seeming strongest.

Conclusions

In the period from 1700 to 1900, the major development in the Robin Hood story came through fiction, and in particular through the historical novel. This was anticipated by a scholarly interest in the Robin Hood ballads, which were now available in collections. This collection of material was the necessary prelude to the advance. Literary men became aware of the Robin Hood ballads and were attracted for a variety of reasons. It is surely not mere coincidence that this was an age of political unrest and revolution, a time when the more radical persons in society sought to find their heroes from ordinary men of their own nation. It should also be noted that the readership for Robin Hood works definitely moved down the social scale; some medievalists and specialists on ballad material now themselves came from the middling and lower ranks of society.

One contributing amateur scholar was Frederick James Furnivall (1825-1910), son of a fairly well-off doctor, who did a great service to the Robin Hood material by assisting in the editing and publication for the first time of the ancient Percy Folio (containing many of the earliest Robin Hood ballads) in its complete and original form. This was done through the Early English Text Society, which Furnivall helped to establish.[87] He was educated at University College, London, and later also at Cambridge. He also founded the Working Men's College in 1854 and sought to play a role in educating working men. He made the interesting comment: 'my chief aim has been throughout to illustrate the social conditions of the English people in the past'.[88] Thus Robin is seen as 'the people's hero'.[89]

Perhaps the major attraction to Robin for writers at this time was the romantic aspect — not so much as regards his relation with Maid Marian as his association with the forest, with nature and the simple life, with freedom from the restraints of normal life. The growing attention to the Middle Ages, together with the romantic attitude that produced Medievalism, encouraged attention to Robin Hood as a subject for fictional works.

The development of the historical novel had a particular significance for the future. The nature of the novel forced a requirement to elaborate the Robin Hood story, to investigate the personal thoughts and motives of the characters, to develop the plots in greater depth. Hence Robin Hood became a less simple figure. Robin was not the central character in Scott's *Ivanhoe* but it was perhaps the single most influential work to bring about this transformation in how Robin Hood was seen by the general public. He became fixed in the Plantagenet period and, as a Saxon, attached to supporting the Saxons against the dominant Normans.

Endnotes

1   See Michael Alexander, *Medievalism*.
2   Alexander, p. 109.
3   Alexander, p. 131.
4   Alexander, p. 220.
5   Thomis, p. 158.
6   Thomis, pp. 157-59.
7   Fowler, p. 132.
8   Knight, *Mythic*, p. 95.
9   Knight, *Complete*, p. 22.
10 See Rev. J. Pickford, 'Life of Bishop Percy', in Hales and Furnivall, I, part ii, pp. xxvii-liv.
11 Dobson & Taylor, p. 1.
12 Dobson & Taylor, p. 36.
13 Fowler, p. 132.
14 Percy, p. 2.
15 Hales and Furnivall, i, part ii, p. xii.
16 Hales and Furnivall, i, i, pp. xx, xxii.
17 Hales and Furnivall, i, ii, p. xix.
18 Hales and Furnivall, i, ii, p. x.
19 Hales and Furnivall, i, ii, p. xiv.
20 Fowler, p. 132.
21 Fowler, pp. 271-93.
22 Fowler, pp. 294-331.
23 Knight, *Mythic*, p. 95.
24 Bellamy, p. 2.
25 Knight, *Complete*, p. 156.
26 Alexander, p. 19.
27 Knight, *Mythic*, p. 96.
28 Dobson & Taylor, p. 54.
29 Bellamy, p. 3.
30 Mary Ellen Brown, 'Mr. Child's Scottish Mentor: William Motherwell'. Pp. 29-39, in Cheesman and Rieuwerts.
31 S. Rieuwerts, 'In Memoriam: Francis James Child (1825-96)', in Cheesman and Rieuwerts, p. 19.
32 Knight, *Mythic*, pp. 116-8.
33 *Ivanhoe*, p. 441.
34 Knight, *Mythic*, p. 110.
35 *Ivanhoe*, Introduction.
36 *Ivanhoe*, Introduction; p. 30.
37 *Ivanhoe*, p. 458.
38 *Ivanhoe*, Introduction.
39 *Ivanhoe*, pp. 329, 432.

40 *Ivanhoe,* p. 62.
41 Knight, *Mythic,* p. 113.
42 Alexander, p. 107.
43 Alexadner, p. 31.
44 Alexander, p. 30-1.
45 Dobson & Taylor, p. 56; Knight, *Complete,* p. 182.
46 Dobson & Taylor, p. 57; Knight, *Complete,* p. 182.
47 Knight, *Mythic,* p. 121.
48 Knight, *Mythic,* p. 119.
49 Knight, *Mythic,* p. 143.
50 Knight, *Complete,* p. 159.
51 Dobson & Taylor, pp. 198-99.
52 Knight, *Complete, p.* 168.
53 Knight, *Complete,* p. 186.
54 Knight, *Mythic,* p. 148.
55 Knight, *Mythic,* p. 132. Percy's real name was John Cundall.
56 Knight, *Mythic,* p. 133.
57 Dobson & Taylor, pp. 243-49; Tennyson, *Foresters..*
58 Knight, *Mythic,* p. 137.
59 Tennyson, p. 90.
60 Tennyson, pp. 76-7.
61 Knight, *Complete,* p. 198.
62 Tennyson, pp. 11-2.
63 Tennyson, pp. 47,91.
64 Tennyson, p. 32.
65 Tennyson, p. 154.
66 Cheesman & Rieuwerts, p. 14, and Dianne Dugaw, 'The Politics of Culture: John Gay and Popular Ballads', pp. 189-98 in Cheesman & Rieuwerts.
67 Dobson & Taylor, p. 45.
68 Knight, *Mythic,* p. 90.
69 Knight, *Complete,* p. 148.
70 Knight, *Complete,* p. 150; Linda V. Troost, 'Robin Hood Musicals in 18th-century London', in Hahn, pp. 251-64, p. 252.
71 Knight, *Complete,* p.150.
72 Linda V. Troost, in Hahn, p. 251.
73 Knight, *Complete,* p. 152.
74 Knight, *Mythic,* p. 136.
75 Knight, *Mythic,* p. 137.
76 Knight, *Complete,* p. 192.
77 Knight, *Mythic,* p. 147.
78 Knight, *Mythic,* p. 148.
79 Bellamy, p. 3; Thierry, *Histoire de la Conquête de l'Angleterre par les Normands.*
80 Bellamy, p. 4.

[81] Bellamy, p. 6.

[82] Knight, *Complete*, p. 23.

[83] Knight, *Anthology*, pp.187-95.

[84] Knight, *Anthology*, p. 190.

[85] Knight, *Anthology*, p. 192.

[86] Knight, *Mythic*, p. 145; Knight, *Anthology*, p. 194.

[87] Hales & Furnivall; see also Peter Faulkner, 'The Paths of Virtue and Erly
English', pp. 144-58 in Simons.

[88] Faulkner in Simons, p. 157.

[89] Hales & Furnivall, i, p. 7.

3

Stuart Ballads

Printing the Robin Hood Ballads

The bulk of our early material on Robin Hood comes in the form of ballads that were printed in the Stuart period. They provide the plots and characters that have dominated Robin Hood stories ever since. They do, however, also have some significant differences from modern versions of the story and that is what we intend to examine in this chapter. It must be remembered also that the ballads in this period themselves differed from the very earliest work on Robin — they added material to the original just as, in modern times, more has been added to the Stuart version. We therefore need to see both transitions.

Some of the ballads of this period were taken from old manuscripts and printed, some were altered and others were invented. However, it is clear that they continued an old tradition in terms of the basic stories about our hero. It is as well to remember that the earliest printed works were themselves published in fairly small numbers and, therefore, only seen by a limited number of readers. It has been fairly said that these early printings had 'the status of a curious de luxe manuscript'.[1]

The ballad printings came in two main forms. The first was as a broadside, that is, usually a single printed sheet. In this form, the work had perforce to be brief and it is clear that some old ballads were deliberately curtailed in order to be used. Nevertheless, it was a relatively cheap form, produced in numbers, and so played a large part in increasing the popularity of the Robin Hood works. The second main form for printed ballads was the chapbook. This was a small booklet of perhaps twenty-four pages, which were bound together. It might contain others things but ballads proved to be a popular subject for these little books. Sometimes, for chapbooks, ballads with a common theme were collected, such as those about Robin Hood. The other possibility with the chapbooks, as against the broadside, was the printing of one longer work. There was also less need to abbreviate the old works that were sometimes now published.

The Ballad Form and its Significance

It was during the Tudor and Stuart period that the bulk of the material that went to forming the legend of Robin Hood appeared. These were the ballads. Some further material, as we shall see later, came from plays. Probably through the accident of survival, the surviving dramatic publications by and large predate the earliest surviving printed ballads. There are surviving printed plays from the sixteenth century, while the early printed ballads come only from the seventeenth century. The plays did fill out the 'biography' of our hero — their nature ensured that. However, it is not clear that the earliest material about the hero's life came in dramatic form. The fact that play texts survive from an earlier period than printed ballads seems to be simply a case of accident. Some of the performed material, in the May games and local celebrations, was undoubtedly early, but it was also insubstantial in content. We may never know for certain which came first, the play-games or the ballads, though the latter have generally been favoured by scholars. The printed play texts come from the sixteenth century onwards. The printed ballad texts come from the seventeenth century onwards. Only a very few earlier pre-printing texts survive in manuscript.

A very few surviving examples of poetic works on Robin Hood were or may have been medieval. We shall save close examination of these early poems to a later chapter. Nothing at all survives that can be shown to be earlier than c. 1450. There are less than a dozen references to Robin Hood of any sort before 1450.[2] The vast majority of literature on Robin Hood was first collected or printed in the period after 1485 when Henry VII, the first Tudor, came to the throne. A few of these items were plays, but in the seventeenth century the vast majority of these were ballads. We do well to remember that the Robin Hood ballads — as we have them — were not aimed at either a medieval courtly audience or medieval local popular listeners but to readers of the Stuart age, who must have been educated, urban, and mostly comfortably off. Almost certainly, their origin had been in quite short works that would be memorised for oral use — primarily either for reciting or for singing. The printed versions came after written versions and written version came after — often long after — the original oral compositions. The distance between the versions is at best difficult to gauge, at worst impossible.

Let us emphasise the point: no surviving Robin Hood ballads were printed before the seventeenth century. The printed ballads may well — and probably do — reflect an earlier existence but the degree to which they repeat it precisely is impossible now to determine. The ballad evidence used in this chapter is the main evidence about Robin Hood in literature and it is from the seventeenth century. On the whole, historians have concentrated on the earliest surviving works because they are seeking to find the origins of Robin Hood — as indeed are we. However, as a result, the major material of the seventeenth century has been relatively overlooked — and yet it is this material that has chiefly formed the picture of the outlaw as we now know it. If we ever do find the original Robin Hood, he will certainly not be Robin Hood as we know him in the twenty-first century. The seventeenth-century ballad material is a vital stage in the forming of the Robin Hood legend.

There were earlier medieval origins of the seventeenth-century ballads. However, for the most part these are now lost, and we have no way of ascertaining the changes and alterations made in most cases. We must look at the evidence as we find it, not as we should like it to be. What this reminds us is that so much of how we now see Robin Hood depends upon additions made over the centuries to an earlier and sparser story. Much of what we see as the Robin Hood story is from the later trappings. There was a medieval version of Robin Hood, a considerably embroidered Tudor and Stuart version, a further embroidered eighteenth- and nineteenth-century version, and then the modern one, which is largely dependent on the inventions of film and TV. Undoubtedly, much of what was accepted as the Robin Hood story is a romanticised version — the good outlaw, the friend of women, robber of the rich to help the poor. Probably we should add the longbow to this list — the weapon romanticised by later ages for our earlier great victories over the French. It will, in due course, be interesting to see how much of this appeared in the earliest works and what has been added later.

The ballad as a verse form is thought to derive from the Italian *ballata*, 'a song, which is sung during a dance'.[3] That, in turn, may be derived from the Roman *ballistea*. The ballad is not a set form as, say, the sonnet. Indeed, there is argument even over whether the ballad must be simply a poem or whether it may be the lyrics for a song. Attempts to define the ballad form include the following. Should it have a traditional structure? Must it have the use of the vernacular? Should there be a necessary base of a simple plot that dominates the whole of a narrative song?[4]

We do not need to become too closely involved in such arguments. For our present purposes, we intend to examine those short works in verse that were either written down in manuscripts or printed in the period after 1485. These, for us, fulfil the description of 'ballads'. The most helpful works for us are those of deliberately collected works about Robin Hood — though, of course, ballads were on a great variety of subjects of which Robin Hood was simply one. Certainly, in many cases, there was a musical form attached to the ballad and sometimes we know the intended tune, though generally only the words survive.

There is also some argument about the social use of the ballads. Were they intended for a literate audience, perhaps courtly, or were they for the ordinary folk, to hear rather than to read? The fact that they were printed in early chapbooks does suggest a literate interest, but the alternative choice of form as a broadside suggests a more popular target. The fact that we so rarely know the author suggests an oral history for most of the ballads, during which authorship has been forgotten. Probably the ballads have also been tinkered with over generations. This is one very important reason why the search for an historical Robin Hood is so difficult — the evidence is rarely in its original form and is not entirely reliable as history for the beginnings of our story.

One suggestion is that the ballad was a particular kind of work deriving from traditional songs.[5] The ballad would then be the result of combining the metrical romances of the later Middle Ages with English folksong.[6] This would see the ballad deriving from medieval minstrels but taking its recognisable form in the fifteenth and sixteenth centuries. One should, however, note that some of the earliest ballads, though printed later, have a fourteenth-century background in terms and situations, which suggests that period for their origin.

Ballads were short pieces of verse, sometimes with a repeated refrain. Although the refrain was far from universal in ballads, it is a sign that at least some of them came from a folksong tradition since the refrain is almost certain evidence that those were words for singing.[7] It is interesting that one of the very earliest popular ballads found in a fifteenth-century manuscript was about a 'Robin' in *Robyn and Gandeleyn* who, though not Robin Hood, also 'lyth in grene wode bowndyn'.[8] It is often argued that some of the earliest Robin Hood works were not ballads since they were recited rather than sung.[9] Nevertheless, most Robin Hood works from the Stuart period, which we are at present considering, were in ballad form.

The ballad was generally based on telling a story. It was a short poem or lyric, sometimes with repeated lines or with a refrain. In the eighteenth century, Thomas Percy had noted the large proportion of the old minstrel works that were from the north and in 'the northern dialect'.[10] Most commonly, the subject matter dealt with the area of the Anglo-Scottish border, which may be a result of chance survival or of regional interest in the form. Thus, early ballad survivals include works on the battles of Otterburn and Flodden and on the hunting of the Cheviot. The border was an area of much disorder and both private and national conflict, which is often reflected in these border ballads.

Ballad Collections

The modern popularity of the ballad and its revival began with the medievalism of the eighteenth and nineteenth centuries, which we previously considered. A by-product of that movement was the collection and publication of old ballads. In the previous chapter, we considered the major collections made during the eighteenth and nineteenth centuries. This was the period when the Robin Hood ballads were drawn together. We have now moved back into the seventeenth century and are getting closer to the earliest works. We shall not need to repeat the examination of the later collections but we must be clear that what they were finding were chiefly works from even earlier collections, from hand-written manuscripts and printed works in chapbooks and broadsides. It is clear that the later collectors chiefly depended upon their earlier counterparts. We now need to look at the condition of such works in the Stuart period and also to note the collections that were made in that earlier period.

We recognised the significance of Thomas Percy's *Reliques*. We saw that it was based on an earlier manuscript collection that came into Percy's hands. This was the Percy Folio, which included a number of Robin Hood ballads in a hand-written manuscript. That manuscript had probably been collected in the seventeenth century and seems to have belonged to Thomas Blount, who died in 1679.

The contents of this collection continue to have significance as it includes early Robin Hood ballads. One point we did not note earlier was an interesting link to Robin Hood in a different way. We recall that the very earliest mention of Robin Hood is in *Piers Plowman*. The relevant line in the B version reads: 'But I kan rymes of Robyn hood and Randolf Erl of Chestre'.[11] It is not clear if this means separate works on Robin and Randolf or if there were rymes connecting the two. It is generally assumed there were probably separate works that were both being condemned. In the Percy Folio, we have another link between Robin and Randolf. The manuscript included, besides ballads on Robin Hood, a life of the second and third 'Randles', earls of Chester, who lived in the twelfth and thirteenth centuries. While on the point, we might notice that another work, recently discovered, the *Forresters Manuscript*, claims that Robin Hood is under the protection of 'Randolph'. The relevant verse reads: 'Randolph kept Robin fifteen winters/ Dery dery downe/ Till he was fifteen years Old'. The mysterious link between these two figures might yet reveal further information on our hero.[12]

Two other important early collections, which included Robin Hood works, were made by the great diarist Samuel Pepys (1633-1703) and in the mid-seventeenth century by Anthony Wood. To realise the importance of these collections we need only to read the modern collection by Dobson and Taylor and note how often the version used comes from a printed version collected by these two. Pepys collected chapbooks and broadsides that included some Robin Hood ballads. Wood also collected broadsides including Robin Hood works. One important item in his collection was the first full version of *The Jolly Pinder of Wakefield*. *Robin Hood's Progress to Nottingham, The Noble Fisherman, or. Robin Hoods great Prize* and *Robin Hood and Maid Marian* are also found in their earliest versions in Wood's collection.

Most of our information on Robin Hood comes from the poems about him. It is known that Robin Hood ballads were printed in the sixteenth century, but they do not survive. The Stationers' Register recorded two possible Robin Hood works before 1600. The first was the 'ballett of Wakefylde and a grene' from 1557-58, which is thought to be a version of the Pinder of Wakefield.[13] The second was the 'ballett of Robyn Hod' from 1562-63. It has been suggested this might be the *Gest* but, as it does not survive, identification from such a broad title is impossible. Our point, in any case, is that although no sixteenth-century Robin Hood ballads survive there is no doubt that they existed. In 1575, we also know that one Captain Cox possessed 'stories' which included some on Robin Hood but, again, we do not know what they were.

The main sources for our seventeenth-century Robin Hood ballads are three in number. The first two are the collections printed as garlands in 1663 and 1670. The garland was simply a collection of related ballads, in this case all about Robin Hood, printed in one little book. A garland usually contained at least a dozen ballads. The third main source is a more recent discovery, the Forresters

Manuscript. We shall quote from these three sources by using modern editions: firstly, where they are included in it, the edition by Dobson and Taylor; secondly for those not in Dobson and Taylor, the Sargent and Kittredge edition of Child's collection; and thirdly the recent edition by Stephen Knight of the Forresters Manuscript.

As so often in history, we think we know all there is to know and that our conclusions are fixed, and then along comes a new piece of evidence to alter the composition of the stew. A major find was made in 1993 of a manuscript that has been dated to the early 1670s.[14] It came to light through a West Country bookseller. It is now known as the Forresters Manuscript, British Library Additional manuscript, BL Add MS 71158.

The collection of ballads in the Forresters Manuscript was written into a book purchased from a stationer and in two hands, one probably that of the collector, the other of a professional scribe.[15] Only a few of the ballads in it were taken more or less directly from known seventeenth-century garlands. Five of the ballads here do not appear at all in the two main seventeenth-century garlands of 1663 and 1670, and most others have some interesting variations. In other words, these are versions previously unknown. The manuscript of 102 leaves contained twenty different Robin Hood ballads and two versions of the Pinder. Two of these ballads were considered better versions than those known, being *Robin Hoods Fishing* and *Robin Hood and Queen Catherin*.[16] Others have significant differences from previously known versions including *The Old Wife, The Butcher, The Pinder (1), The Bride, The Sheriffe* and *The King*.

The Forresters Manuscript was probably made with the intention of using the material to print a new garland that never actually came into being. It probably took much of its material from manuscript ballads rather than from printed broadsides. The better texts contained in it are too long to have been printed in broadsides. It is probable that the unknown collector of this manuscript, called the 'supervisor' by its editor, intended to print a new garland that would be better than that published in 1663 — which indeed it would have been.[17] He was 'serious, scholarly and creative in both compiling and redacting the Robin Hood tradition'.[18] It is just possible that the initials 'W. F.' on the cover were those of the collector.

It is probable that the appearance of the 1670 garland in print was enough to discourage yet another Robin Hood publication and the idea of using the Forresters collection was then dropped and the manuscript left to be forgotten for three centuries, though, in the view of the modern editor, if printed this 'would have been the best of the garlands'.[19]

The seventeenth century saw the printing of many Robin Hood poems. The oldest known broadside ballad (not about Robin) was printed in *c.* 1513.[20] Some poems were published as broadsides, that is, single sheets containing a short work. This was the main form of publication for the early Robin Hood ballads. The form itself, the cheapest form of printed work, suggests a popular readership. Oliver Cromwell's acquisition of power and the imposition of Puritan ideas resulted in the banning of ballad singing and hence of related publications.[21] In 1656, fiddlers or minstrels, who performed in alehouses, inns and taverns, or even offered to do so, were to be treated as 'rogues, vagabonds, and sturdy beggars'.[22] Therefore the period of publication of early Robin Hood ballads was of a restricted time. In fact, the broadside was in decline as a popular form of printed matter already before the ban.

The following period saw the publication of many little books of collected poems in the form of garlands, also known as 'penny-merriments'.[23] The first Robin Hood garland to survive appeared in 1663.[24] It included seventeen poems. These garlands were especially popular in the eighteenth century when the Robin Hood collection had increased to include twenty-seven poems. The other major seventeenth-century Robin Hood garland is that of 1670. The garlands were usually composed by collecting individual works from broadsides. Sometimes, however, the garland version of a ballad survives where a broadside one does not.

We have seen already that these early broadsides and garlands, together with a few manuscripts, were used in the eighteenth and nineteenth centuries for new collections and publications. A problem with virtually all early printed versions of the ballads is the 'editing' that often then occurred. It often involved altering spellings and, even more dangerously, the text for 'improvements'. Hence, we find that a single Robin Hood ballad might well exist in several early forms, none of which is definitive. Modern editing seeks to avoid the 'improvement' policy of earlier editors, but resolving differences is often difficult. Where available, we shall rely on the printed version in Dobson and Taylor as a modern and reliable source — accepting that variations exist, especially when more than one early version of the ballad survives.

The Robin Hood Ballads

The nature of the Robin Hood ballads is worth thinking about for a moment. Not many modern anthologies of old poetry include the Robin Hood ballads — if they are seeking only a selection of best poems. Critics do not place them on the same level as say Langland or Chaucer. We must admit that in general the Robin Hood poems are not great literature, they did not seek to be that. If you read the Robin Hood ballads, what you are struck by is not the beauty of the language and the brilliant use of similes or adjectives or phrases. Your interest is held rather by the stories, and this is their point — to tell a good tale, often humorously. Like all good stories, they move along at speed and keep focused on the plot.

We need to examine the Robin Hood ballads in a general way before looking into their details and significance. Dobson and Taylor reckoned there were thirty-eight traditional ballads, of which they selected fourteen to include in their *Rymes of Robyn Hood*.[25] They list these thirty-eight works with their eighteen variant titles in a useful appendix.[26] Three of these ballads are thought to be early in origin and possibly medieval, that is, *Robin Hood and the Monk*, *Robin Hood and*

Guy of Gisborne and *Robin Hood and the Potter*. We shall accept this dating for now and look at those three works in the following chapter on the Middle Ages. Otherwise, here in these ballads lies the bulk of our interest for the present, the thirty-five poems about Robin Hood with their variant versions that appeared in the seventeenth century or later.

There may be some argument over the exact total number of the different ballads but we shall make a start with this collection. We shall attempt to analyse these works in a series of different ways, looking at their chronology together with the information they provide on the life of Robin Hood, the make-up of Robin's outlaw band, the gallery of villains or enemies of Robin, the main plots and themes, and any unusual elements to be detected.

The Chronology of the Robin Hood Ballads

It is this ballad material, dating primarily from the seventeenth century, from which the bulk of evidence on early Robin Hood comes, that we mean to look at now. There is some discussion over the poetic form of this work. We have chosen, for the present, to call them all ballads, though some would dispute this label for some of the works. In essence, we are looking at short poems in rhyming verse. These were sometimes collected together to make up little books, usually on a related subject. Others survived as individual works. Quite often, they were oral works recollected in memory and only printed sometime after their beginnings. Usually, we do not know when that beginning was, even to the century, and hence our difficulty in knowing which works were genuinely medieval in origin. These orally memorised verses are obviously in general the most important for historical evidence. Other works may be seen as either Tudor or Stuart rewriting of older works or newly written poems. In only a few cases do we know the name of the author of the works under consideration.

Among the most popular ballads of the fifteenth and sixteenth centuries were the rhymes of Robin Hood.[27] The 'rymes', mentioned by Langland in the fourteenth century, may not have been songs or ballads. None survive from that period, so we cannot be sure of the nature of those rhymes. They may have been close in form to those of the following two centuries. It is also possible that he meant verse used as commentary for May-game presentations. This latter possibility is enhanced by Langland's criticism, in moral and religious terms, of popular taste. There is a strong similarity between Langland's disdainful comment and the later remarks against Robin Hood made by various churchmen, such as Latimer. It does, however, give a clue to the nature of those 'rymes' — they were of a nature to upset churchmen and they were seen as popular.

It is virtually impossible to know for certain the nature of the earliest works. Given the history of medieval verse and of early ballads, it seems most likely that the earliest Robin Hood works were recited rather than sung. The work on the monk is called a 'talkyng'. One can quote such lines as 'now speke we of Roben

Hode' or the much repeated 'lythe and lysten' — all indicative of spoken rather than sung words.[28] What we do know is that the early works were popular. The popularity was obviously important since it led to the subject being chosen for many early sung ballads, multiplying the information on our hero: 'yf thou might have a song that is good,/ I have one of Robyn Hode'.[29]

When a work's author is known it is clearly useful in being able to date the work and know its origin. We do know the authorship of a few Robin Hood works, albeit mostly fairly late in time. Laurence Price wrote both *The Famous Flowr* and *Robin Hood's Golden Prize*, while Martin Parker produced *A True Tale of Robin Hood*.

The Main Plots and Themes in the Ballads

The Robin Hood ballads are not generally seen as great literature. The characters are not filled out. There are often obvious heroes, such as Robin, and villains, such as the sheriff, but we are given little personal information even about them. The poetry is sometimes good but rarely great — more like the lyrics of modern popular songs than the work of say T. S. Eliot or Seamus Heaney. The main attraction of the Robin Hood ballads is usually a fast-moving action plot, often with touches of humour — hence the later appeal for cinema and TV. The plots are frequently repetitive, such as forcing someone to dine and pay for their meal, or a match between two men — a familiar story given a different twist or different characters to perform it. Because the plots tend to be repetitive, we shall take the main themes and just look at one or two examples of each.

A) COME AND DINE

Robin Hood and the Bishop

One of the common plots in the ballads is that an outlaw, usually Robin, invites an individual, often by force, to come and dine with the band — and then they have to pay for the privilege. It is a way of presenting highway robbery and theft as a kind of pleasant joke. Often the victim is a churchman, shown little favour in the ballads. Such is the story of *Robin Hood and the Bishop of Hereford*, which is virtually the same ballad as *Robin Hood and the Bishopp* in the Forresters Manuscript.[30] The Forresters version is older than any printed version, the first of those being only as late as 1754, in a garland.

There may be some readers who have not yet tackled the original ballads; this is understandable. They are easily enough available to students and scholars but mainly in scholarly editions. They are in a somewhat archaic English, though a little effort soon overcomes this and modern editions usually explain the more difficult words and phrases. We cannot, in a book of this nature, give the poems in their entirely, but we hope the reader will be drawn to them. We can, however, just give a quick taste. Here is the opening of *Robin Hood and the Bishopp*.

> Som will talke of Lords and Knights
> And som of Barrons Bold
> But ile tell you how Robin Hood sarud [served] the Bishop
> When he Robd him of his gold.
>
> Robin he walked in merry Barnsdale
> Al in a morning of May
> News came to him the Bishop of Heriford
> Came rideing a long that way.[31]

In the ballad then, Robin walked 'in merry Barnsdale' and saw the bishop of Hereford riding along. Robin tells Little John to slay a deer on which the bishop shall dine and for which he shall pay. Little John suggests that six outlaws, together with himself and Robin, should dress up as shepherds. This group is then found celebrating over a deer they are about to eat. The bishop is invited to dine but prepares instead to arrest the men for killing the deer. He plans to take them to the king since they have killed 'King Richards game'. Robin calls the bishop hardhearted and blows his horn, with the result that fifty archers appear. Robin says 'the King hath made an oute Law of mee/ For killing his dear'. The bishop is forced to dine and pay with £300 of gold they find in his baggage. Robin also makes him sing a Mass and dance with him to music as he holds his hand.

B) Match and Disguise

One of the major plots in the ballads is that of a match, usually between Robin Hood and a rival. This story may take many forms but only rarely does Robin Hood win. The most common outcome is that, after a Titanic struggle, Robin either yields or halts the fight. Impressed by the ability and valour of his opponent, Robin usually then invites him to join the outlaw band. Sometimes, the match ballads have a match followed by Robin taking on the clothes and occupation of his opponent.

The Jolly Pinder of Wakefield

The Jolly Pinder of Wakefield is one of the best-known match ballads.[32] A pinder was a manor official who was responsible for impounding stray animals. The pinder story was used in Robert Greene's play of 1592, George a Greene, who is a pinder. The ballad of the pinder appears in the Percy Folio, as well as in a seventeenth-century broadside and in two versions in the Forresters Manuscript. The first example in the latter (Pinder 1), is a fuller version, since all of the early part of the ballad is lost from the Percy Folio, while the broadsides are shortened versions for single sheet printing. It may be, however, that the Forresters version is a late rewriting by its supervisor.[33] This must remain an open question.

There is no certainty as to how the pinder George a Green entered the Robin Hood tales — whether originally in an early ballad, adopted from a separate tradition of his own ballads or through Robert Greene's drama. A pinder ballad with George in it was almost certainly in existence in the mid-sixteenth century since the Stationers' Register for 1557-58 lists 'A ballet of Wakefylde and a grene'.[34] George a Green had appeared in an Elizabethan play about the pinder or pinner by Robert Greene. George may have originated as a character in May games at Wakefield itself.[35]

In the broadside, the pinder tells Robin and his two friends that they are trespassing and must turn back. They refuse and fight all day until Robin calls a halt. In the Forresters Manuscript, the pinder has a 'batt' on his back, that is, some form of club. Robin fights against him with a sword from eight in the morning until sunset. This then is an example of the 'match' plot. The pinder fights so well that Robin invites him to the greenwood. Again, as a brief taster, we quote a little from the surviving part of the Percy Folio version.

> But wilt be my man?' said good Robin,
> And come and dwell with me?
> And twise in a yeere thy clothing be changed
> If my man thou wilt bee.[36]

In the Forresters Manuscript version, the pinder, when invited to join the band, says he will think about it and come to 'barnes dale' if he agrees. They then repair to the pinder's house where his wife, Genney, provides the means of celebration.

The second Forresters version (Pinder 2) is more like the broadside version though of relatively 'high quality'.[37] When Robin and his two friends are trespassing across a cornfield they meet the pinder. He tells them 'turne againe turne againe', which sounds rather like Dick Whittington. He leaps back 30 feet and they fight all day until Robin invites him to join the band. His answer is that he will after Michaelmas, once he has collected his fee for his work.

Other ballads that might be compared to that of the pinder are those where Robin has a match with a shepherd and a beggar. We will not detail every single ballad, as there is much repetition in terms of the plot. One notes from these variations that the different versions of the various Robin Hood ballads are often much more than simply copies with the odd difference. They speak strongly of oral works that have survived in different forms and then been written down, probably with further changes. Always, it is the basic plot that holds the clue to their origin. The story comes first.

Robin Hood and Urban Tradesmen

There are a whole series of ballads about Robin having a match with an urban tradesman, be it potter, tinker or tanner. The potter ballad is one of the earliest and we shall look at that in a future chapter. Again, we shall not detail each of these ballads but take one as an example, in this case that of the butcher.

Robin Hood and the Butcher is a variant on the match plot, but this time the dominant theme is that of borrowing a disguise.[38] This ballad appears in the Percy Folio, in a broadside and in the Forresters Manuscript. There are some interesting differences between the versions. The Percy Folio ballad is, inevitably, fuller than the broadside, and the original has obviously been abbreviated when printed in broadside format.

In the forest, Robin meets the butcher on his way to market. The butcher's dog flies at Robin's face and Robin kills it with his sword. The butcher is angry and takes up his staff. They then fight. A section is missing in the Percy Folio. Clearly, however, the butcher impresses Robin in the fight and our hero then offers him something in exchange for his cart and meat. We then find Robin pretending to be a butcher and speaking to the sheriff's wife.

> 'I am a younge bucher', sayes Robin,
> You fine dames am I come amonge;
> But ever I beseech you, good Mrs Sheriffe,
> You must see me take noe wronge.[39]

Robin sells off the butcher's meat at a very cheap price and sells out. There is another gap in the Folio. Robin leads the sheriff into the forest where he claims the animals are his. He blows his horn and fifty archers appear. There is another gap. The sheriff goes home and his wife suggests he has learned a good lesson. Unlike many later versions, the sheriff here is a sensible man and neither violent nor vindictive. He agrees with his wife 'I have learned of thee' and says Robin 'shall never be sought for me'.[40]

The later broadside version of the butcher ballad, though shorter, fills in the gaps of the plot. There is no violent killing of the dog. Robin buys the meat and goes to Nottingham as a butcher. Robin and the local butchers dine with the sheriff. Robin says he has animals he can sell to the sheriff and leads him to the forest. Robin tells Little John he has brought the sheriff to dine, for which the latter has to pay with the gold he has brought. We have here then, as quite often, a combination of the 'dine' and the 'match' plots.

There is also a version of 'the Butcher' in the Forresters Manuscript, which is interesting, because it does not have the gaps of the Percy Folio and is longer than the broadsides. In this version, Robin kills the butcher's dog, without provocation and in a brutal manner. Robin fights with a sword against the butcher, who has only a staff, which seems somewhat unfair. Again, this theme is fairly common, perhaps the point being to show what a good fighter the opponent is.

There are several other match plots setting Robin against urban tradesmen. It seems likely that one well-known plot was employed to please or interest that trade. One may suggest a ballad performed at some gild function. The minstrel might use a well-known plot but alter the trade of the opponent concerned. On occasion, gilds probably financed the printed versions. It is worth noting that, although the trade of the opponent might alter from ballad to ballad, the town concerned is always Nottingham. This suggests that the plot was already well known and Robin's association with Nottingham was too strongly recognised to alter. It is, for example, on the way to Nottingham that Robin meets his match in *Robin Hood and the Tinker*.[41] Yet another urban tradesman opponent was the tanner. There are several versions of *Robin Hood and the Tanner* from the seventeenth century, all very similar. It appeared in a broadside in 1643, in the garland of 1670, as well as in the Forresters Manuscript.[42] In the Child version of the ballad, the tanner is from Nottingham and is called Arthur a Bland. He meets Robin in Sherwood Forest. Robin, tongue in cheek, introduces himself as a forester and accuses Arthur of stealing the king's deer. Arthur answers bluntly:

> For they sword and thy bow I care not a straw,
> Nor all thine arrows to boot;
> If I get a knop upon they bare scop
> Thou canst as well shite as shoote.

Robin primly tells him to 'speak cleanly'. They fight until Robin calls a halt. Arthur proves to be a relation of Little John and joins the outlaw band.

Famous Matches

Nowadays, it is a familiar plot to have Robin fight with an opponent who then becomes a well-known member of his band. The ballad we have just considered, which is about Arthur a Bland, is one such poem, but Arthur is rather less well known than the two figures we now consider. Interestingly, the match ballads about them are both quite late. *Robin Hood and Little John* is probably a late ballad but it has certainly joined the canon of well-known plots.[43] It is another of the match plots. The first reference to it was made in 1624. It was sung to the tune of *Arthur a Bland,* sometimes called *Hey down, down a down,* and the rhythm has an almost modern air with the double rhyme in the fourth line.

We follow the chapbook version used by Dobson and Taylor. This ballad claims that Robin was twenty when they met. John is described:

> Tho' he was call'd Little, his limbs they were large,
> And his stature was seven foot high;
> Where ever he came, they quak'd at his name,
> For soon he would make them to fly...
>
> They happen'd to meet on a long narrow bridge,
> And neither of them would give way. [44]

Robin then draws his bow but when John, who has only a staff, accuses him of being a coward he agrees to fight with staves. It is a mighty struggle. Finally, John hits Robin on the head and then knocks him in the brook. Robin then acknowledges that John is brave and calls up his band, including Will Stuteley. They offer to duck John but Robin forbids them. Robin then invites John to join the band, which he does. He introduces himself as John Little and it is Will Stuteley who suggests they alter it:

The words we'll transpose, so wherever he goes,
His name shall be call'd Little John.[45]

The match between John and Robin is the one that has been most used in modern times, except perhaps for that between Robin and Friar Tuck.

Our other major outlaw figure is Friar Tuck. In this case, earlier ballads about an unnamed cleric seem to have been adapted to introduce Tuck with a match story. One of the most famous match plots is the first meeting of Robin Hood and the friar.[46] Its earliest appearance is in the Percy Folio. There is also a seventeenth-century broadside version printed in Dobson and Taylor and, in fact, quite a few other seventeenth-century examples including garland collections. There is another version in the Forresters Manuscript.[47]

The story was clearly known before the period of the surviving copies as it was used in Elizabethan drama and no doubt existed even before that. Oddly, by the 17th, the friar is from Fountains Abbey, which was in fact a Cistercian monastery, housing monks and not friars. There must be a suspicion that the original character was a monk. One suspects that, as so often happens, an early plot has been altered over time. One should also note that the friar in the earliest version, the Percy Folio, is not named, though the poem was later given the label of *Robine Hood and Ffryer Tucke*. We may take it that originally the character was not called Friar Tuck or given any name except that of a friar.

In the Percy Folio version of the friar ballad, we set off in 'the merry month of May'. Once more, in this manuscript there is a considerable section missing. Robin declares he must see 'that cutted friar'. We have discussed 'cutted' and 'curtail' already and noted that it probably refers either to his hair or his habit. Robin goes to Fountains Abbey and meets the friar. He asks to be carried over the water. In this account, the friar seems to see it as a good deed and takes Robin on his back. But then the friar draws a sword and demands that Robin carry him back, which he does. Robin, in turn, then forces the friar to take him back again:

Then Robin Hood wett his fayre greene hoze,
A span above his knee;
Says, 'Beare me ore againe, thou cutted f[riar].'[48]

Here follows the next unfortunate gap. Robin's men then come at the call of his horn and the friar asks, in return, to be allowed to whistle, which he does. Fifty savage dogs respond and the friar prepares a fight between each outlaw and a dog and between himself and Robin. Robin, however, now suggests a halt, to which the friar agrees. The end is missing.

The seventeenth-century broadside version fills some of the gaps. Will Scadlock refers to the 'curtal friar in Fountains Abby' — again not naming him. Robin and the friar meet and, after the crossings, the friar throws Robin in the water. The outlaws and the dogs are called. Little John suggests the compromise. The friar is invited to join the band. In the broadside version, John kills ten of the dogs with his bow before a halt is called. This is more similar to the Forresters version than that in the Percy Folio. In Forresters, he is called a 'cortial' or 'cortiall' friar — clearly the same as curtal.[49] Again, he is not named and comes from Fountains Abbey. As in the broadside, Little John shoots ten dogs before peace is made. One constantly notes that earlier versions tend to contain more brutal violence against both men and beasts.

It seems most likely that the match with the friar began as a match with a monk who joined the outlaws. Later, when Friar Tuck became a popular figure in the legend, probably originally through the play-games, he was given the part in this plot. The match over the water with Friar Tuck has now become one of the most familiar of all Robin Hood stories.

C) Disguise Plots

There are almost as many ballads that use a theme of disguise as those of a match. Several ballads, as we have seen, use both match and disguise — after the match with an opponent Robin exchanges clothes and then pretends to be the potter or butcher or whoever. Usually, the disguise plots have Robin dressing up as someone else to fool the sheriff.

Robin Hood and the Butcher

Robin's most common disguise is that of an urban tradesman selling goods that can be taken to Nottingham. *Robin Hood and the Butcher* is one such ballad. As we have seen in the Forresters version, after the fight Robin buys the butcher's meat and goes in disguise as a butcher to Nottingham. Robin, disguised as the butcher, sells off his meat five times more cheaply that the other traders. After accompanying the sheriff to the forest and taking his cash, Robin sends him home with just 2s from his £500. The ballad ends when the sheriff's wife says she will give her husband money to make up for his losses and he says Robin then will be welcome 'whether hee cum to thee or to mee'.

Robin Hood's Fishing

This is a ballad that seems separate from the other in its setting — both of town and activity — and is a kind of one-off plot of 'Robin goes to sea'. In different versions, we are taken to Whitby or Scarborough. The ballad also introduces a foreign element with a French ship as the enemy — the only main ballad with this background. The same plot appears under several ballad titles, including *The Noble Fisherman, or Robin Hood's Preferment*. It appears in the *Forresters Manuscript* as *Robin Hood's Fishing* and is where he pretends to be a fisherman called Symon of the Lee — rather a watered down version of the disguise plot![50] This latter is the fuller form of the ballad. In it Robin goes to Scarborough where he stays in a widow's house near the sea. She owns a ship and he promises to serve her for three years. The men fish with line and bait but do not catch much; Robin wishes he were back in Plumpton Park. Then, a French warship approaches. Robin

boasts that he could settle it with his 'bent bow'. The Master is scornful but Robin
has himself tied to the mast and with two shots hits the French steersman and then
his replacement. They board and capture the ship where they discover £1,200 in
gold. Robin keeps half for himself and his men, and gives half to the widow. He
promises to build a chapel with his money, 'and it shall stand on Whitby strand'
with a priest to say mass. Whether this comes from the writer knowing the name
of Robin Hood's Bay or is a real explanation who can say? The priest and the
mass suggest a pre-Reformation origin. It does remind us that elsewhere Robin
was said to have founded a chapel in Barnsdale.

The Golden Prize and the Priests

In *Robin Hood's Golden Prize*, Robin puts on another unusual disguise as a
friar. The golden prize ballad is seen as a variant of the forresters ballad, *Robin
Hood and the Preists*. There are some signs of antiquity in this latter version, in
the rhyme, the language and perhaps in the anti-clerical attitude. However, others
have seen it as a seventeenth-century creation.[51] In the priests version, Robin
dresses as a friar who fights against two monks. They deny they have money but
Robin searches them and finds gold. He gives them some but keeps the rest. In a
not-very veiled way of criticising the behaviour of those in orders, he makes them
swear not to lie again, not to tempt maids, not to go with other men's wives and
to aid the poor.

D) Cross-dressing Plots

Robin Hood and the Old Wife

In the various ballads, Robin sometimes takes on most unlikely disguises, including
some as women. There is a clearly comic element in this approach. It is not too
surprising that, in more modern times, Robin Hood has been a popular subject
for pantomimes. In the Forresters ballad, *Robin Hood and the Old Wife,* which is
a version of *Robin Hood and the Bishop,* Robin dresses as an old woman.[52] The
story begins with a line reminiscent of the modern saying 'between a rock and a
hard place' with 'Betwixt a Cragg and a stony Rock'. Robin falls asleep and wakes
to find the sheriff and his men riding towards him. Robin runs to the house of an
old woman whom he has previously helped with money for clothes and shoes.
She changes clothes with him. She dresses as Robin and holds his bow. Incredibly,
the sheriff is fooled and carts her off to King Henry (unnumbered). Robin Hood
escapes still dressed as an old woman. His men eventually recognise him because
of his beard! The old woman finally convinces the sheriff she is not Robin but a
woman by telling him to 'lift vp my legg and see'. Later, Robin returns her clothes
and gives her £20.

Robin Hood and Maid Marian

The cross-dressing leads to some pretty incredible plots. Another such, *Robin
Hood and Maid Marian,* was printed in a broadside. In it Robin is the earl of

Huntington. He then disguises himself as the outlaw Robin Hood and goes to see Marian, who falls in love with him. Marian is described as more beautiful than Jane Shore. Jane was the mistress of Edward IV, thus placing this ballad in an unusually late period. It might be a clue to its date of origin. Marian then, for some odd reason, dresses as a page boy to go and seek out 'Robin Hood'. When they meet as 'Robin Hood' and a page boy they do not recognise each other and, in fact, fight — so this becomes another rather odd variation on the match plot as well. They fight with swords for over an hour, during which both are wounded. Robin finally calls a halt and suggests the page boy join the outlaw band. Marian, at last, recognises Robin by his voice and they kiss. They live together in the greenwood.

E) ARCHERY COMPETITIONS

Robin Hood and the Sheriff

Robin and the outlaws participating in an archery competition, usually set up by the sheriff, has become a popular modern plot. One also finds more private archery contests between the outlaws. Unlike the match plots, in archery competitions it is usually Robin who is the victor. The archery contest is found in the seventeenth-century ballads. The story appears in variant versions, as in *Robin Hood and the Sherriffe* in the Forresters manuscript and in *Robin Hood and the Golden Arrow*.[53] Apart from the relevant story in the long medieval poem, the *Gest,* which we shall examine later, the Forresters version of the sheriff ballad is the oldest known version and would not otherwise have entered this chapter since the first printed form was only in a late garland of 1740. This reminds us that even late printings may well have much earlier origins.

We are told in the *Robin Hood and the Sherriffe* ballad that Robin has just returned to the greenwood from fishing (the previous ballad in the collection). During his absence, Little John says they have captured gold and silver plate from a servant of the sheriff. The sheriff believes Robin to be dead as he has been away so long but is now confronted by the outlaws and told that Robin is alive. The sheriff is forced to dine off his own plate and then asked to pay for the pleasure. He says 'I haue noe store of chinke' but they find £15 in his baggage. They send him home. He then goes to London to King Richard, who tells him he must capture the outlaws. The sheriff plans to trap them by holding an archery competition. The prize is an arrow with a silver shaft, gold head and feathers. One of the outlaws, David of Doncaster, warns that it will be a trap, but Robin calls him a coward. They do, however, change into clothes of varied colours, not their usual green — Robin himself in red. One hundred and forty of them turn up and between them win the prizes without being recognised. Robin wins the arrow. They get away safely, but Robin is somewhat miffed that the sheriff does not know how he has been fooled. Little John suggests they write a letter to tell him and shoot it into Nottingham attached to an arrowhead — which they do. The sheriff is suitably angry (and clearly an idiot).

The plot of *Robin Hood and Queen Catherin* is basically around an archery competition.[54] The Forresters version is reckoned to be 'one of the most important discoveries in the Forresters manuscript'.[55] It is seen as the first known version to make sense of this story since too much is omitted from broadside versions and too much lost from the Percy Folio. In Percy the king is Henry (unnumbered). He is not named in the Forresters version either but it is assumed that the queen is probably Katherine of Aragon and he is Henry VIII. We have some unusual place-names and personal names in this ballad. The deer are said to be in 'Dalum-Lee', a place found once elsewhere.

In the ballad, Queen Katherine sends a page to find Robin so that she can employ him and his outlaws in an archery competition against a team representing the king. They take on other names, and Robin becomes Loxley. Privy counsellors mentioned are Sir Richard Lee and the bishop of Hereford — so one suspects a late concoction of known names from other ballads. The outlaws win the contest, Robin splitting Tempest's shaft in three and Clifton (Little John) splitting the willow wand.

As we shall see shortly, the ballad about Robin and the foresters contains a similar archery competition.

The Biography of Robin Hood in the Ballads

The ballads did not initially set out to provide a life of Robin. They are mostly stories set within a very short time span. Any attempt at a 'biography' is, therefore, to a degree artificial. It has been tried many times over the years. The earliest poetic attempt was in the medieval work known as the *Gest* — probably compiled from separate ballads. This poem has Robin's death but is hardly written in autobiographical form. It is simply a number of separate stories stitched together. The basic plot of most ballads is not concerned with the life of Robin but with an episode. Many of these plots have a common theme. One theme is a fight or match with an individual who then joins the outlaw band. A second theme concerns the capture of an individual who is brought to a feast in the forest for which he must then pay. Other plots have an archery competition or a clash with a villain, such as the sheriff. We shall examine these repeated themes later in the chapter but will now concentrate only on elements reflecting the progress of Robin's life.

ROBIN HOOD'S BIRTH, BREEDING, VALOR AND MARRIAGE

Robin Hood's Birth, Breeding, Valor and Marriage is a pretty odd ballad in many respects.[56] It is certainly a fairly late addition and no doubt it deliberately set out to fill an obvious gap — Robin's early life — in much the same way that modern films do. We are told he was 'born and bred' in 'Locksly town, in Nottinghamshire'. He was the son of a forester. Robin's mother is named as Joan and is the niece of Sir Guy 'a Coventry knight'. She had a brother called George Gamwell of Great Gamwell Hall.[57]

ROBIN HOOD AND THE FORESTERS

Apart from that about his birth, the first biographical plot in the ballads concerns how Robin Hood became an outlaw. There are two versions of this. The first is *Robin Hood's Progress to Nottingham* and the second, from the Forresters Manuscript, is the first version of *Robin Hood and the Forresters*.[58] These two ballads have significant differences. Knight believes the Forresters ballad version dates from 'the 16th century at the latest'. In this, Robin is brought up by one Randolph, not a name found elsewhere. One's mind immediately springs to the *Piers Plowman* connection between Robin and Randolph, earl of Chester. Knight argues that the name Randolph is introduced here from knowledge of that medieval poem. There is, however, no evidence either way, and we shall keep an open mind. The ballad says Randolph looked after Robin for his first fifteen years. At this age, Robin goes to Nottingham. On the way, he meets fifteen foresters who tease him. He is heading for an archery competition set up by the king. One forester picks a fight and wrestles with Robin, and is surprised to find that the boy beats him. Robin then shows his 'birding bow', saying that he has two even better ones 'at home at Merry Loxley'. Robin boasts that he could shoot a deer that is 200 yards away. He does so. The foresters then say they will buffet him, and, to prevent this, Robin, with a somewhat over the top reaction, proceeds to shoot fourteen of them. The fifteenth does a runner but is also caught. The town of Nottingham is raised against Robin, who returns to Loxley where he and Randolph celebrate by getting drunk. In this version, therefore, the ballad does not take us on to outlawry, though it produces a pretty good cause for it.

ROBIN HOOD'S PROGRESS TO NOTTINGHAM

In *Robin Hood's Progress to Nottingham* Robin is also fifteen — suggesting at the least a common origin for the two works. The similarity of plot and of several lines in the ballads shows that these are not entirely separate works. Probably they both derive from a lost common original. In this ballad, Robin goes to Nottingham and meets fifteen foresters, this time drinking. There is to be a shooting match. Robin shows off his archery by hitting a mark and killing a hart. They tell him to go or they will beat him. Again, Robin reacts by shooting fourteen of them and then hits the last as he runs. Nottingham is raised against him; in this version, Robin flees to the greenwood.

Robin Hood's love life is obviously tied up with Maid Marian. As we have seen, she appears in the ballad of *Robin Hood and Maid Marian* from a seventeenth-century broadside.[59] Marian does appear in a few other seventeenth-century ballads, though not very frequently. One such is *Robin Hood's Golden Prize* (otherwise 'Robin Hood and the Preists') where she is Maid Marion.

Robin Hood's Birth

Less obviously and less well known, Robin also has a love relationship with one Clorinda in *Robin Hood's Birth*. This ballad is certainly out of the ordinary, dealing with Robin's early life and giving him a family. In it, Clorinda is the 'queen of the shepherds', which suggests that the origin here might be the French works about the Robin who is *not* Robin Hood. Robin and Clorinda are in love, but he has to take to the woods. Robin is impressed by her ability to shoot deer with a bow. After Robin and Little John have fought successfully against eight yeomen, she says 'put up thy sword, Bob'. They encounter men dancing a morris and singing. Sir Roger, the parson of Dubbridge, marries them. The singer of the ballad promises:

> And then I'll make ballads in Robin Hood's bower
> And sing em in merry Sherwood.[60]

Robin Hood's Death

The ballad known as *Robin Hood's Death* obviously deserves an important place in this section.[61] We shall reserve a fuller examination until later, as it deserves to be seen as one of the earlier works. The plot in general is, however, often used and appears in several garlands. Basically, Robin goes to a nunnery and is tricked by the prioress, in cahoots with an enemy of Robin's into being bled. He is so weakened that he dies.

The ballad was included in the Percy Folio as *Robin Hoode his Death*. Unfortunately, when this valuable manuscript was saved from burning this ballad was in the part already damaged. It is calculated that about half of the original version was lost.[62] There is a version of the story in the medieval poem the *Gest*, though the latter is very brief on the event. This means that all the earliest versions of the plot are incomplete. We have, thereby, lost forever, it seems, some vital material, such as why the old woman cursed Robin or what Robin's last words were. The story is also found in the Stuart period in printed garlands. These later works were also shorter than the original Percy version would have been and omit the old woman and the villain Red Roger. Nevertheless, they help to fill out what must have been the original plot.

The other major source for Robin Hood's death is the Forresters Manuscript ballad *Robin Hood and the King or Robins Death*.[63] The editor considered it a 'major ballad', 'in many ways the most interesting and most impressive of the texts in this collection'.[64] It was probably intended to be the final work in a garland that was never published. Its account of the actual death is quite brief but a little longer than that in the *Gest*. It has some connection with all the other main accounts. King Richard and his men are dressed as monks and go to Fountains Abbey and Barnsdale. Robin meets them and believes the king to be an abbot. Robin says he is loyal to the king but the 'abbot' brands Robin Hood as a traitor. Robin blows his horn and 140 men appear. Robin drinks with the king and explains his hostility to clerics. The king then reveals his identity and Robin asks pardon, which is granted. Robin is invited to court. They go on to Nottingham where the people, at first, are fearful, believing them all to be outlaws. For thirteen years they had lived in fear of Robin Hood. Then the king reveals himself to them and all is well. Robin promises to restore the plate he has stolen. They go to court and Robin is restored to the peerage. He then lives at court for three years, after which he asks to leave. He goes to Kirklees 'monastery'. In this version, the friars are responsible for killing Robin by bleeding him to death. The prioress puts up a stone epitaph, which is not detailed in the ballad.

An eighteenth-century garland about Robert, earl of Huntington, gave a version of Robin's death that fills in some of the gaps and may have come from a version of the death ballad.[65] It does not, however, include the old woman who cursed Robin for a reason still unknown or the villainous partner of the prioress called Red Roger. The one major addition is the now familiar story of Robin shooting his bow from the deathbed and saying that where the arrow lands 'There shall my grave digged be' — which is done.[66]

An Early Attempt at Biography: Martin Parker

An oddity in the Robin Hood material is a poem by a known balladeer, Martin Parker, called 'A True Tale of Robin Hood'.[67] It was first mentioned in the Stationers Register for 1632. Parker was probably born in the first year of the seventeenth century and died in 1656. He was a prolific ballad writer and tackled many subjects other than Robin Hood. He clearly knew the current ballads, including the *Gest* and some ballads now lost.

In the *True Tale*, 'Robbin Hood', otherwise Robert, is the noble 'Earle of Huntington'. Parker places the story in the time of Richard I. The abbot of St Mary's is Robin's enemy who has caused him to be an outlaw. Clerics in general are Robin's foes and often charged for dining with him. According to Parker this was justified, since monks and friars filled the country with bastards in those days. Robin aids the poor, the helpless, widows and orphans. He would do no woman wrong. The abbot of St Mary's is captured and set back to front on his horse. He appeals to the king to deal with the outlaw and a price is put on his head. King Richard then goes to the Holy Land. Robin's enemy here is the bishop of Ely as chancellor rather than Prince John. Robin survives until the king returns and comes to Nottingham. Robin appeals for pardon by letter. While the king debates this, some of the outlaws go 'Unto the Scottish king'. Before the pardon can be given, Robin dies due to the treachery of a friar, rather than a prioress, blamed for bleeding him to death. Parker adds an epitaph, written by the prioress of Kirklees, for Robert, earl of Huntington, who 'lies under this little stone', known as Robin Hood and an outlaw for thirteen years. It is dated 1189, in the reign of Richard I.

The truth is then that the seventeenth-century ballads do not give a great deal of information on any biography of Robin. They are episodes and incidents with little about his life and background. Parker's 'life' is clearly a mish-mash of the poems and plays about Robin that he knew. It has little claim to being an historical life of Robin Hood. It seems to be an invention sprinkled with tit-bits of ideas from the poems.

The Main Members of the Outlaw Band in the Ballads

The most prominent and virtually ever-present member of the outlaw band, then and now, is Little John. He is presented as the closest to Robin. They do argue at times but John is always reliable. He is frequently the spokesman for the band. In the friar ballad he tells the latter 'I am Little John, Robin Hoods man'.[68] There is a ballad in a chapbook version called *Robin Hood and Little John*. It is not thought to be an early ballad and is one of those using the match plot. In the death ballad, John is the one present at Robin's final scene in the priory at Kirklees and carries out Robin's last request.

Another outlaw who appears frequently is Will Scarlet, though his name appears in various forms, such as Scathelock, Scathlock, Scarlock or Scadlock as well as Scarlet or Scarlett. In the 'Pinder', the two outlaws with Robin at the start of the ballad are John and Scarlet. The name in early poems seems to appear more often in the Scathelock or similar form rather than Scarlet. We may take this as a pun of the 'Bill the Burglar' type — Scathelock meaning break the lock or burglar.

There are several named outlaws who, in various ways, are confused with Will. The confusion is by now almost too involved to ever decipher. Will Stutely is a member of the band, less familiar in modern versions. There is a separate seventeenth-century ballad about him, *Robin Hood Rescuing Will Stutly*. Otherwise, the only relatively early reference to him is in *Robin Hood and Little John* when he is among the outlaws who answer Robin's blast on the horn. In this ballad, it is Stutely who alters the name from John Little to Little John. There is also some confusion between Will Scarlet and Will Stutely in the ballads. The ballad called *Robin Hood Rescuing Will Stutly* is the same as that of Robin and Will Stutely in the 1663 garland and is virtually the same work as that in the Forresters Manuscript called *Robin Hood and Will Scathlock*.[69] Indeed, in this latter manuscript someone has added a later note against Scathlock on the title page as Stutely. The origin and significance of the confusion is by no means clear. A possible explanation is that this was originally one character called Will Stutely (also at times confused with Gamwell and Allen a Dale). He was nicknamed Scathelock for his criminal activities. The name was later transformed to a more familiar sounding surname as Scarlet.

A further confusion with Will Scarlet comes with the entry of yet another character, Gamwell. This introduces a relative of Robin's and has been much used in modern tales. The ballad in question is *Robin Hood Newly Reviv'd*, which is from the seventeenth-century garlands, appearing as *Robin Hood and the Stranger* in the Forresters manuscript.[70] It is also very similar to *The Bold Pedlar and Robin*

Hood.[71] In the various versions, the stranger eventually names himself as Gamble Gold, Gamwell, Maxfield and Loxley — in other words, it is quite a muddle. The Gamble name is almost certainly based on the Gamwell version. It is widely thought that the name Gamwell originated in the old works about Gamelyn or Gandelyn. There is indeed yet another ballad called *Robin and Gandelyn* that has some similarities, but the Robin in it is not Robin Hood.

In the forresters ballad, the stranger meets Robin on foot in another 'match' plot. He is a well dressed, 'deft young man'. He shoots a deer at some distance with a yew bow. He and Robin face up to each other and then fight. He says he is from Loxly and his name is 'young Gamwell'. He has killed his father's steward and come to seek his relative, Robin Hood. He says his mother is Robin's sister. Little John appears and offers to fight Gamwell but Robin prevents it and says that Gamwell will join the band and be 'My Chief man next vnto thee'. He adds 'And Scathlock hee shall bee'.

The miller's son gets variously named. In the *Robin Hood and the Curtal Friar* and *Robin Hood and Queen Katherine* he is Midge. In the forresters fryer ballad he is Mitch. In *Robin Hood and Allen a Dale* he is actually called 'Nick the miller's son'. But he also appears under the more familiar title of 'Much the miller's son'. In several early ballads, he is one of only a handful of named outlaws and so seems to belong in the company of Little John and Will.

The ballad of *Robin Hood and Allen* (or Allin) *a Dale* is unusual. This may be because we only have relatively late garland versions.[72] A reference from *c.* 1600 suggests that the plot might originally have concerned Will Scarlet (Scarlock) rather than Allen. Supporting this idea is Allen's costume in the ballad, which is 'scarlet red'. Allen is met by Little John and Midge, the miller's son. Allen raises his bow towards them but goes with them to Robin. Allen has no money — only 5s and a ring for his wedding. The girl he plans to marry has been forced to accept a wealthy old knight. Robin then hastens to the church where the wedding is to take place and plays the harp before the bishop who is to conduct the ceremony. Robin sees the old knight and the beautiful girl and declares it is 'not a fit match' but the bishop refuses to marry her to Allen. Robin blows his horn for his men. He takes the bishop's coat and puts it on John who then conducts the wedding service and they all return to the greenwood.

Friar Tuck is a regular member of the modern band. The curtal or cortial friar in the ballad is actually not named, and 'Tuck' is thought to be a relatively late addition to the band. However, he does appear in some of the ballads, including *Robin Hood and the Bishop* and *Robin Hood's Golden Prize* (otherwise *Robin Hood and the Preists*). He is consistently said to come from Fountains Abbey, which was, of course, a Cistercian monastery for monks and never a priory or base for friars.

The Main Villains in the Ballads

The sheriff of Nottingham and Prince John are the common enemies of Robin in modern times. Guy of Gisborne also often features in one form or another nowadays. Guy only features in one ballad, which is an early ballad we shall look at in the next chapter.

The sheriff of Nottingham is a villain who appears in both early and late works. He is Robin's most constant enemy. In the butcher ballad, Robin says that the sheriff is after his head. In this ballad, however, the sheriff is not particularly villainous — and this is true of several of the early works. He is more the dupe of Robin's trickery, having to pay for forest animals that Robin has claimed belong to him as a butcher. Sometimes, the sheriff suffers the 'come and dine' trick and has to pay for his meal before being released. The sheriff is also married to a wife who flirts with Robin and shows a sense of humour in persuading the sheriff not to hold a grudge. There are other ballads, though, where the sheriff is simply the enemy, and there are some in which he is killed by Robin or another of the outlaws. The variety of plots suggests that we are not looking at some historical account — if it was a real sheriff and the same man then he can only have been killed once and in one way! Again, as with Guy of Gisborne, we shall look at the earliest sheriff ballads in a later chapter.

Other villains do appear. One of the most interesting comes in the ballad of the death of Robin. Robin is tricked by two underhand characters. The first is his cousin, the prioress of Kirklees, who bleeds him with his consent but deliberately lets blood to the point of death. Her companion in crime, in what is virtually the murder of Robin, is Roger. In *Robin Hoode his Death* this villain is called Red Roger. Unfortunately, one of the missing sections of this work in the Percy Folio probably contained more explanation about Roger's role. In the garland version there is no male villain to assist the prioress. At any rate, in the Percy version Roger finishes off the weakened Robin with a blow from a sword in his side. Though fatally weak and wounded, Robin still manages to retaliate and slices Roger between head and shoulders, killing him. Robin himself then expires.

In none of the early poems is Prince John the villain, even when Robin is ennobled as the earl of Huntingdon. He does not even appear. John has entered by another door, through the plays. Of course, once the period for Robin's activities was moved into the Plantagenet era then John became an obvious villain to use.

Locations in the Ballads

The ballads provide our main knowledge of where Robin operated. They are mostly short pieces but they sometimes name the location and setting of the story. When there is a town it is nearly always Nottingham, as in *Robin Hood's Delight, Little John a Begging, Robin Hood and the Bishop,* as well as the butcher ballad and in those about the tanner, the tinker, Little John and Allen a Dale.

Occasionally, the reference is to Nottinghamshire, as in *Robin Hood and Allen a Dale*. In *Robin Hood's Birth* we find an unusual reference to 'Locksly town, in Nottinghamshire'. It is nearby, we assume, where stands Great Gamwell Hall. Along with Nottingham, Sherwood is the forest most often mentioned by name. Of the thirty-three ballads printed by Child, only three mention Barnsdale (in Yorkshire) but no less than seventeen refer to Nottingham and/or Sherwood.[71]

London does sometimes get a mention, though this is usually the sign of a late ballad, as in *Robin Hood and the Prince of Aragon* and *Robin Hood and Queen Katherine*, where even the background period is Tudor. In the latter case, Finsbury Field also gets a mention. Not surprisingly, *Robin Hood's Chase*, another late effort with a rather silly travelling plot, takes us around the country to Nottingham, Sherwood, Yorkshire, Newcastle, Berwick, Carlisle, Lancaster and London. 'Robin Hood's Birth' has place-names not found in other works with a 'Titbury town' and a parson who comes from Dubbridge.

Many ballads mention Yorkshire place-names. The pinder ballad has the central character as the pinder of Wakefield, otherwise George a Greene. The first of the Forresters Manuscript ballads about the pinder both names him as George a Greene and says he is from 'yorkesheir'. Other Yorkshire names appear frequently. In the death ballad, Robin meets his end in Kirklees priory. The curtal friar is said to come from Fountains Abbey. The fishing ballad locates in the port of Scarborough and has Robin promising to build a chapel in Whitby. From the Forresters Manuscript we see that the Yorkshire place-name of Barnsdale was known and used in the ballads of the bishop of Hereford (*Robin Hood and the Sheapard*) and the pinder. It is almost certainly behind the name 'Barons dale' in *Robin Hood and the King*. One outlaw in the sherriffe ballad is called David of Doncaster and the villain, Roger of Donkesley, is probably also intended to be of Doncaster.

A fair number of ballads refer to Lancashire place-names. Plumpton Park may be one of these and is mentioned, for example, in the fisherman ballad when Robin remembers chasing deer there. Some have thought that the Lee of Sir Richard at the Lee could be in Lancashire. There is little doubt that the main place names are northern.

All of the above is to be expected — Nottingham, Yorkshire and, to a lesser extent, Lancashire. The ballads are mostly set in the greenwood, though the location is not always named. When it is, it is usually Sherwood, as, for example, in *Robin Hood's Delight*, *Robin Hood and Queen Katherine*, *Robin Hood's Chase*, *Robin Hood's Birth* and the butcher ballad, as well as those of the tanner and the Scotchman.

Less usual, and in many ways less important, are the more exotic or distant places mentioned. Perhaps the silliest of the main ballads is 'Robin Hood's Chase'.[74] It was almost certainly composed in the seventeenth century as a sequel or alternative to *Robin Hood and Queen Katherine*. Robin and his men shoot in a match before the king as the team for the queen. In this ballad, the king is angered by their success. There follows a rather ridiculous chase with Robin leading the king and his men a dance via Nottingham, Yorkshire, Newcastle, Berwick, Carlisle, Lancaster, Chester and so back to London. When the king arrives, the queen begs him to pardon the outlaws and he yields.

To sum up then, in the seventeenth-century ballads the most common locations for Robin are Nottingham and Sherwood Forest. In the basic stories he does not travel far from that region. The only other major locations in these works are the northern counties of Lancashire and particularly Yorkshire. It is only in the 'travel' ballads, such as the chase ballad, that he gets much further.

The Period in which the Ballads are Set

The seventeenth-century ballads place Robin Hood in two reigns. Rarely, and usually only in late works, we find the period of Richard the Lionheart. King Richard appears in the sheriff ballad. A number of other ballads mention a King Henry (without number), who seems — usually, at least — to be Henry VIII and seems to reflect the common tactic of ballads of placing their stories in a more recent background. King Henry alone, though, is the most inconclusive of all monarch names if it is unnumbered since there are no less than eight possibilities! It is one reason why placing a real Robin Hood is so difficult. A King Henry appears, for example, in the old wife ballad.

Conclusions from the Ballad Evidence

It is not quite time to assess the full value of the ballads. We yet need to view the other major evidence, including the poems that are earlier than the Stuart age, but we can conclude that it *is* major evidence. There is more evidence in quantity in the ballads that have survived from this age than any other. Some critics are less convinced than others of the value of these ballads. One important modern scholar, for example, sees these ballads as 'secondary to the plays and games'.[75] However, we shall reserve our judgement. The very bulk of the ballad evidence where sources are so scant is certainly significant in itself.

The most immediate thought is that the Robin Hood of seventeenth-century ballads is not so very different from the modern version. He is an outlaw and a hero. He is involved in various plots that are still familiar to us, such as on fighting matches against potential members of the band or individuals. He can change clothes with in order to go in disguise and he invites enemies especially to dine in the forest so he can demand payment for the feast. The chief location, as now, is Nottingham and Sherwood. The main villain is the sheriff of Nottingham. The background period does vary but is not usually specific. In these ballads, the background age is less important to the stories than it has become since.

One general conclusion that we can now reach is to note how each period translates Robin in terms of a dominant medium. In the modern age, it has been cinema and TV. In the eighteenth and nineteenth centuries, it was the historical novel, operas and musicals. In the seventeenth century, it was the printed ballad. In order to fit this medium, Robin's tales from the Stuart age were mostly fairly brief — the length of a song or a poem — and initially printed on a single sheet for wider popular consumption and, perhaps, performance. As Robin becomes a popular figure there are efforts to fill out the stories and make some sort of biography. The ballads thus provide now an early life, an explanation of his outlawry, and accounts of his birth and death.

Robin was always a figure to appeal to the lower classes but never to any one group in isolation. Clearly, he would appeal to those who were oppressed in society and also to those more fortunate persons who could have sympathy for the victims. The multiplication of urban middling men in the ballads must say something of the audience appeal — to potter, butcher, tinker, saddler or pinder. Politically, Robin was likely to appeal to rebels and revolutionaries — to opponents of oppression in its various forms. In the ballads, the oppressors are presented as those who use power, such as the sheriff, and those who seek gain, such as the monks. This is the main reason for Robin's clashes with the church authorities, including the curtal friar and the abbot. The hostility to the prioress is rather different but her hypocritical sexual laxity is given as a reason for the reader to oppose her from the start. Robin was too much a figure of comedy and crime to appeal much to a Puritan nature. Men of the age knew that he had figured prominently in the May games, with their accompanying fights, fun, and drunkenness so scorned by Puritans.

Robin was not presented as a revolutionary in politics. He frequently defers to the king and is happy to aid a poor knight; it was injustice rather than the overthrow of the *status quo* that spurred him on. Perhaps, middle class and moderately liberal men were the most likely to buy the printed works about him. Robin was very much an English hero or perhaps British would be the safer term. The early works on Robin, unlike most poetic works that derive from the medieval period, were always in the English language and never in French or Latin. By the seventeenth century, as English clearly became the dominant language of new literature, Robin was a natural subject.

Appendix to Chapter Three: the Seventeenth-Century Ballads[76]

This list does not include early works that do not appear in seventeenth-century ballad publications or manuscripts. Nor does it include works that were only printed in the eighteenth century. The few earlier works thus omitted will be examined later. Where the same (though usually with differences) ballad appears under different title in the Forresters Manuscript, this is shown together with the other title, separated by a forward slash (/).

1. *The Jolly Pinder of Wakefield*. Percy Folio; Garlands 1663 and 1670; and Broadsides; Forresters – two versions.

2. *The King's Disguise and Friendship with Robin Hood*. Broadside. */Robin Hood and the King or Robins Death*. Forresters.

3. *Little John a Begging (Little John and the Beggars)*. Percy Folio; Garlands 1663 and 1670. */Little Johns Begging*. Forresters.

4. *The Noble Fisherman, or Robin Hood's Preferment*. Broadside; Garlands 1663 and 1670./*Robin Hood's Fishing*. Forresters.

5. *Robin Hood and Allen a Dale*. Pepys; Broadsides. */Robin Hood and the Bride*. Forresters.

6. *Robin Hood and Guy of Gisborne*. Percy Folio.

7. *Robin Hood and Maid Marian*. Broadside; Wood.

8. *Robin Hood and Queen Katherine*. Percy Folio; Garlands 1663 and 1670. */Robin Hood and Queen Catherin*. Forresters.

9. *Robin Hood and the Beggar I*. Broadsides; Garlands/ *Robin Hood and the Begger*. Forresters.

10. *Robin Hood and the Bishop*. Broadside; Garlands 1663 and 1670. */Robin Hood and the Old Wife*. Forresters.

11. *Robin Hood and the Bishop of Hereford./ Robin Hood and the Bishopp*. Forresters.

12. *Robin Hood and the Butcher*. Percy Folio; 1640 Broadside; Forresters.

13. *Robin Hood and the Curtal Friar*. Percy Folio; Broadside 1660. */Robin Hood and the Fryer*. Forresters.

14. *Robin Hood and the Golden Arrow. /Robin Hood and the Sherriffe*. Forresters.

15. *Robin Hood and the Peddlers* (Pedlars). Manuscript *c.* 1650.

16. *Robin Hood and the Scotchman*. Added to Robin Hood Newly Revived. Broadsides; Garlands.

17. *Robin Hood and the Shepherd*. Garlands 1663 and 1670. */Robin Hood and the Sheapard*. Forresters.

18. *Robin Hood and the Tanner*. Garlands 1663 and 1670; Broadsides including 1643; Forresters.

19. *A New Song to drive away cold Winter, Between Robin Hood and the Jovial Tinker*. Wood; Pepys; Broadsides. */Robin Hood and the Tincker*. Forresters.

20. *Robin Hood Newly Revived, or His Meeting and his Fighting with his Cousin Scarlet*. Wood; Garlands 1663 and 1670; Pepys. */Robin Hood and the Stranger*. Forresters.

21. *Robin Hood Rescuing Three Squires from Nottingham Gallows*. Percy Folio.

22. *Robin Hood Rescuing Will Stutly* (Stutely). Broadsides; Garlands 1663 and 1670. */Robin Hood and Will Scathlock*. Forresters.

23. *Robin Hood, Will Scadlock and Little John, or A Narrative of their Victory Obtained against the Prince of Aragon*. Pepys.

24. *Robin Hood's Birth, Breeding, Valour and Marriage*. Pepys.

25. *Robin Hood's Chase, or A Merry Progress between Robin Hood and King Henry.* Garlands 1663 and 1670; Broadsides; Forresters.
26. *Robin Hood's Death and Burial.* Percy Folio.
27. *Robin Hood's Delight, or A Merry Combat Fought between Robin Hood, Little John and Will Scarlock and Three Stout Keepers in Sherwood Forest.* Wood; Broadside; Garlands. /*Robin Hood and the Forresters 2.* Forresters.
28. *Robin Hood's Golden Prize, Showing how he Robbed Two Priests.* Broadside; Garlands 1663 and 1670. /*Robin Hood and the Preists.* Forresters.
29. *Robin Hood's Progress to Nottingham, Where he Slew 15 Foresters.* Wood; Garlands 1663 and 1670. /*Robin Hood and the Forresters I.* Forresters.

Endnotes

[1] J. Simons, 'Romance in the 18th-century Chapbook', pp. 122-43 in Simons; p. 124.
[2] Maddicott, p. 278.
[3] Percy, p. 58.
[4] For example see James Moreira, 'Genre and Balladry', pp. 95-109 in Cheesman & Rieuwerts, p. 97.
[5] Fowler, p. 7.
[6] Fowler, p. 18.
[7] Fowler, p. 40.
[8] Fowler, p. 36; Dobson & Taylor, p. 7.
[9] Fowler, pp. 10-3.
[10] Percy, p. 25.
[11] *Piers Plowman, B,* p. 331, l. 395.
[12] *Forresters,* p. 2.
[13] Dobson & Taylor, p. 47.
[14] *Robin Hood, the Forresters Manuscript.*
[15] *Forresters,* the description of the ms by Hilton Kelliher, pp. xxii-vi.
[16] *Forresters,* p. ix.
[17] *Forresters,* p. xviii.
[18] *Forresters,* p. xxi.
[19] *Forresters,* p. xxi.
[20] Dobson & Taylor, p. 47. Although the title is similar this is not the same plot as in *Robin Hood and the Bishop* as found in the 1663 garland (which is similar to *Robin Hood and the Old Wife* in the Forresters Manuscript).
[21] Dobson & Taylor, p. 47.
[22] Percy, p. 57.
[23] Percy, p. 58.
[24] Dobson & Taylor, p. 51.
[25] Dobson & Taylor, p. ix.
[26] Dobson & Taylor, pp. 281-85.

[27] Fowler, p. 65.

[28] Fowler, p. 67.

[29] Fowler, p. 69.

[30] *Robin Hood and the Bishopp, Forresters,* no. 7, pp. 38-43, compares to *Robin Hood and the Bishop of Hereford,* Child, no. 144, pp. 340-41. *Robin Hood and the Bishop* is in Child, no. 143, pp. 338-40 and compares to Robin Hood and the Old Wife, *Forresters,* no.3, pp. 10-5.

[31] *Forresters,* p. 39.

[32] Dobson & Taylor, pp. 146-49.

[33] *Forresters,* p. 62.

[34] Dobson & Taylor, p. 147.

[35] Dobson & Taylor, p. 147.

[36] Dobson & Taylor, p. 149.

[37] *Forresters,* p. 68.

[38] Dobson & Taylor, pp. 150-57; *Forresters,* pp. 44-51.

[39] Dobson & Taylor, p. 153.

[40] Dobson & Taylor, p. 154.

[41] Child, no. 123. pp. 307-9; *Forresters,* no. 14, *Robin Hood and the Tincker,* pp. 86-91

[42] Child, no. 126, pp. 305-7; *Forresters,* no. 18, pp. 117-22.

[43] Dobson & Taylor, pp. 165-71.

[44] Dobson & Taylor, p. 167.

[45] Dobson & Taylor, p. 169.

[46] Dobson & Taylor, pp. 158-64, compare Child, no. 123, *Robin Hood and the Curtal Friar,* pp. 297-300.

[47] *Forresters, Robin Hood and the Fryer,* no. 11, pp. 71-6.

[48] Dobson & Taylor, p. 160.

[49] The meaning of curtal, cutted and the variants is not certain. It has been suggested as referring to the monastic haircut, or to a shortened cut gown, or to one who kept a monastic vegetable garden. The latter is the most likely and underlines the probability that the original figure in this story was a monk and not a friar.

[50] *Robin Hood's Golden Prize,* Child no. 147, pp. 347-48; *The Noble Fisherman (Robin Hood's Preferment,* Dobson & Taylor, pp. 179-82; *Robin Hoods Fishing, Forresters,* no. 4, pp. 16-22.

[51] *Forresters,* no. 12, pp. 77-80; p. 77.

[52] *Forresters,* no. 3, pp. 10-5; Child, no. 143, pp. 338-40.

[53] *Forresters,* no. 5, pp. 23-33; Child, no. 152, pp. 358-60.

[54] *Forresters,* no.9, pp. 52-61; compare Child, no. 145, *Robin Hood and Queen Katherine,* pp. 341-46.

[55] *Forresters,* p. 52.

[56] Child, no. 149, pp. 350-54.

[57] *Forresters,* p. 103. Gamwell in the *Forresters* version is said to be not from Gamwell but from Loxley and to be the son of Robin's sister (unnamed) and hence his nephew.

[58] Child no. 139, pp. 330-32; *Forresters,* no.1, pp. 1-5.

[59] Dobson & Taylor, pp. 176-78.

[60] Child, no. 149, pp. 350-54; p. 354.

[61] Dobson & Taylor, pp. 133-37.

[62] Dobson & Taylor, p. 133.

[63] *Forresters,* no. 17, pp. 105-16.

[64] *Forresters,* p. 108

[65] Dobson & Taylor, pp. 137-39.

[66] Dobson & Taylor, p. 138.

[67] Dobson & Taylor, pp. 187-90 gives part; Sargent & Kittredge, pp. 362-68.

[68] Dobson & Taylor, p. 164.

[69] Child, no. 141, pp. 334-36; *Forresters,* no. 15, pp. 92-7.

[70] Child, no. 132, pp. 309-11; *Forresters,* no. 16, pp. 98-104.

[71] Child, no. 132, pp. 316-17.

[72] Dobson & Taylor, pp. 172-75.

[73] Holt, p. 179.

[74] Child, no. 146, pp. 346-47; *Forresters,* no. 19, pp. 123-26.

[75] Stephen Knight, 'Which Way to the Forest?', pp. 111-28, in Hahn, p. 123.

[76] Commencing with the list of 38 pieces listed by Dobson and Taylor, Appendix I, pp. 281-85. In addition so far as possible the first date of printing or dating from a manuscript collection has been given.

4

Tudor and Stuart Plays

We now peel back to include a slightly earlier period, that of the Tudors (1485-1603). In the Tudor and Stuart period together, most of the early evidence on Robin Hood appeared in plays as well as ballads. The evidence from this period is absolutely basic. There is hardly any medieval evidence. What there is we shall look at in the next chapter. There is, however, a mass of evidence from the period from 1485 to the end of the Stuart dynasty. Probably the ballads printed in this period, which we examined in the previous chapter, are the major evidence, but we also need to look at the plays about Robin Hood that survive. Some historians searching for Robin Hood have ignored or played down the importance of the evidence from drama. It has been suggested that Tudor and Stuart playwrights were much influenced by the ballads they knew for plots and content of their dramas and, therefore, that the plays are only of secondary significance.[1]

Some plays are undoubtedly based upon ballads but there are three important reasons for studying them in their own right. The first is that some plays were almost certainly in part based upon lost ballads. The second is that the texts of some of the plays survive from an earlier period — that of the Tudors — than the ballads, which, as we have seen, were printed in the Stuart age. The third reason is that there is another thread of Robin Hood material, probably not from ballads and linked directly to performances, including those for local May revels or games. The earliest printed plays provide important evidence.

It is not at all certain which came first in origin, the ballad or the play. David Wiles has suggested that the games 'often inspired the creation of ballads'.[2] It is a bit like the chicken and the egg, given the paucity of evidence. It is, in effect, impossible to make any clear statement about which came first — the ballad or the game. It is true that some play manuscripts do predate ballad manuscripts but this may simply be due to accidents of survival. It is, at any rate, certain that games and performances played an early part in building the Robin Hood legend.

The number of references to early performances of plays and games about Robin Hood is also interesting when compared to all the other Robin Hood evidence. Of 260 references before 1600, no less than 136 are concerned with such performances.[3] One thing is clear: the evidence from the games and plays is too early and too important to neglect.

Robin Hood in May Games and Local Entertainments

From the late medieval period and into the Tudor times, local entertainments played a major role in country pursuits. At certain times, one could expect popular entertainment in the form of pageants and plays to be offered to the local populace. These may have begun as visual presentations by clerics to give religious instruction to the people. By the end of the medieval period, the Church was becoming concerned about some of the lay elements in such entertainments, including low comedy.

The only 'text' for such performances is the late medieval piece probably associated with the Pastons. We shall examine this in the next chapter. We do not, therefore, know the spoken words of the Tudor play-games. There is, however, a great deal of evidence about when and where performances were given, and it is easy enough to read between the lines of comment and criticism to image a recreation of the kind of performances. What we are looking at here are not honed performances to a silent and attentive audience. These were performances to a holiday crowd in holiday mood. Part of the performance consisted of a moving pageant or parade — not unlike modern carnival processions. There would be local people in costumes as well known figures — King Arthur, St George or, of course, Robin Hood. As they moved along, there would be music and dancing, often including Morris dancers. As they still do, they would sometimes draw in spectators for a whirl or dance and kiss one of the local girls. Flora Thompson vividly described such rustic entertainment from her own memory of the late nineteenth century. Here, the boys and girls carried a doll known as 'the lady'. As she suggested, this might have been a corruption of earlier Christian practice to represent the Virgin Mary — or possibly it could stem from even earlier pagan beginnings. It could provide one explanation of the link between Robin Hood and the Virgin Mary — 'our Lady'.[4] For such occasions, the Robin Hood legend drew together characters not initially involved but easily recognisable. A character accompanying Robin in female costume, whether a male or female inside it, was easily known to be Maid Marian. A fat jolly man in a shortened robe, perhaps with a special hair-do, was obviously Friar Tuck. These characters played out little acts as they went along. Others of the band held boxes and collected coins from the crowd, which were to go to the upkeep of the local church. There would be a stopping point where the crowds knew they should collect to see the final performance. It was normally a local open air space, perhaps the market square or the churchyard. Here the characters would perform for public entertainment. There might be a few words spoken but this was not the meat of the act and is surely the reason that texts do not survive. What mattered were recognisable activities, such as the matches — perhaps a wrestling match between Robin Hood and Little John, a match with staves between Robin and Friar Tuck or possibly a sword-fight between Robin and the sheriff. Sometimes, these events ended with a repast in the local church — a good reason again for a Robin Hood story of coming to dine with him. Basically, the Robin Hood play-games were for holidays and not to be taken too seriously. Sometimes they were accompanied by a degree of rowdiness, sometimes even the odd outbreak of violence, sometimes by over-the-top levity or flirtation. Usually, however, they were simply good fun and ended up with a useful contribution for the local church — just as local modern carnivals include collections for charity.

Local lords and the royal court were patrons of dramatic entertainments and, increasingly, so were the urban authorities and the gilds. Pageants and plays thus became associated with certain religious festivals and times of holiday. Stratford-upon-Avon, for example, had a pageant of St George and the Dragon, which was paid for by the local authority until there were efforts to stop it in the 1560s. In this case, they used the church for performance, while St George appeared upon a horse and led a dragon that belched flames and smoke. A buffoon was also involved.[5]

Robin Hood became a popular subject for local celebrations. Before 1600, there are over 100 references to Robin Hood play-games.[6] Often, these took the form of public performances by local players, though we also find semi-professional groups who moved about to perform in several locations. In 1532, 4d was paid by New Romney to the 'Robyn hode players of Hythe'.[7] In many places, local figures, often of some standing, were expected to perform — and even fined if they did not.[8] The role of the local authorities was often important. In the early reference to a Robin Hood play at Exeter in 1427, a man was paid to play Robin before the mayor. It seems to have been common practice that a performance would be given before the local officials in advance of any public performance – perhaps with an element of censorship involved.

There is certainly a connection of such performances with the month of May and with 1 May, an occasion for local celebrations. Such local shows go back to at least the first half of the thirteenth century. It seems probable that Robin Hood in performance was first linked with the local May celebrations rather than with specifically religious occasions. The summer games were conducted by a Summer Lord. The various figures incorporated in the shows seem often to have gradually merged, and Robin's role became increasingly greater with his growing popularity.

By the time we hear much detail about Robin Hood plays and games, it is clear that they were by no means restricted to the month of May, let alone its first day. In 1565, there is a reference to 'the may which was the 10 of June'.[9] The only real limit for outdoors performance seems to have been the time of year when such shows would be possible in the weather conditions, that is, from spring to autumn, usually beginning from Whitsun.

Robin Hood also appeared in mumming plays. The usual format for these plays was to introduce a series of characters in turn, each performing some brief act of drama — possibly a fight. The characters did not speak but would commonly have a speaker to explain what was happening. Such a play was often linked to a local festivity that included feasting. Various characters were featured. The hobbyhorse seems initially to have been part of the winter celebrations, possibly deriving from pagan sacrifice of animals, often by this time concerning a man dressed in an animal skin.[10]

One cannot but wonder here about the link between Robin Hood and Guy of Gisborne in the original ballad where Guy appears in a capel — or horse hide. It is not difficult to imagine that the pagan man-animal transformed into the villainous Guy. This seems yet another hint that the local plays may have preceded the ballads, the horse hide covered actor transforming into the ballad character. The frequent use of a disguise plot in the ballads also seems quite possibly to derive from a theatrical origin. The use of masks or costumes that cover the individual was common in the dramatic performances. The practice of disguising in public was often a cause of complaint, presumably because it was sometimes used to cover some dubious and possibly obscene activities. In 1418, in London, 'mummings, plays, interludes or any other disguisings' were forbidden.[11] In 1479, Bristol forbade people going about with 'closed visageds'.[12] The disguisings, however, a vital part of mumming and local games, continued and became a vital part of masques in the Stuart age.

The evidence for Robin Hood performances is quite widespread in the Tudor period. Robin Hood, along with other characters connected with him, was often mentioned in the local performances. At Croscombe, Somerset, in 1476, one Richard Willes was paid for playing Robin Hood.[13] In 1498, in the same county, the corporation of Wells paid towards an entertainment about Robin Hood accompanied by dancing girls and church ales. At Kingston-on-Thames from 1507, the churchwardens accounted for payments towards similar entertainments, which included costumes and props.[14]

Little John, Maid Marian and a friar are mentioned at Kingston as well as Morris dancing. Morris or Moorish dancing had an entirely separate origin but became part of late medieval English local entertainment. Types of performance and the individual characters merged through time. Morris dancing linked to the play-games. Marian and Friar Tuck joined Robin Hood. It is not surprising that plays, games and Morris dancing combined for celebrations.

Maid Marian may have originated as Murrian (the Moorish one) from the Morris dancing.[15] On occasions, Marian was played by a man, as, for example, one 'trimly dressed up in a cast gown and a kercher of Dame Lawson's, his face handsomely muffled with a diaper-napkin to cover his beard, and a great nosegay in his hands'.[16] It is possible that Robin's love began as a Moorish man! In the games, Marian was at first connected to the fool and then to Friar Tuck rather than to Robin. The friar in the games was presented as a lecher and a fool. Munday would later refer to 'merry morices of Frier Tuck'.[17] However, the French Marian seems to predate the Morris connection. David Wiles states with conviction that 'the Robin Hood game is older than the morris dance'.[18] One notes that the French Robin (not Robin Hood) appeared in the thirteenth century in a play in France, *Le Jeu de Robin et Marion,* by Adam de la Halle.[19] The title of this work is also interesting, meaning 'the game'. Through the May games, Maid Marian became linked forever to the Robin Hood stories, though she almost certainly had a separate, and possibly French, origin.

The first reference to Morris dancing in England is only in 1494, and its popularity came after Robin Hood games had passed their peak.[20] That does not preclude some association between all the elements in the popular mind and certainly the Robin Hood games and Morris dancing often occurred together. There is an Elizabethan reference to 'the Summer Lord with his may-game or Robin Hood with his morris dance going by the church'.[21] Morris dancing, like Robin Hood games, had some impact on the new professional theatre. Will Kemp was probably involved with the play called *The Mad Man's Morris*.[22] This rather muddling confusion over the connections between Robin, Marian, Friar Tuck, play-games and Morris dancing leads us back to the conclusion that various trends gradually fused through the practice of local entertainment.

It may well be that these popular local occasions used the old ballads and employed the same materials. The local entertainments preceded any formal dramatic performance upon a stage for a paying audience. Mention of the various characters shows that the main bulk of the narrative of Robin Hood stories was already familiar by Tudor times, though we know little about the actual content of the early performances. From our knowledge of medieval religious plays, it is probable that some of these shows did have simple plots and dialogue. Certainly, in London, 1559, at a May-game there was a procession with various characters, then Morris dancing and then 'Robyn Hode and lytull John, and Maid Marian and frere Tuke, and they had spechys rond a-bowt London'.[23] One element in the games and the ballads brings us back to the difficult question of which of them came first. This is the use of a combat or match. Combat games were popular for entertainment at all social levels, from tournaments to wrestling and archery contests. In the 'Cotswold' games played in the West Country, we hear of running, cudgel, leaping, wrestling and throwing competitions.[24] Such public matches were known before Robin Hood games. The Lord of Misrule (or the mocking king) always lost — as the inevitable procedure of the misrule practice. Robin seems to have taken over this regal role in his games. One of the basic plots in many Robin Hood ballads, as we have seen, is that of the match between Robin and another individual.

The very earliest dramatic script for a Robin Hood play-game is that from Norfolk, probably associated with the Pastons. The text is very brief, little more than listing a series of matches between Robin and his opponent. It has often been suggested that the ballads inspired these dramatisations but Wiles may well be right in suggesting the reverse: that the games came first and they inspired the ballads. We shall return to this question. The combat element was one cause of the rowdiness associated with Robin Hood games. An element, on the contrary, that could be encouraged by the authorities was the archery competitions, which would encourage ability in that sport — most useful for military purposes. There are sixteenth-century examples of town authorities deliberately organising Robin Hood events to encourage archery.[25]

The popularity of the local entertainments is certain. They generally occurred on Sundays or religious festivals. This was inevitable as being the only time when most people were free to attend. There was much clerical criticism of plays or games on Sunday and church festivals that competed with church services. Plays often took place in the churchyard or even inside the church. As early as 1244, Bishop Grosseteste had banned plays that took place in May or autumn and clashed with religious occasions.[26]

Complaints about rowdiness and indecency increased as Puritanical views developed. There were fears that the entertainments could even be anti-religious. Stephen Gosson thought that 'May-games, Stageplaies, and such like... Nurce up Idolatrie'.[27] The games and celebrations certainly gave licence to behaviour that broke the normal rules. Men might capture women and ransom them — and vice versa.[28] Young couples might disappear into the woods. There is little doubt either that the local celebrations could be of a sexual or even indecent nature: men and women who 'kiss sometimes upon the grass, and sometimes in the hay'.[29] A Latin record at Wells in Somerset connects 'the time of Robynhode' with dancing girls.[30] The Stuart poet Milton still thought of May as the month 'that doth inspire/ Mirth and youth, and warm desire'.[31] The straight-laced Puritan Philip Stubbes condemned 'young men and maids, old men and wives [who] run gadding overnight to the woods, groves, hill and mountains, where they spend all the night in pleasant pastimes'.[32]

This side of the games brought growing condemnation from the increasingly puritanical element in the English Church. Archbishop Grindal complained about activities including 'dance and play' in 'church or churchyard'.[33] In 1549, Bishop Hugh Latimer was annoyed to find no congregation attending to hear his preaching on a Sunday. He was told the reason was that it was 'Robyn hoodes day' and the parish had 'gone a brode to gather for Robyn Hoode'.[34] His comments give some idea of the establishment view of Robin — 'a traitor and a thief'.[35] In Latimer's case, reflecting the opinion of the Church authorities, the criticism was because the congregation preferred the Robin Hood games to the 'ministration of God's word'.

Condemnation did not come only from ecclesiastics either. In 1528, the Lord Warden of the Cinque Ports banned Robin Hood games in the Kent and Sussex towns under his authority. In 1536, Sir Richard Morison wrote to Henry VIII complaining about the 'plays of Robin Hood, Maid Marian, Friar Tuck: wherein, besides the lewdness and ribaldry that is opened to the people, disobedience also to your officers is taught' about the criminal outlaw who 'for offending the laws should have suffered execution'.[36] The Scottish parliament banned Robin Hood games in 1555, though this was not entirely successful since further action had to be taken against performances in 1561, and again in 1579.[37]

Often there was a sort of charitable link when the players would go around collecting money for the Church. Local records make clear that this was a widespread practice and raised respectable amounts — not unlike the collections made at modern carnival processions. The growing popularity of Robin Hood in these events might partly have resulted from the financial success. At Kingston-upon-Thames, for example, in 1506, the gathering by Robin Hood was almost twice that of the game king.[38]

The performances did, however, also mean expenses for players, costumes, musicians, drums, bells, shoes for the dancers, food and drink, sometimes even fireworks or a horse. Badges were specially made to represent 'livery' and were sold to spectators — again very like getting a badge or sticker nowadays for contributing to a charity collector. Certain respected local groups performed in several locations. One group, in 1562, visited ten local parishes.[39] This was often following a procession rather than a play, with characters in costume as easily recognisable figures — Robin, his men, a friar, Marian. The records from Kingston-upon-Thames show that the friar was clothed in distinguishing white and Marian in a hooded cloak. The methods of collection were sometimes a bit over the top and led to complaints from the church itself. Robin Hood and his outlaws could be an excuse for collectors to 'capture' spectators and charge them for release. At Exeter, already in the fourteenth century, there were complaints that the performers dragged men from their houses, including clerics, in order to extort money 'under colour of a game'.[40]

In 1497, at Willenhall, 'Robin Hood' (the player) was taken before Star Chamber for his activities, which included some local feuding and knocking men down.[41] The consuming of over thirty gallons of alcohol at one such event in 1508 suggests at least one cause of rowdy behaviour. Several celebrations were called Robin Hood Ales. The feasting and drinking also sometimes took place within the church building. The growing Puritanism in English Christianity caused embarrassment at any link between the Church and the Robin Hood games.

The authorities had other reasons to be apprehensive about Robin Hood games. The name of the outlaw had obviously become associated with certain political ends, not least giving justice to the poor. There would, over the years, be various rebels who were likened to or chose to call themselves Robin Hood. More often, however, it simply seems to have been a case of games either getting out of hand or being used an excuse to show discontent with the *status quo*. A well-known instance had occurred in 1441, and by the Tudor period there was clearly a wish to stop the practices altogether. In 1549, the summer fair at Wymondham in Norfolk, which included a play, turned into a rebellion against enclosure when Robert Kett's followers gathered there under an old oak. John Knox referred to other troubles in Edinburgh caused by popular disregard for regulations against Robin Hood games.

Robin Hood games and entertainments were also popular in Scotland, including May games, as at Edinburgh, Aberdeen and Perth. The puritanical opposition to Robin Hood and such entertainments was probably even stronger in Scotland than in England. The prohibitions were invariably aimed against popular gatherings that might have irreligious, anti-social, political or even criminal outcomes. As in England, the Church in general was becoming critical of these games. The Roman Catholic Mary Queen of Scots also banned Robin Hood events in 1562. She was confirming a decision by the Scottish Parliament and probably seeking to mollify its views rather than expressing any personal distaste. Nevertheless, she was, to a degree, backing the authoritarian view that Robin Hood represented opposition to the powers that be.

In England, though, by the reign of Henry VIII, Robin Hood had become part of courtly entertainment. Popular gatherings were being suppressed but courtly celebrations were clearly exempt. In 1510, King Henry and eleven of his nobles burst into Queen Katherine of Aragon's chamber dressed in Kendal green and wearing hoods, while bearing bows, arrows, bucklers and swords, 'like outlawes, or Robyn Hodes men'.[42] It is worth noting that the event ended with 'certain daunces and pastime made'.[43] Five years later in 1515, again in May, Henry and Katherine were at Shooter's Hill on their way to Greenwich when they were met by 200 men dressed in green under a 'Robyn Hood', who led them into the greenwood to a bower where they dined on venison and drank wine. The 'outlaws' made a show of their archery.

It is obvious that by this time Robin Hood games with Robin and his band were recognised by everyone in the country and accepted at the highest level. Only the growth of Puritanism and a new authoritarianism halted this widespread popularity. Certainly, in the Tudor period it was difficult for playwrights to criticise monarchy, even in the person of Prince and later King John. The ennoblement of Robin and his support for Richard the Lionheart proved an eventual solution to this problem, however unhistorical in terms of the original Robin that might be.

The Robin Hood games did not entirely die out following the Puritan attacks, even though taken up by ecclesiastical and secular authorities. They lingered on in some areas through the seventeenth century. An interesting performance was recorded at Linton in Scotland in 1610 when George Ker of Linton played Robin, the local innkeeper was Little John, a shepherd played the sheriff and a ploughman played the lord or abbot. We know about this performance because the ecclesiastical authorities brought charges against those involved. They were first ordered to repent and then excommunicated in 1611. The following year, the performers apologised and were allowed to attend church again.[44] One still finds the odd example of games being performed, even during the Protectorate.

What seems most likely is that the old popular May games, which often included Robin Hood as a character, endured into the sixteenth century. As the number of performances began to decline, many of their characteristic aspects and ideas were taken up by authors writing for the new public theatre and the court. There are various references in the new plays in which Robin Hood appears to May games and strongly suggests the continuity from one form to the other. This is true of the early 1560 play about Robin Hood and the friar, of Ben Jonson's *Sad Shepherd* and even the seventeenth-century Restoration play *Robin Hood and his Crew of Souldiers*. A further example is the popular story of the pinner of Wakefield, who joined Robin in a famous ballad. He too was a subject for May games — in 'his many May games which were to be seene Yearly presented upon Wakefield greene', and he too (as George a Greene) became the subject of a play for the theatre.[45]

Tudor and Stuart Plays and Theatres

The employment of Robin Hood as a character in medieval play-games made him a well-known figure and a natural subject for the burgeoning public theatre of Tudor times. The use of Robin Hood in drama blossomed at the very end of the sixteenth century. The likely reason is that once the subject had been introduced in this way its popularity was apparent. The state of the Robin Hood legend was such that it had already been current in local performances and was broad enough to allow all sorts of inventions and embroidery for the new purpose-built theatres in London.

There was also a clear transition from the country games and processions to the theatre plays. The very design of the new theatres owed much to the old mobile stages, temporarily constructed stages, and open-air arenas, with a stage that could be almost surrounded by spectators. Dances, mimes and music played a major part in theatre performances as they had in the old entertainments. Sixteenth-century plays were still tied quite closely to the idea of games and general entertainment, as one commentator wrote, a 'variety of pleasure' that included 'garish apparel, masks, vaulting, tumbling, dancing of jigs, galliards, moriscoes, hobby-horses'.[46] Many plays of the Tudor period incorporated such entertainments. Jigs, country songs and dances were often performed following a play as afterpieces. They were also introduced at the heart of plays. The great comedian Richard Tarleton, who had a catchphrase 'Here we are again', was noted for physical performances as well as spoken comedy and was said to love maypoles.[47] Sword fights and combats were common on stage, and the appeal of a Robin Hood plot is easily apparent. It is, however, also true that the literary quality of plays was increasing and that action alone was no longer sufficient.

The connection with the professional theatre did not make Robin Hood any more acceptable to the Puritanical brigade. Like the games, the theatre plays were soon condemned for their 'lewde jigges songs and daunces'.[48] The building of the Fortune theatre was opposed because it was feared there would be an 'increase of base and lewde people and divers other disorders'.[49] Philip Stubbes condemned 'filthy plays and bawdy interludes' — bemoaning the fact that people flocked to see them while the churches were 'bare and empty'.[50] There clearly were saucy remarks made on stage. William Johnson, for example, was the person referred to in the line 'Time caused my Willy to come to the court', and 'A groom of her chamber my Willy was made'.[51]

A visitor to London in 1590 confirms this criticism of the audiences for drama. He planned to see a play at the theatre and 'found such concourse of unrulye people that I thought it better solitary to walke in the fields'.[52] The groundlings (who had to stand on their feet to watch plays) were known on occasion to become rowdy and were often crushed close together at a popular play.[53] One doubts that the spectators were all literary-minded intellectuals. Some were the 'stinkards... glewed together in crowdes' that a disapproving contemporary looked down his nose at.[54] Shakespeare's porter in *Henry VIII* spoke of 'the youths that thunder at a playhouse, and fight for bitten apples.[55] Theatres were seen as places that encouraged anti-social behaviour — as in a comment from 1580 where they were reckoned to be the scene of 'great affrays, assaults, tumults'.[56] Apart from their worrying political and religious content, plays were noted for saucy and lewd remarks. One notes that plays previously performed on public stages had to be censored for court performance.

Crowds at the theatres also attracted cutpurses. It was apparently the practice if such a cutpurse was caught at a play to shame him by tying him up on stage to public view. It has been suggested that the frequent closing of London theatres sometimes used the plague as an excuse rather than the true reason.[57] On the other hand, there was money to be made from the theatres and various London businessmen became involved. There is also little doubt of the popularity as an entertainment, and even the crown and the nobility valued this. Popular plays and crowded theatres were, therefore, very welcome to some. Probably secular London in general wanted control rather than suppression.[58]

Church criticism of certain plays had begun well before this period. In 1352, the bishop of Exeter had prohibited 'lewd plays' in that city.[59] Town authorities became increasingly censorial about what was performed. Interludes, which began as entertainments during the interval of feasting, were a cause for concern and were often forbidden in the sixteenth century. Strolling or travelling actors were treated as vagabonds unless they could prove noble patronage. In 1572, the earl of Leicester's players appealed to their lord for protection, to 'now vouchsafe to retain us as your household servants and daily waiters', with livery and licence as heretofore.[60] Hence, the development of several acting companies under the protection of great lords.

Under Elizabeth, scripts and printed versions of plays were subject to censorship, and there were harsh penalties for transgressions in actual performances. Again, the anti-authoritarian nature of Robin Hood stories, with their implied criticism of secular authorities and grasping prelates could be problematic in an age of growing censorship. The anti-clerical elements in Robin Hood were generally easy to maintain as being of the former Catholic era in England, but the political nature of outlawry and opposition to authority was less so. This was, no doubt, important in reinventing Robin as a noble with good moral character, with stress laid upon his support of good King Richard.

From medieval times, performance of plays had depended considerably on royal and noble patronage, and that situation did not alter. In the late fifteenth century, as many as fifty lords had their own players.[61] Richard III was the first English king known to have supported a group of players.[62] In the Tudor age, the best companies were those of royalty or of such figures as the Lord Admiral and the various earls. It seemed an easier way to assert government control. Lords had to seek licences in order to employ players in their livery. But less elevated patrons also had their place. Local town authorities were also supporters of performances, and local guilds often supplied their own performers as well as all the trappings necessary for a show.

Before the rise of the new permanent specialist theatre buildings, plays were performed in any suitable building or outdoor site, from town halls to tithe barns and village greens. Pageants and performances at local celebrations often made use of a temporary stage, for pageants generally a small travelling stage on wheels — a 'pageant-cart' or 'play-wagon'.[63] In the West Country, it was the practice to use earth amphitheatres in open fields for performances. Robert Willis, who was born in 1564, wrote of the players at Gloucester and how his father took him to the play 'and made me stand between his legs, as he sat upon one of the benches'.[64] London was, at times, hostile to the rise of professional actors, and in 1554, London prohibited 'that players should have or should make their living in the art of playing'.[65] Opposition from the city of London authorities forced the theatre companies to find places to perform that were outside the city boundaries. One site, at Newington Butts, made use of an old archery ring, probably 'a booth within a fenced "place" '.[66]

The first of the new purpose built theatres, actually called the Theatre, opened in Shoreditch in 1576. It was soon followed by the Curtain the following year and, in due course, by others, such as the Globe, the Swan and the Fortune. These structures were partly open to the air and were used for daylight performances, usually beginning at about three in the afternoon. Most of the new theatres were of circular shape or similar, surrounding a stage. The Fortune was different in being 'sett square... fower score foote of lawful aseize square everye waie', and three storeys in height.[67] A foreign visitor found the new theatres to be 'peculiar houses'.[68] These new Elizabethan theatres were very much a feature of their own age. The Theatre itself was the longest to endure, for eighty-three years.[69] Robin Hood plays were written chiefly for the Rose theatre and were a part of this flourishing but brief episode in the history of English drama.

Performance in the first purpose-built open air theatres was obviously affected by the weather and not always ideal. Nor were these often hastily constructed buildings always safe. Collapse was not unknown and there was a famous fire at the Globe. Henslowe noted that by 1600 the Bankside theatres had become 'verie noisome for resorte of people in the winter tyme'.[70] Like sports stadiums they could also annoy neighbouring residents by the noise that arose from them.

Understandably, plays were also performed indoors in local and noble halls, in the Inns of Court and at the royal court. In such venues, they might also be put on in the evening by candlelight. In the Jacobean period would come professional indoor theatres not unlike our modern concept. For Shakespeare's company their indoor theatre was in an old dissolved priory at Blackfriars. The profits from professional theatre could be considerable and attracted businessmen and speculators. It also allowed some actors and playwrights to become sharers in the theatres and thus in the profits. Shakespeare, for example, made enough to return to his hometown of Stratford, where he restored the family fortunes lost by his father and bought the second largest house in the town.

Plays in the age of Shakespeare for theatre performance needed to be of about five-act length. This meant that the old ballad stories, such as those about Robin

Hood, though often having useful plots, did not, on their own, possess sufficient content for a play. They needed to be embroidered and enlarged. The lengthier literary dramas now expanded considerably on the stories of Robin Hood, mostly through new invention and addition.

Information on Lost Plays about Robin Hood

With the development of Tudor theatre, Robin was introduced as a minor figure in several plays, and a major character in a few. It is clear that more plays about Robin Hood were written in Tudor times than we possess. There are various mentions to lost plays. In 1594, for example, we read in the Stationers' Register of 'a pastorall plesant commedie of Robin Hood and Little John' — sadly not preserved.[71]

There is also evidence in Philip Henslowe's famous 'diary'. We shall mention this source several times. It was kept by a man much involved in theatre business — an organiser, a financier and father-in-law of the great actor Edward Alleyn. Henslowe paid for theatre goods, made loans to theatre people, acted as a banker to acting companies, hired actors, paid writers, received money paid by visitors to the theatres and organised the building and repair of theatres — paying for such things as boards, nails, lime and sand or for 'mackinge the throne In the hevenes'.[72] Fortunately, he also kept a good record of his dealings in a book now known as Henslowe's Diary. Many of the payments related to props and costumes, including 7s 6d for repair to a coat eaten by rats.[73] Among the costumes paid for were a friar's gown, a green gown 'for Maryan' and 'the fryers trusse in Robin Hoode'.[74]

Henslowe kept a detailed record of his 'diary', which is really an accounts book. He also mentioned another lost play called *Robin Hood's Penn'orths*.[75] This too is in the register, where it is listed under 1600-1 and attributed to William Haughton.[76] In 1601, it was performed by the Lord Admiral's Men.[77]

Plays that Mention Robin Hood

The widespread knowledge of Robin in Tudor times is made clear in many of the dramas of the time, chiefly the comedies. Shakespeare himself never wrote a play about Robin Hood, but he did mention him on occasion. *Henry IV Part I* names Maid Marian and in *Part II* Silence sings of 'Robin Hood, Scarlet, and John' — clearly from the known ballads or play-games.[78] In the opening scene of *As You Like It,* Charles, the wrestler, says that the duke lives in the forest of Arden and 'many of his merry men with him; and there they live like the old Robin Hood of England', which he compares to 'the golden world'.[79] For Shakespeare then, Robin Hood seems to be something from a remote and sentimental English golden past.

Plays in Which Robin Hood Appears

EDWARD THE FIRST

There are fuller references in some plays to Robin Hood. George Peele's *Edward the First, sirnamed Edward Longshanks* (or *The Famous Chronicle of Edward I)* was printed in 1593 and included a Robin Hood game. It was probably performed in 1590.[80] The Welsh prince who is the hero claims 'I'll be Master of Misrule, I'll be Robin Hood'.[81] His associates are to play Little John, Friar Tuck and Marian. Here, as David Wiles sees it, Maid Marian is also an 'idealised May Queen'. Mortimer, who plays the potter in the play, claims that with Robin absent the friar 'will lick his Marian./ So will the Potter if he can' — which does not sound too idealised![82] Indeed, the friar goes on to sing a love song to her. Mortimer sings *Blithe and Bonny*. He also sings a rather silly song to Marian:

> Friar, a ditty
> Come late from the city
> To ask some pity
> Of this lass so pretty.

The friar then mocks this verse. He and the potter fight with staves. The play probably used the story of Robin Hood and the potter.[83] The debt to play-games is very obvious and is good evidence of the link between those rural entertainments and the more professional Tudor theatre. Knight suggests *Edward the First* may have made use of the two plays printed by Copland.[84] Perhaps the most interesting thing about this play is that it associates Robin with Edward I, an almost unique link of period — and by no means an impossible one. As a work of literature, however, it leaves much to be desired

GEORGE A GREENE

George a Greene, the Pinner of Wakefield was printed in quarto form in 1599, some time after Robert Greene's death in 1592. It was described as from a 'confused and mutilated copy' and is a poor edition with abbreviated scenes.[85] When the quarto of the play was found it was seen to have two comments on authorship added to it, in different hands. One said it was 'written by... a minister who act[ed] the piners part in it himself. Teste W. Shakespe[re].'; if this was correct then it would seem to dismiss the idea of Greene as author. However, the second comment was 'Ed. Juby saith that ye play was made by Ro. Gree[ne]' — and this has generally been thought more likely to be true.[86] Edward Juby was a playwright and actor of the time. *George a Greene* had also been entered earlier, in 1595, in the Stationers Register as an interlude, usually a short piece. It may actually have been performed as early as 1588.[87] It had also been mentioned by Philip Henslowe in his diary in 1593, when it was performed at the Rose. Five performances were noted during 1593 and 1594.[88]

It is worth taking a little time to look at the writers who were attracted to the Robin Hood story in this period. Robert Greene, the probable author of *George a Greene,* was born and brought up in Norfolk but spent most of his life in London. He was not of high birth, probably the son of a saddler, born and baptised in 1558.[89] Greene received a university education at Cambridge where he gained a BA in 1578 and an MA in 1583, probably at St John's and then Clare Hall.

There are many uncertainties about Greene's private life. He married the daughter of a gentleman and had a child by her. He seems to have moved to London, leaving his wife in Lincolnshire, possibly in 1586 — an interesting parallel with the life of Shakespeare. A good deal of rather malicious detail about Greene is to be found in the printed writings of Gabriel Harvey.[90] According to Harvey Greene kept a woman (Em Ball) who was 'a sorry ragged queane' and sister of the notorious low-life Ball, 'surnamed, cuttinge Ball', whom Greene employed.[91] By her, according to Harvey, he had a 'base sonne' known as Infortunatus Greene.[92] Greene may also have married a second time to Isabell Beck, possibly a bigamous relationship.[93]

Greene told of his own life in his *Groats-worth of Witte,* and *The Repentance of Robert Greene* written on his deathbed.[94] He admitted to various sins, lewd living, relations with whores and low-life characters. A contemporary described Greene 'with ruffianly haire' and unseemly clothes, often swearing, always moving because he was in debt, having to pawn his belongings and frequenting 'filthy hauntes'.[95] Yet another acquaintance referred to him as a follower of Machiavelli — not as a compliment — while Thomas Nashe commented on his long red beard shaped like a steeple and not trimmed, a man whose only worry was to raise enough money to buy wine.[96] In fact, most of his contemporaries, like Harvey, saw him as 'vile Greene', the 'Dog of spite'.[97] Though his prose may contain an element of fiction there can be little doubt that in outline he gives a true picture of his ups and downs, his dissolute life, his relationships, his regrets, and his ambitions.

The Repentance of Robert Greene, Maister of Arts is a straightforward statement of his final repentance on his deathbed. He confessed: 'I began to followe the fithines of mine owne desires'. He went to Cambridge and spent his time with 'wags as lewd as my selfe'. He now, after six years without seeing her, asks his wife to forgive him. A letter found after his death asks her to forgive his many wrongs and his adultery. He says he now suffers from 'vlcerous sores', which suggests he may have contracted venereal disease. A note at the end of the printed *Repentance* tells how he was sick for a month with a pain in the belly which became swollen, as did his heart and face. He called on God throughout this time. On his last evening, he managed to walk to his chair and back, and then from nine in the evening lay on his bed. Robert Greene died on 2 September 1592. According to Harvey he died of a surfeit of pickled herring and Rhenish wine.[98]

There have been doubts over the authorship of *George a Greene* but Robert Greene seems the most likely author. The fact that it was played by another company than his usual one is not serious since we know on another occasion that Greene earned money by selling a play (*Orlando Furioso*) twice to different companies.[99] The actor Edward Juby had attributed it to him and we know Greene was a prolific writer

— some forty plays may have come from his quill.[100] The play *George a Greene* seems mainly based on the ballad about Robin Hood and the pinner — though Robin is a relatively minor figure with the pinner, George a Greene, taking centre stage — hence we have included it here in the section on plays that mention Robin.[101] In this group it is perhaps the most important as its main inspiration seems to be a Robin Hood ballad. Apart from Robin Hood, other characters in the play include Maid Marian, Will Scarlet and Much the Miller though, perhaps oddly, not Little John — who is simply mentioned. Interestingly, it is set in the reign of a King Edward, who is not numbered but has been generally identified since as Edward IV.

The play opens with a rebellion in the north — where Lancastrian risings had indeed occurred in the fifteenth century and where Robin's name had been taken by the rebel leaders of both Redesdale and Holderness. There is, however, little attempt to make the historical background realistic. Robin, in the play, does not enter until some way in and is loyal to King Edward. The play gives a Yorkshire setting to Robin, with scenes set in Bradford and Wakefield. George is the yeoman pinner from 'merry Wakefield', noted for his staunch support for the king and his fighting ability. George is in love with Bettris (Beatrice) whose father, Grime, is opposed to her marrying a lowly pinner. James, King of Scotland (presumably James III if Edward is Edward IV), is beaten by King Edward and then accompanies the latter through the rest of the play. George confronts the rebel lords and states his view: 'a poor man that is true,/ Is better than an earl, if he be false'. There is, then, some comic disguising when George's boy Wily (Willie) dresses as a woman. The 'woman' then becomes the 'love' of the presumably short-sighted Grime — all this in rather pantomime style. George, in turn, disguises himself as an old man to tell the lords' fortune — that the king will beat them. George's identity is revealed and he fights the lords. The two he captures are sent on to King Edward.

At last, in act four scene two, we meet Robin, Marian and the outlaws. Marian vows she will not lie with Robin until he has beaten the renowned pinner, so they all set off for Wakefield. George sees them crossing a cornfield and tells them to go back. They refuse and he says he will fight them even if they be 'as good as Robin Hood' and his men. George fights the men in turn. He defeats Will Scarlet, then Much the miller's son and finally fights Robin — until the latter stops the contest and reveals his identity. He invites George to become his man and George asks them all to dine. Then we switch to the kings (in disguise) who, on their way, meet the shoemakers of Bradford who insist they must trail their staves. Then enter Robin Hood and George (also in disguise). George taunts the kings for yielding to the shoemakers and acting as 'base-minded peasants'. George fights all the shoemakers and beats them. Then everyone reveals their true identity. George and the outlaws ask pardon of the king who grants it. George rejects the offer of a knighthood but says he would rather marry Bettris. Grime tells them he will allow the marriage if he can marry Wily – who then reveals himself as a boy. Grime gives in to it all. Clearly, Greene has based his work on the ballad about the pinner but has transformed it through developing the pinner's part. Linking this play to later pantomime is irresistible.

Plays about Robin Hood

Apart from one survival from 1475, which we shall examine as medieval, there are no plays surviving before the reign of Elizabeth I. The other two major early Robin Hood play survivals came from c. 1560 and were published together by William Copland with his edition of the *Gest*.[103] They were *Robin Hood and the Friar*, and *Robin Hood and the Potter*, both apparently based on the relevant ballads. Copland introduces the work as 'a newe play for to be played in Maye games very plesaunte and ful of pastyme' — so there is no mystery about the type of work and its connections. The fact that he calls it a play rather than two plays, suggests that they were meant to be performed together. Play-games were not confined to one plot. These plays are relatively crude and, like the medieval play about the sheriff, seem to have depended in performance largely upon action to the sketchy dialogue. Also like that work, they may have been two parts of a single play for performance. They might together be the work entered in the Stationers' Register in 1560 as 'the play of Robyn Hoode'.[104]

ROBIN HOOD AND THE FRIAR

The play about the friar has claims to date from an early period. The publication says it is a new play 'verye proper to be played in Maye Games' and may well be a written down version of such a performance — the writing has no great literary claims. Robin Hood acts as the presenter who explains the situation and gives a commentary. Friar Tuck (Fryer tucke) is named as the 'stoute frere' and has the famous match with Robin at a stream. Tuck describes himself as 'a jolly fryer'. The friar says he has come to seek a good yeoman: 'In Bernisdale men sai is his habitacion/ His name is Robyn hode'. Robin admits that he has never loved friars and calls his adversary a 'lousy frer'. Meeting a friar or a fox in the morning will lead to a bad day — it would be better to meet the devil. This sounds more like genuine repulsion and hatred of friars than a jest. Robin notes that there is no bridge and tells the friar 'Over this water thou shalt me bere'. Tuck takes him on his back and then throws him in the water. Then they fight with staves. Robin blows his horn and the outlaws appear clothed in Kendal green. The friar then whistles for his dogs. Their number is reduced, no doubt for reasons of performance, from the fifty in the ballad to just three (thought to be humans acting as dogs). After their clash, Robin asks the friar to join his band, for gold and fee. Then Robin produces a woman (a lady free) whom he offers to the friar — clearly expressing what he sees as the mendicants' reputation for holy behaviour! Some have thought this female was Maid Marian but she is not named in the play. The friar exclaims 'Here is an huckle duckle' and describes her as a 'trul of trust, to serue a frier at his lust,/a prycker, a prauncer, a terer of shetes/a wagger of ballockes when other men slepes'.[105] Child chose to omit these rather improper lines from his edition of the work.[106] In conclusion, the friar promises to dance with her in the mire. This conclusion suggests descent from the old play games.

Robin Hood and the Potter

The other early surviving play in the pair, *Robin Hood and the Potter,* may have been intended for performance after an interval, as a second part after the friar play. It also dates from *c.* 1560 and seems to be based on a ballad.[107] In the manuscript, the play may not be complete and seems to lack an ending, though it probably concluded with a Morris dance and may not have required a textual conclusion. Indeed, it seems to be the text for a May-Game play.[108] The link to the potter ballad is even clearer than in the case of the friar play because here we do have the early surviving ballad.

The potter play begins like a ballad with Robin saying 'Lysten to [me?] my mery men all/ and harke what I shall say'.[109] The opening dialogue is between Robin Hood and Little John. In fact, the dialogue at times follows the words of the ballad, so the borrowing is well nigh certain. The play seems to have been written by the same author who composed the friar play. Here, the potter's boy, Jacke, is trying to get to Nottingham and has lost his way when he meets Robin and Little John. Robin bets John £20 that he will make the potter pay for passage. Robin provokes the trader by dropping and breaking some pots — again not demonstrating a particularly pleasant character. He insults the potter by calling him a cuckold. The potter is, unsurprisingly, annoyed and calls Robin a 'naughty knaue'. He swears he is not even married. He refuses to pay passage to go on his way. Robin defends his demand by saying he is chief governor under the greenwood tree. He calls on Little John to fight the potter and John promises to 'rappe hym on the snoute'. They fight with sword and buckler. Here the script concludes, either incomplete or leaving the actors to finish with actions rather than words.

Two Plays by Anthony Munday

Anthony Munday (1560-1633) was a prominent Elizabethan and Jacobean playwright noted for his ability in plotting. We may agree with Tracey Hill that his contribution has 'long been underestimated'.[110] He was a prolific writer, though, unfortunately, only a handful of his plays survive. In 1597 alone, he wrote, or contributed to, at least twenty-six plays.[111] Munday was born and bred and lived and died as a Londoner, the son of a freeman of the drapers who was a practising stationer. Anthony was apprenticed to a London printer and became a freeman of the city. Mundays were common among the boy choristers and performers in London and that was probably the start of his theatrical career. His father died while Munday was only eleven and he was referred to as an orphan, though his mother seems still to have been alive.[112] Munday married Elizabeth (elsewhere called Gillian) and had five children.[113]

Anthony Munday led a busy and varied life. He travelled to Rome in 1579 where he entered the English College as a scholar. He probably became an actor for the earl of Oxford, and was referred to as a 'stage player'.[114] He also worked for the government as a 'messenger', in fact employed by the government as a spy and used against Roman Catholics though he may himself have been of that belief. He made enemies by his role in several denunciations, arrests, tortures, trials and executions of Catholics. The Protestant minister Giles Wigginton thought Munday 'seemeth to favour the Pope and to be a great Dissembler'.[115]

Munday wrote various works, including prose, poetry, commentaries on religion and politics, and plays. He wrote several pageants for the lord mayor's show for which he was called on one occasion a 'peaking pageanter'.[116] He was hard up and wrote for a living. On one occasion, he was accused of stealing £40 from a widow's house that he had searched on the pretext of her Catholicism.[117] He has frequently been belittled as a 'hack writer', one who 'would do anything for money' but has recently attracted more scholarly attention and is beginning to emerge as a more important contributor to Elizabethan and Stuart literature.[118]

Interestingly, it seems likely that Shakespeare and Munday worked together with others for Henslowe on the play about Thomas More. Munday sought patronage where it seemed most sensible, from nobles, privy councillors, companies or eminent citizens of London. In his later years, he spent much time revising the work of his former friend, Stowe, on London. Munday died in 1633.

Again, we find a somewhat eccentric character involved in contemporary political writing, who found Robin Hood interesting. No doubt, he was partly attracted to the popular ballads about our hero and their connection with Nottingham. Munday wrote the only two plays of the period with Robin Hood as a primary figure that were performed on stage.[119] They are, in effect, a two-part life of Robin. It is perhaps worth noting that Robin Hood had been popular in the May games that were now under attack from Puritans, and thus to choose him as a hero might be construed as taking a religious standpoint.[120] Queen Elizabeth referred to the Catholic Irish rebel Feagh McHugh O'Byrne as 'a base Robin Hood'.[121] King John, who is a villain in the Munday plays, had become for a time something of a hero to Protestants because of his battle with the pope.

Both of the main works on Robin Hood by Munday were entered in the Stationers' Register on 1 December 1600 and printed the following year. The name Robin Hood did not appear in their titles, only that of Robert Earl of Huntington — who, of course, was Munday's ennobled Robin Hood. The plays were probably written and first performed in 1598, the year in which Philip Henslowe paid Munday £5 for 'a play boocke called the firste part of Robyne Hoode', and a little later for 'the ij partes of Robart Hoode'.[122] The two plays were put on during the year 1598 at the Rose.[123] The payment of £5 for the second play was shared with Henry Chettle, who also did some work on 'mending' the first part before performance at court — probably checking to make sure there was nothing to cause embarrassment before the queen.

THE DOWNFALL OF ROBERT, EARL OF HUNTINGDON

The court performance in 1598 was recorded as 'by the earl of Nottingham's men twice, who played The Downfall of Robin Hood, and for this they are rewarded at the rate of £10 a play'.[124] This is almost certainly Munday's play though, interestingly, called Robin Hood rather than Robert earl of Huntington. It is also worth noting that it was performed by the earl of Nottingham's players. The earl of Nottingham was Charles Howard, the Lord Admiral and a patron of the theatre. Howard was made Lord Admiral in 1597, only a few months before the first payment was made to Munday for his play about the downfall of Robin Hood.[125]

This first play about Robin Hood by Munday was printed in 1601 as The Downfall of Robert, Earle of Huntington, afterward called Robin Hood of merrie Sherwodde. There seems to be either some hurried writing that was not corrected or else some careless editing for print. The hero is 'Robin the good,/ Calde Robin Hood'.[126] He has transformed to Robin from the earl of Huntington. There is some confusion over names of the characters. Friar Tuck at one point says he promised a play of Robin Hood about how 'Greeneleafe robbed the sheriff' — though Greenleaf does not appear again. In the play, Maid Marian appears but, confusingly, also as Matilda: 'Maide Marian' — 'No Marian, but Fitzwaters chast Matilda'. Marian is said at first to be the daughter of Lord Lacy but later her father is Fitzwater. Marian's father Fitzwater remarks 'I wonder why her name is changed thus'. Robin explains that she is called Maid Marian because 'she liues a spotlesse maiden life'. The confusion is multiplied when on one occasion our heroine is named as 'Marilda'.[127] The play claims to be historical but some of the characters involved did not play the part given them here in the reign of King Richard.

The play begins in the time of Henry VIII when it is decided to put on an historical play about Robin Hood — which is thus a play within a play. The presenter, Skelton, reports that the young man 'Is our Earle Robert, or your Robin Hoode'. Note that Robin is not the dispossessed earl or the claimant to the title but the actual earl. Robin even refers to himself and Marian as 'Sovereigns', that is, rulers — a harking back to the May King and Queen tradition.[128] The play begins with the entrance of 'Robert, earle of Huntington, leading Marian'.[129] Sir John Eltham takes the part of Little John and acts as the earl's steward. Much the Miller's son is referred to as a clown, reminding one of play-games. There is a certain amount of slapstick, including a scene between Little John, Warman and his wife, who is given odd rustic pronunciations. The bishop of Ely appears dressed as a woman, a 'bearded witch'. Oddly, Will here becomes two characters, brothers, using both of the early versions of the name (one is Scarlet and the other Scathlock), who have been outlaws in Barnsdale. Robin has been outlawed through his uncle Gilbert de Hood, the prior of York. The traditional Yorkshire origin of Scarlet and Scathlock is retained, though the outlaws settle in 'merry Sherwood'. There is also a sheriff of Nottingham and reference to Nottingham's red cliffs. In fact, a number of northern places are mentioned, including Blythe, Southwell, Tickhill, 'merry' Mansfield, Bradford, Wakefield, Leeds, Rotherham and Huddersfield. An interesting and unusual place-name is that of the nunnery as Farnsfield — a place that does indeed exist in Nottinghamshire near to Southwell. The villains include Sir Doncaster and Warman.

The play within a play about Robin Hood is set in the time of Richard the Lionheart, with Prince John ruling England in his absence and seeking Marian for himself — from love. Robin exclaims 'for now begins the game' — suggesting a connection with the play-games. The play has references to 'jests' of Robin Hood, 'merry morisses' of Friar Tuck and 'pleasant skippings up and downe the wodde'. There are several instances of combats or matches, including one in which Fitzwater knocks down Prince John and a mention of a wrestling day at Mansfield. There are also a series of disguisings, including the bishop of Ely as a woman and Prince John as an outlaw in green. Skelton quotes the famous saying 'many talk of Robin Hood, that never shot in his bowe'. John's mother, Henry II's wife, Eleanor of Aquitaine, claims to have loved Robin Hood. The play ends with the appearance of Richard the Lionheart. He restores Robin and Fitzwater, returns Marian to Robin and pardons John, who is repentant — for the time being. Robin invites the king into his bower — reminiscent of the actual invitation extended to Henry VIII. Skelton claims that the play is unfinished and a second part 'shall presently be penned' about Robin's death and 'faire Matildas Tragedie'.

The Death of Robert, Earl of Huntingdon

Munday's second play on the outlaw hero was *The Death of Robert, Earle of Huntington, otherwise called Robin Hood of merrie Sherwodde,* on which Henry Chettle probably collaborated. Henslowe paid Chettle 10s 'for mendinge of Roben hood for the corte'. Munday also probably made use of the recent 1594 poem *Matilda, the Faire and Chaste Daughter of Lord R. Fitzwater* by Michael Drayton. The printed title of the play continues *'with the lamentable Tragedie of chaste Matilda, his faire maid Marian'*. Again, the play is set in the later part of Henry VIII's reign and is presented to the audience by the character Skelton. Again, there are errors that suggest hurried work. Thus Queen Eleanor is addressed near the end as 'Isabell'. Robin dies at the end of the first act, having been poisoned. This death is not the traditional one planned by the prioress. The guilty parties here are the prior of York and one Sir Doncaster. Robin asks to be buried at Wakefield underneath the abbey wall with bow, arrows, sword and a cross at his side.

The play is primarily concerned with the effects of Robin's death. Much of it is about Marian seeking to escape the clutches of John, now king. Marian has been granted Robin's lands by King Richard (and become Matilda again) but with that king dead she is chased by the lustful John. She seeks help and then decides to enter a nunnery, but even the abbess is prepared to collude with John. A monk tells her 'the King must lie with you', and the abbess says it will be alright because 'no bodie shall see'. The nunnery will receive cash for the exchange. At this, Marian/Matilda gives up hope of escape and exclaims 'would I were deade'. When John's evil servant Brand comes to her with poison, Marian is only too glad to commit suicide and finally escape the king. Brand is undone by his own acts and also commits suicide. King John ends by showing repentance and promises 'I will be better than I yet haue beene' — not difficult perhaps.

Given the connection between the Bruce family (members of which were kings of the Scots) and the earldom of Huntingdon, the introduction into the play of Old Bruce and Young Bruce has some interest. There are muddles, as in the first play. Young Bruce is also called Young Fitzwater (and thus Marian's brother) — but at various moments in the play he is called Fitzwater's cousin or nephew! He is also the eldest son of Old Bruce. Another point to note is the appearance of the character Rafe of Chester, reminding us of the *Piers Plowman* link between Robin Hood and Randolf, earl of Chester.

Munday's was arguably the most important work of the period for its effect on the Robin Hood legend — though Knight believes Martin Parker and the ballads contributed more.[130] To a degree, Munday took the tale back to its origins, including probably a reading of the *Gest*. He had borrowed from various sources, including the ballads, Drayton, and the George a Greene play. Munday's dual work made an impact in its own right, notably in the emphasis on Robin's nobility as earl and the role of Maid Marian. He also chose the Plantagenet period for his setting. Perhaps the most effective part of Munday's effort was the transformation of Robin from a criminal outlaw to an honourable noble — a supporter of royalty, not a political rebel.

This second Robin Hood play by Munday also includes a 'maske', which involves no spoken words but consists of a procession and then a dance when the male characters each take a lady partner — though Matilda refuses at first to partner King John and is then handled roughly by him. This is much in line with suitable occasions at court and probably the work of Chettle. Munday did later write a stand-alone masque, the *Metropolis Coronata*, for the aldermen on the occasion of Lord Mayor's Day in London in 1615. The entertainment took place on barges on the Thames as well as on land with a procession. The main theme was the myth of Jason and the Argonauts but at the end of the line came Robin Hood and his men in green, carrying a slain deer. This work shows that Munday was not much troubled by historical accuracy. Munday here revived Robin as Earl Robert de la Hude, the son of Henry FitzAylwin.[131] Robin and the outlaws sing a song proclaiming them as servants of the mayor. Among Munday's other works perhaps a passing mention should be made of *John a Kent,* in which the characters include Ranulphe Earl of Chester and his daughter Marian.

Look About You

Another play of the period was *A Pleasant Commodie called Looke About You*, which is anonymous. It was performed by the Admiral's Men. The play begins with the entrance of Robin Hood who is the earl of Huntington.[132] This play was probably influenced by Munday's work. He may even have co-written it. Other possible authors suggested are Antony Wadeson, Henry Chettle and Thomas Dekker – but there is no clear evidence. The play has been deemed 'entertaining balderdash'.[133] It is certainly broad comedy. At one point Robin enters dressed in

Lady Marian Faukenbridge's gown, with 'night attire on his head'. It is set in the Plantagenet period but this time in the reign of Henry II.

The Sad Shepherd

Ben Jonson was probably the greatest of the Tudor and Stuart playwrights attracted to the Robin Hood tales. Like the others in this group, he had a lively career. He got into serious trouble when he killed the actor Gabriel in Hoxton fields. At the time, he was described as a bricklayer rather than a playwright.[134] For the killing he was imprisoned and branded on the thumb. In time, he recovered to become a respected court poet who regularly wrote masques for court performance for the early Stuarts. He was in demand for Christmas masques and described himself as a poet who was 'a kind of Christmas engine'.[135] The Jacobean masque was something like a pantomime and court performances could be chaotic. When The Masque of Blackness by Ben Jonson and Inigo Jones was performed, one member of the audience was horrified to see the queen and her ladies blacked up in order to perform. There was a great crush to get in and see, and no doubt some of the courtiers were drunk. A table covered with food for the banquet was overturned. One lady 'lost her honesty... being surprised at her business on the top of the terrace' — make of that what you will.[140]

The production of masques, which were popular entertainments, with songs and dances rather than serious drama, gives an interesting link to the old May games in which Robin Hood had often featured. Jonson also wrote a now lost pastoral called The May Lord while staying with William Drummond in Scotland. Jonson introduced Robin Hood into his poetry and into the unfinished play called The Sad Shepherd: or a Tale of Robin-Hood, probably written in the 1630s, possibly in the last year of his life, 1637. He suffered a stroke and was seriously ill by then. The unfinished work was found among Jonson's papers after his death. When his posthumous works were printed, the play was considered 'too much worth to be laid aside'.[141] Perhaps Jonson found the subject something of an escape — it has a lively simplicity lacking in some of his work. Jonson may have been inspired to favour Robin Hood by a dislike for sheriffs. It was said that he had a strong resentment against one Sir W. Wiseman and prevented him becoming a sheriff by remarks made to King James I.[142]

The Sad Shepherd: or A Tale of Robin-hood was unfinished with only two-and-a-half acts completed, perhaps halted by Jonson's death. It was printed in 1641. Some critics have thought it an earlier work, ignored because he abandoned it.[143] In the manuscript, Jonson provided a prose outline of the contents intended for each act — so one can reconstruct the play. It has some literary merit, seen by one recent writer as 'without doubt the single most distinguished literary treatment of the Robin Hood legend'.[144] The play was edited and completed when produced for the stage of Drury Lane in the eighteenth century but made no great impact. The completion, made by F. G. Waldron in 1722, has been published in modern times — but our present interest is in Jonson's original work.[145]

The Sad Shepherd has much traditional Robin Hood material. It is set in the Vale of Belvoir in Sherwood Forest, which Jonson visited during the 1630s. We are told at the start 'The SCENE is Sher-wood' with reference to Robin Hood's bower and his well. Jonson's patron, the earl of Newcastle, was also Lord Warden of Sherwood Forest. Jonson consistently calls his hero 'Robin-hood' with the hyphen, reminiscent of Robinhood surnames. The play takes place in June and has been described as 'an English fairy tale'.[146] The cast includes both Will Scathlock and Scarlet — as brothers. Maid Marian, Friar Tuck, Little John and Much also appear. Less familiar characters are George a Greene; Maudlin, the witch of Papplewick; and Puck-Hairy, otherwise Robin Goodfellow. Jonson was probably having fun with various tales known to him. Although the witch does not appear elsewhere in Robin Hood tales, Papplewick in Yorkshire does have a connection. Firstly, it was said to be where Alan a Dale married, and secondly, it is close by Robin Hood's Stable at Pappelwick Hall and a Robin Hood's cave.

The play has Robin bringing folk to 'the Jolly Bower/ Of Robin-Hood' and referring to hornpipes, tambourines, 'Songs, and Dances in the Wood'. There is reference to treading country dances and games.[147] It is clearly influenced by the games and masques of the period, not least in Robin's role, which is chiefly as a master of ceremonies. Marian is unequivocally referred to by Robin as his mistress. They have an unprecedented quarrel but it is soon patched up. The witch, Maudlin, pretends to be Marian to trick Robin and makes the outlaws give her their slain deer. As a result, Marian becomes unpopular with the outlaws. She denies the action but is only shown to be telling the truth through Robin. He seizes the false Marian by the belt, which breaks, and 'Marian' turns into Maudlin. In many ways, the play centres round Marian more than Robin and introduces more subsidiary and normally unrelated characters than is common, including Maudlin the witch, Karol, Clarion, Amie, Lionell, Lorel, Earine, Clarion, Aeglamour, and Puck or Puck-Hairy. Even if completed, it would not have been Jonson's greatest work but it has an interesting and complex plot, plenty of lively action and some excellent poetry. Robin himself, however, is a somewhat colourless character.

In addition to surviving plays, there are some records of theatrical business associated with Robin Hood. Perhaps the most interesting is found in Henslowe's diary. Here we find mention of props, including one 'hatte for Robin Hoode' and one 'hobihorse'.[148] The hobbyhorse suggests that in the professional theatre the playing of Robin Hood was still associated with trappings familiar from the old games.

Robin Hood and His Crew of Soldiers

After the English Civil War, the interest in Robin Hood declined. This was partly, no doubt, from the puritanical suspicion over the play-games. Robin was not to be taken up again in drama in a significant way until the eighteenth century. Puritanism got a grip on May games and theatrical entertainment, all scorned.

The Restoration of the Stuart monarchy did also see a restoration of some public pleasantries. The very ceremonies of Charles II's Restoration saw a reappearance of Robin Hood.

In Nottingham, in 1661, a comedy called *Robin Hood and his Crew of Souldiers* was performed on the very day of Charles II's coronation, 23 April: 'this happy Coronation, which is this day to be celebrated'.[149] It was printed in London the following year. This play is set in a bower and, given the circumstances, seems to have derived from the old play-games. Its political message is clear, with the outlaws transformed into royal supporters, though Little John does complain that the sheriff is marching 'to reduce us to loyalty and the miseries of an honest life'. Robin claims that his past position has 'melted into loyalty'.[150] The sheriff's messenger announces a pardon. Will says they must now give up venison in favour of crusts and mouldy cheese. The messenger insists that a good man cannot think it a loss of freedom to 'obey the commands of his Prince'. Robin says that he sees in his men, as in himself, 'shame and true penitence for their fore-past Crimes'. They end with a song to the health of the king.

Conclusions

David Wiles has claimed that the plays and games of this period were more representative of popular opinion and creative activity than the ballads.[151] Certainly, at their peak these performances and processions, often organised by local officials, were widespread and engaged the interest of ordinary people. They brought in locals as performers and virtually the whole local population as spectators. These activities come under many names — revels, sport, plays, games, ales, pageants, dances, gatherings — but they cover the same sort of ground: local performances for public celebrations.[152] The general idea was to have a gathering of the local community for fun and games, including dancers who 'set and turn about,/ Change sides and cross, and mince it like a hawk;/ Backwards and forwards, take hands then, in and out' until midnight.[153]

Perhaps oddly, the regions most engaged in these activities when Robin Hood appeared were not as one might have anticipated. There are virtually no records of them north of Nottingham, except in Scotland. They were common in the valleys of the Thames and Severn and in the West Country, but not in Wales.[154] David Wiles has compiled a list of references to Robin Hood plays in the early period before 1600.[155] The results are fascinating. There are no references from Yorkshire, Nottinghamshire, Derbyshire or Lancashire — where one might most expect to find them from locations mentioned in the early ballads. There are some Midlands' references but most come from East Anglia and the South. It clearly suggests that these were the areas where the plays were most popular.

The importance of these entertainments in the localities is reflected in surviving documents. Local councils had to fund and often organise the performances. Although, in the end, religious attitudes were largely responsible for the decline and disappearance of the games, the Church had earlier been often responsible for their flourishing. The churchwardens' account book for Kingston-upon-Thames is a fascinating record of local expenses.[156]

One question on consideration of the dramatic evidence from this period is the extent to which it confirms the ballad evidence and, on the other hand, the extent to which it contrasts with it. It is interesting that the characters of Maid Marian and Friar Tuck seem to differ in the games from their traditional figures. Both indeed appear earlier in the games in connection with Robin than they do in the ballads and this may have been their means of entry to the latter. In the games, Marian can be a troll, a 'lady free', or a May Queen, and was sometimes played by a man.[157] Friar Tuck is generally a figure of fun, clownish as well as lecherous. There were games involving an abbot as the chief figure, for example at Willenhall in 1497 or Shrewsbury under Henry VIII, and this may be another source of the eventual friar character.[158] Often in the games, Tuck, rather than Robin, is Marian's partner, especially in dances. One cannot but feel that their link to Robin comes through these games, especially as the games become transformed into more literary dramatic pieces. Shakespeare's Falstaff still saw Marian as possessing an immoral character. It may well be that the initial association between Robin Hood and both Maid Marian and Friar Tuck was in the processions and games in local villages, where Robin Hood games, May games, play games, greenwood celebrations, Moorish dancing and various other elements were easily welded into one procession and entertainment, and increasingly confused into closer relationship.

We have earlier pointed out the possibility that the games and plays came before the ballads. There is no certainty about this, in either direction. The surviving evidence is too unclear. The problem is that the earliest versions are usually printed versions and clearly printed long after their origins. This is true especially of the ballads. Equally, the play-games were not of a nature to demand much printed — the dialogue was not the vital component. However, since the general conclusion of critics is that the ballads came first, it seems wise to balance this with such thoughts as why the Robin Hood ballads contain so much that seems to originate from the play-games, such as animal skin disguise, disguising in general, combat matches, dancing and music, and other elements that are quite likely to have had their origin in public performance. We tend to side with David Wiles and give emphasis to the importance of play-games at the beginning of the making of the Robin Hood legend.

Perhaps even more important in the long run is the effect of the popularity of Robin Hood as a subject for stage drama in this period, which itself grew out of the old play-games. It was here that the most enduring impact was to be made. The work of Anthony Munday is especially important. In 1598, Munday was called 'our best plotter' by Francis Meres — though this may be a pun on his spying activities as well as his authorial achievements.[159] His works were not, perhaps, the greatest dramas of the age, but his contemporary reputation for excellent plotting was deserved. In the phrase of Stephen Knight, Munday imagined 'a new biography for Robin Hood'.[160] There have been various additions and changes to the Robin Hood legend since the time of Munday but his basic 'biography' has survived. Munday was obviously aware of the popular ballads of his day, though he only made limited use of them. Whether he gained information from now lost sources, or invented elements not previously recorded, we cannot know. It is of some interest that in his play about Sir John Oldcastle, Munday refers to Oldcastle's steward Harpoole owning a book about Robin Hood.[161]

Our Robin Hood owes a great deal to Munday's Robin Hood – the noble earl of Huntington (or Huntingdon). Why Munday chose this particular noble title is an interesting question. There were historical earls of Huntingdon, though none that match Robin Hood. The earldom had been held for some time by members of the Bruce family, which produced kings of Scotland. Is it mere coincidence that Munday has a Bruce family in his Robin Hood plays? There was an actual earl of Huntingdon in Munday's own period in Henry Hastings. Hastings was Lord President of the North and 'the most Puritan of all the nobles'. He was related to the royal family and other important nobles. He was married to the earl of Leicester's sister, Katherine, and an ally of that earl. They rode alongside each other at the funeral of Philip Sidney. Hastings was descended from Edward III and was 'the nearest Protestant male in line'.[162] There were claims that Leicester planned to make him Elizabeth's official successor. When it was feared that Elizabeth might die of smallpox, Hastings was seen as a possible successor by the Protestants. Munday was taking a risk in making Robin into Huntingdon when Elizabeth's Huntingdon had a claim to the throne, though Huntingdon remained firmly loyal to Elizabeth. He had been recognised as earl of Huntingdon by Elizabeth in 1561.

Munday set Robin in the Plantagenet period of Richard the Lionheart and John. It is Munday who turns Prince John into the Robin Hood villain. We should take seriously the possibility that Munday, who was at least a Catholic sympathiser, chose Robin Hood for much the same reason that others have since: to make a political point about resistance to authority. In Munday's plays, Prince, and later King, John *is* a villain, chiefly because of his lusting after Marian and the lengths to which he is prepared to go to get her. He is forgiven more than once, but he persists. In the play, Leicester refers to him as 'This Goblin of the night'; Hubert calls him 'this wanton king, repleat with crueltie'; while to Bruce he is the 'tyrant Iohn'. Even John's mother, the queen, refers to his 'unkingly lust and crueltie'. Munday, who made many contributions to the development of the Robin Hood legend, may then be credited with turning Prince John into the chief villain. In Munday's second play there is an odd reference to writing in Saxon during this Plantagenet period and this may have started a further distortion in the legend of turning Robin into a Saxon hero against the Normans.

Munday also makes Robin a protector of women. His outlaws are told they must not abuse women but use them well and 'lustful thoughts expel'. The outlaws shout in reply 'we like it well'.[163] No lewd gambolling here then as in the play-games! They are told the rules of the band include to 'never do the poor man wrong', and not to spare 'a Priest, a usurer, or a clarke'. Here, more than anywhere, we see the origins of the Robin of modern cinema and television. He is no longer simply the costumed figure of the play-games but becomes an individual with a history and a character.

There is no doubt that Munday contributed largely to the modern nature of Robin Hood stories — the nobility, the period and the royal villain. Yet, oddly, given that Munday was noted as the 'pageant poet' who wrote ballads, he did not introduce the most obvious ballad plots into his plays — no Guy of Gisborne, no tinkers or potters, no forced dining and no archery competitions.[164] What we can say, is that the Tudor and Stuart dramas transformed some aspects of the Robin Hood stories but did not incorporate all the elements with which we are now familiar.

In this period, the ballads may have been the main source of information on Robin Hood. The plays are often surprisingly different from the ballad tales. Yet in some ways, the Robin Hood plays have had a greater impact in the long run. When we come to modern times, as we have seen, the visual media has taken over as the main vehicle for the transmission of Robin Hood stories to the general public. The dramatists of the Tudor and Stuart period had much the same problems as the writers of films. The existing stories had to be elaborated and expanded. Modern visual versions have borrowed a good deal from the early plays. These plays were themselves following the old tradition of play-games. One element of importance was the action involved — the matches and competitions. Plays for the theatre, however, also needed more complex plots and to develop the thought processes of the characters, turning them into more rounded individuals.

The other major conclusion about these Robin Hood dramas relates to the political attitude of the writers. Why did they select Robin Hood as a subject? Our answer to this question lies in a consideration of the dramatists concerned. As we have seen, three writers in particular chose to write plays in which Robin played a major part — Anthony Munday, Robert Greene and Ben Jonson. Munday was probably a spy, certainly involved in secret political manoeuvrings, unpopular even among his own kind. Greene was from an ordinary background, disinherited by his father. He deserted his wife and child and had an illegitimate child. He was ashamed of his own life and misdeeds, of which he repented, and turned to religion and the hope of salvation. Ben Jonson knew his own talent and felt that he was undervalued by his contemporaries. His main ambition was to write serious classical-style plays but they proved unsuccessful. Jonson came from a lowly social background.

All three of these men knew that the profession of playwright was not thought respectable. Each sought to make a mark by other means. They knew they were outsiders in their world, belonging neither to the ordinary people nor to the nobility and the court. It does not take a great deal of working out to see that Robin Hood would be an attractive subject to such men — an outlaw, an outsider, a threat to authority.

Robin Hood and Robert the Bruce

A particularly important conclusion from this chapter has to do with the development of Robin into the aristocratic earl of Huntingdon. We have seen that the work of Anthony Munday was especially significant in this respect but the origins of the idea remain obscure. We cannot pretend to solve the puzzle but we can offer at least one possibility.

The connections between the aristocratic Robin Hood and the great Scottish hero Robert the Bruce, who became King of the Scots, are surprisingly numerous. First and foremost, the Bruce family, over a long period, held the earldom of Huntingdon in England. Second, the Bruces had Scottish connections and were at times opposed to the English establishment. Robert the Bruce was, for some time, a famous outlaw. In political songs, the Bruce, as he was known, was called 'kyng of somere' and 'King Hobbe'. In his early life, he was as much an Englishman as a Scot and indeed has been called by a leading modern historian 'essentially a Yorkshireman'.[165] The name Robert in the period was synonymous with Robin. Another point of interest is that in the early poem of the *Gest* Robin claims to the king that he had built a chapel at Barnsdale — surely only someone of considerable standing could have done that?[166] The Bruce family, as earls of Huntingdon, held Barnsdale in Rutland, which Stephen Knight has suggested might be the Barnsdale of the poems rather than that in Yorkshire.[167] Gisborne also has a connection. The Bruce family had founded the house of Guisborough in Yorkshire in 1130 and that was commonly known as Gisborne. The chronicler Walter of Guisborough, for example, called it 'Gysseburne'. Two leading members of the Bruce family were buried there. We would not claim that Robert the Bruce was the original Robin Hood but he probably contributed to the Robin Hood story. There was a later poem about 'The Bruce' but perhaps there was an earlier one now lost that provided material for the Tudor playwrights who turned Robin into the earl of Huntingdon. It cannot be proved but we suggest that a lost work on Robert the Bruce was known to those in the Tudor and Stuart period who contributed to the Robin Hood legend. They added material relating to Robert the Bruce as they turned Robin Hood into a noble.

Endnotes

[1] See Gerald Porter, 'Telling the Tale Twice Over: Shakespeare and the Ballad', pp. 165-78 in Cheesman & Rieuwerts.

[2] Wiles, p. 2.

[3] Knight, *Complete*, p. 100, quoting Lucy Sussex.

[4] Thompson, p. 186.

[5] *Minutes, i.*

[6] Knight, *Mythic*, p. 9.

[7] Wickham, *Medieval*, p. 148.

8 Wiles, p. 12.

9 Wiles, p. 4.

10 Wickham, *Medieval*, p. 131.

11 Wickham, *Medieval*, p. 172: 'any manere mommyng, pleyes, enterludes, on any other disgisynges', from an edict of the mayor and aldermen of London.

12 Wickham, *Medieval*, p. 161.

13 Dobson & Taylor, p. 39, from *Church-Wardens' Accounts of Croscombe*, IV, 1890.

14 Dobson & Taylor, p. 39, from the *First Report of the Royal Commission on Historical Manuscripts,* London, 1874, p. 107.

15 Knight, *Complete,* p. 104.

16 Wiles, p. 5, as described by Nashe.

17 Knight, *Mythic,* p. 58.

18 David Wiles, 'Robin Hood as Summer Lord', pp. 77-98 in Knight, *Anthology,* p. 90

19 Wickham, *Medieval,* p. 142.

20 Wiles, p. 4.

21 Wiles, p. 6.

22 Henslowe, p. 92.

23 Dobson & Taylor, p. 40, from *The Diary of Henry Machyn,* Camden Soc, 42, 1848, p. 201.

24 Byrne, p. 215.

25 Wiles, p. 32.

26 Bradbrook, p. 20.

27 Hamilton, p. 20.

28 Byrne, p. 213.

29 Wickham, *Medieval,* p. 142, quoting Beaumont and Fletcher

30 Wickham, *Medieval,* p. 143.

31 Wickham, *Medieval,* p. 142 from Milton's *Ode to the Morning Star.*

32 Byrne, p. 213.

33 Wiles, p. 14.

34 Dobson & Taylor, p. 39, from Latimer's *Seven Sermons before Edward VI* , ed. E. Arber, London, 1869, pp. 173-74.

35 Wiles, foreword.

36 Wiles, p. 53.

37 Knight, *Mythic,* p. 52.

38 Wiles, p. 68.

39 Wiles, p. 8.

40 Wiles, p. 15.

41 Wiles, p. 15.

42 Dobson & Taylor, p. 42.

43 Knight, *Complete,* p. 110.

44 Wiles, p. 29.

45 Collins, *Greene,* p. 165.

[46] Bradbrook, pp. 96-7.

[47] Bradbrook, pp. 164-5.

[48] Wood, p. 118.

[49] Hill, p. 132; Chambers, *Elizabethan Stage,* IV, p. 327.

[50] Bradbrook, p. 75.

[51] Bradbrook, p. 173.

[52] Hotson, p. 298; Bradbrook, p. 103.

[53] Hotson, p. 227.

[54] Hotson, p. 298.

[55] Hotson, p. 301; *Henry VIII,* Act V Scene IV.

[56] *Minutes,* iii.

[57] Hill, p. 113.

[58] Hill, p. 119.

[59] Bradbrook, p. 20.

[60] Bradbrook, p. 53.

[61] Bradbrook, p. 25.

[62] Bradbrook, p. 27.

[63] Hotson, p. 62.

[64] *Minutes,* ii.

[65] Bradbrook, p. 45.

[66] Bradbrook, p. 62.

[67] Henslowe, p. 301 (?), muniment no. 22.

[68] Hotson, p. 306.

[69] Hotson, p. 306.

[70] Henslowe, pp. 288,290.

[71] Dobson & Taylor, p. 43 and n. 4.

[72] Henslowe, p. 7.

[73] Henslowe, p. 184.

[74] Henslowe, Appendix 2.

[75] Dobson & Taylor, p. 43 and n. 4; *Henslowe's Diary,* ii, p. 215.

[76] Knight, *Complete,* p. 116.

[77] Harrison, iii, p. 188.

[78] *Henry IV Part I* Act III Scene I, *Henry IV Part II,* Act V Scene III.

[79] *As You Like It,* Act I Scene I.

[80] Wiles, p. 82.

[81] Wiles, p. 20.

[82] Wiles, p. 84.

[83] Dobson & Taylor, pp. 43-4 and P. 44 n.1.

[84] Knight, *Complete,* p. 118.

[85] Collins, *Greene,* p. 163.

[86] Greene, *Mermaid,* p. 400; Collins, *Greene,* p. 161.

[87] Knight, *Mystic,* p. 49.

[88] Knight, *Complete,* p. 116.

[89] Crupi, p. 3.

[90] Harvey, ed. Harrison.

[91] Harvey, p. 20; Crupi, p. 9.

[92] Crupi, p. 9.

[93] Crupi, p. 10.

[94] Greene, *Groats-worth* and *Repentance*.

[95] Crupi, pp. 10-11.

[96] Crupi, p. 12.

[97] Harvey, pp. 37, 86.

[98] Harvey, p. 13: 'a surfeit of pickle herringe and rennish wine'; Crupi, p. 27.

[99] Crupi, p. 19.

[100] Crupi, p. 18.

[101] Greene, *Mermaid,* pp. 398-452.

[102] Dobson & Taylor, p. 208.

[103] Knight, *Complete,* p. 101.

[104] Wiles, p. 76.

[105] Dobson & Taylor, no. 20, pp. 208-14; Wiles, pp. 72-9.

[106] Dobson & Taylor, pp. 215-9.

[107] Dobson & Taylor, p. 216.

[108] Wiles, p. 76.

[109] Hill, p. 1.

[110] Hill, p. 122.

[111] Hamilton, p.xix, his mother died in 1599.

[112] Hamilton, p. xxii.

[113] Hamilton, p. xx; Hill p. 122.

[114] Hamilton, p.65.

[115] Halliday, p. 60.

[116] Chute, *Jonson,* p. 80.

[117] Chute for example on 'money'; Hill and Hamilton give a more favourable view.

[118] Dobson & Taylor, pp. 220-30.

[119] Hamilton, p.130.

[120] Hamilton, p. 131.

[121] Dobson & Taylor, p. 221.

[122] Harrison, ii, p. 328.

[123] Harrison, ii, p. 324.

[124] Hamilton, p. 130.

[125] Dobson & Taylor, pp. 226,227.

[126] Hill, p. 60; *Death, l.* 762.

[127] Wiles, p. 49.

[128] Dobson & Taylor, p. 223.

[129] Knight, *Complete,* p. 122.

[130] Knight, *Complete,* p. 129.

[131] Dobson & Taylor, p. 44.

[132] Knight, *Complete,* p. 132; from M.A. Nelson, p.161.

[133] Henslowe, p. 286.

[134] Chute, *Jonson*, p. 291.

[135] Lee, *Dudley Carleton*, pp. 68-9.

[136] Chute, *Jonson*, p. 345.

[137] Aubrey, p. 182.

[138] Knight, *Complete*, p. 139.

[139] Dobson & Taylor, p. 231; for the play see pp. 231-6

[140] See Greg's edition of *The Sad Shepherd*.

[141] Chute, *Jonson*, p. 344.

[142] Greg, p. 135.

[143] M.A, Nelson, 'The earl of Huntington: the Renaissance Plays, pp. 99-121 in Knight, *Anthology*, p. 99.

[144] Dobson & Taylor, pp. 237-42.

[145] Knight, *Complete*, p. 144.

[146] Wiles, p. 2.

[147] Wiles, p. 3.

[148] Byrne, p. 220, quoting Nicholas Breton.

[149] Wiles, pp. 3-4.

[150] Wiles, pp. 64-6.

[151] Wiles, pp. 68-70 prints extracts from the accounts.

[152] Wiles, p. 39.

[153] Wiles, p. 25.

[154] Harrison, ii, p. 306; Hamilton, p. xxii.

[155] Knight, *Mythic*, p. 61.

[156] Hill, p. 174; *Oldcastle*, IV, iii.

[157] MacCaffrey, *Shaping*, p. 75.

[158] Nelson in Knight, *Anthology*, p. 115.

[159] Hill, p.75.

[160] Barrow, p. 29.

[161] *Gest,* Dobson & Taylor, p. 111.

[162] Knight, *Mythic*, p. 5 and elsewhere.

5

Medieval Poems and Plays

The Medieval Poems

We are reaching the nub of the question now as we approach as closely as we can through literature to the origins of Robin Hood. It is near to certain that there were more poems about Robin Hood in existence in the Middle Ages than we know about. The direct evidence of actual surviving ballads or poems from before the Tudor period is extremely slight. It has been reckoned that only eleven ballads on any subject come from manuscripts earlier even than the seventeenth century.[1] Pollard has pointed out the similarities in plot and outlook between the earliest Robin Hood works and several other poems from the late Middle Ages, including *The Tale of Gamelyn*.[2] This helps to increase the possibility that many works only printed later may have had medieval origins. We have, however, reserved for examination in this chapter only those few poems that are even definitely medieval or most likely to be.

Dobson and Taylor suggest that the Provençal *ballada* was the origin of the ballad form and that this form was not used for Robin Hood material at all until the sixteenth century. This definition would mean that none of the medieval works were properly ballads. We shall not, however, restrict ourselves quite to this degree. We shall consider the poetic works on the potter and the monk, that on Guy of Gisborne and that on Robin's death. They were early Robin Hood poems and most commentators do see them as ballads.

Maurice Keen, among others, considers the works on the potter, Guy and the monk as especially early.[3] He also points out that although even the early ballads come only from the fifteenth century, they reflect an older world.[4] Keen's own choice of likely background period for this handful of poems is the fourteenth century. Our other medieval work is the *Gest of Robyn Hode,* which is certainly not in ballad form but is a lengthy poem. For our purposes, in seeking the truth about Robin Hood and his legend, the content of the early works is more significant than the specific definition of their poetic form. It is possible that none of these early works were for singing but were recited, which might be the main charge against them being ballads.

We shall later examine the references to Robin Hood works made during the medieval period and see that they precede *any* actual surviving works by almost a century, but for now let us at least look at these earliest poems. Several commentators have thought that the works that survive from the late medieval period show evidence of earlier origins, despite their relatively late date of survival in manuscript collections or in print. J. R. Maddicott, for example, suggests that the vocabulary in them belongs to an earlier period, at the very least before 1400. He suggests an origin in the first half of the fourteenth century. To Maddicott, the content of the *Gest* shows 'strong evidence for an early-fourteenth century origin'.[5]

Even in this handful of examples, we do not have any certainty over the dates of origin. We have narrowed the cases as nearly as possible on the basis of good evidence and opinion but there is not absolute certainty in every case. We shall discuss each in turn, the evidence for it being medieval, its content and its significance. In all cases, our knowledge is incomplete. We have no idea who composed any of these original works from this period and can only guess at important matters, such as the location of the author or the original date of his creation. Thomas Percy thought that the early ballads were in northern dialect and this seems generally to be right.[6] One of the most respected of modern scholars, Stephen Knight, has dated the *Gest* as written by 1500, *Robin Hood and the Potter* at about 1500 and *Robin Hood and the Monk* at about 1450.[7]

In any case, there must have been early works that were either not written down or whose written form does not survive. Undoubtedly, some of the works we have already examined, which survive first from the Tudor and Stuart period, had medieval origins now lost. The very earliest actual surviving work is a short piece of only three and a half lines. It was written in a Lincoln cathedral manuscript dated to *c.* 1400-1425. Brief as it is, it tells us that already by 1425 part of the Robin Hood tradition was established. It begins: 'Robyn hod in scherewod stod'.[8] It adds that he wore a hood, a hat, hose and shoes and carried twenty-four arrows — and that's it. Thomas Ohlgren points out that the Lincoln lines are not in ballad metre and this is interesting as the oldest actual surviving fragment of Robin Hood verse.[9] It has also been identified as being in a North Midlands dialect. A verse with similar content survives from the middle of the fifteenth century. It begins with the same line except 'Robin in Barnsdale stood'.[10]

The Robin Hood works are notable for being in the English language. Still in the late Middle Ages, educated persons tended to look down on works in English as not being quite the thing; Latin was the language of the learned and the educated. After the subjection of Anglo-Saxon to Norman French, English popular poetic works began to emerge again from the twelfth century. English lyrics and carols developed in the thirteenth century and increased in popularity through the Middle Ages.[11] The popular ballad was influenced by these forms and itself emerged in the final century of the medieval period. As an oral form, however, it may well have had an earlier existence that cannot be proven. References to Robin Hood works begin in the fourteenth century though the works themselves do not survive until later. There is doubt over whether the few surviving Robin Hood works from the Middle Ages are rightly called ballads at all. It may well be true that they were intended for reciting rather than singing.[12] E. K. Chambers saw the earliest Robin Hood works as 'recited minstrelsy' and 'rymes' rather than songs.[13] Thus, in the poem of *Robin Hood and the Monk* one hears it called a 'talkyng', as 'Now speke we of Roben Hode'.[14] The length of the *Gest* and its division into sections called fyttes argues against its being sung. It is, however, equally clear that as ballads developed they were sung, and the majority of the Robin Hood works we have so far examined *were* ballads: 'But yf thou wylt have a song that is good,/ I have one of Robyn Hode'.[15] In the view of David Fowler, it was during the fifteenth century that English folksong and metrical romance were worked together to produce the new form, 'a type of narrative song which we now call the ballad', with a stanza as a refrain.[16]

In this chapter, we shall look at a few major Robin Hood works that are generally thought to be the earliest. These include the *Gest* and the works on the monk and the potter. Less certainly quite so ancient, but arguably so, we shall also consider the works on Guy of Gisborne and on Robin Hood's death. For our purpose, the content rather than the form of the works is the main interest. We note that these early poems, like the early dramas, reflect aspects of medieval attitudes and thought. The subject may be an outlaw and his band but the poems respect moral virtues and religion. We discover that, from the beginning, Robin has some of his later attributes, including generosity to those who deserve it and care for the vulnerable in society. He may be a kind of thief but he is not presented as covetous, greedy or deliberately criminal. No one is going to think of outlaws as godly. Robin may not respect greedy or immoral religious individuals but he always respects Christianity and especially the Virgin Mary. Robin, though, especially close to the Virgin Mary, is said in the *Gest* also to have built a chapel to Mary Magdalene in Barnsdale — perhaps a hint at the need of repentance for a sinner.

1: The Gest of Robyn Hode

This work has often been seen as the most important single poem about Robin Hood, at least since its significance was fully recognised in the nineteenth century. It is also the most singular Robin Hood poem. Gray has suggested that it seems 'to defy precise categorization'.[17] There is considerable difference of opinion over its poetic merit as against its importance for details of the Robin Hood story. One critic, for example, considers it no more than 'a minor work'.[18] It is not a ballad nor is it a traditional romance. It has been called a 'popular epic'.[19] Bessinger questions whether it is a 'short epic or long ballad'.[20] Unlike most ballads, it is lengthy. It is broadly accepted as medieval and has been called 'the encyclopedia of the medieval Robin Hood'.[21] The printed versions that we have vary and were clearly adapted by different individuals. Matheson, after a close examination of the matter, believed that the original poem was probably the work of a northerner and possibly a Yorkshireman.[22]

There has been debate over who the *Gest* was intended for. It addresses both yeomen and gentlemen, so this is one clear answer. Holt has argued that it was more of a courtly work. The length and form tend to back the argument that it was meant for a minstrel to perform and such performance would most likely be for an upper class knightly audience.[23] Robin does act in a courtly manner towards women and the poor, with courtesy to all who deserve it. There is, though, also an equally clear picture of Robin and his men as yeomen heroes. One interpretation is that there were original separate shorter works aimed at a yeomen audience but that the author of the *Gest* combined them in his own way for a more upper class group.

Holt has argued that the problems in its plot are thirteenth rather than fourteenth-century.[24] He considers it the 'earliest' of the Robin Hood texts.[25] Maddicott believes that, from its vocabulary and content, it must be from '1400 at the latest' and prefers a date in the first half of the fourteenth century.[26] Maddicott also selects the fourteenth century for the subject matter of the poem, specifically suggesting 1334-38. Ohlgren, Ayton and Pollard favour a similar date.[27] However, no early manuscript survives to give a certain answer to the problem, and it probably was first printed only in or around 1500.[28] Child dated it between 1492 and 1534 and most would now accept the earlier date as more likely.[29] The poem does not survive in manuscript form and the earliest printed version known about has been lost. It was popular and survives in seven printed versions produced in London, York and Antwerp during the century from 1495. One reason for an early date of the original work rather than its printed form is the apparent early nature of the English.

A different approach, and one of the most interesting recent suggestions about the *Gest,* is that of Thomas Ohlgren, who speculates that the work was intended for recitation at a gild function.[30] He suggests that it may have been commissioned in the fifteenth century for the annual election dinner of a London gild, possibly the drapers. His argument includes pointing out the use of terms, such as master, brethren, and draper, in the poem. There are also several mentions of cloth. The outlaw band is presented as serving Robin as their master, with references to apprenticeship and the giving of liveries. There is no evidence that the poem was used by gilds though the possibility exists. Even if it was used in this way, this does not necessarily show its absolute origin — it could have existed already and been turned to such a purpose.

John Bellamy has suggested that one can see influence upon the *Gest* from other medieval poems, in particular from the story of Gamelyn.[31] This would suggest that the *Gest* is later than these influences. Bellamy points out some similarity in phrasing between the *Gest* and the *Tale of Gamelyn*. He has also made efforts to identify characters in the *Gest* from real life, but we shall return to these thoughts later.[32]

We follow Ohlgren in his revised dating of the surviving printed versions.[33] He argued that the edition printed by Richard Pynson of *A Lytell Gest of Robin Hode* from *c.* 1495 was the oldest. It was printed in London and only survives in fragments now kept separately. The fragment known as the first Douce fragment is now seen to be from a copy of Pynson. This is a leaf printed on both sides and previously used by a binder as a waste sheet. It is mutilated, with a hole in the middle, and has damage from torn corners and cut margins. It is now identified as part of fytte 8 of the poem. The Pynson edition has been generally dated to *c.* 1500 but Ohlgren believes it is probably earlier and suggests the 1490s.

The poem was also printed as the *Lytell Geste of Robyn Hode* by Wynkyn de Worde in London, perhaps as early as 1492 but possibly also as late as 1534.[34] One surviving sixteenth-century printed version, the Lettersnijder edition, *A Geste of Robyn Hode,* is now held in Scotland at the National Library in Edinburgh but probably was produced in Amsterdam by the Dutch printer Jan Van Doesborch between 1510 and 1529.[35] The type was cut by Henric Pieterszoon Lettersnijder and that font was used by several printers. There remains a doubt as to the actual printer of this version, though it was certainly printed in Amsterdam. A second version is now held in Cambridge. It has been seen as the oldest edition and much used. Following Ohlgren, however, we find it is 'an incompetent copy' of Pynson, and a 'poorer version' than that of Wynkyn de Worde. Another edition, the *Mery Geste of Robyn Hoode*, was printed in England in *c.* 1560.

The fact that there are so many early printed versions, seven already by the mid-sixteenth century, suggests there may have been an earlier beginning for the work. It was Joseph Ritson who revived interest in the *Gest* with his collection and comments and thus established its significance for scholars.[36] We shall use the version of Dobson and Taylor based mainly on the Lettersnijder and Wynkyn de Worde publications.[37] No doubt future editions will make more use of the Pynson version.

Thus, the medieval origin of this work, though widely accepted as early, is not one hundred per cent certain. One point worth making is that this poem was reprinted several times in the sixteenth century whereas, as we have seen, most Robin Hood printed poems appeared only in the seventeenth century and the other few early works were not reprinted until that century either. The *Gest's* significance is not to be questioned but it still poses many questions. A reasonable conclusion is that, in its surviving form, it was probably written in the earlier fifteenth century and printed in about 1500.

One constant cause of discussion about the *Gest* is the construction of the work, which is more complex than the normal ballad. It is not a ballad and in some ways is more akin to a medieval romance or epic. Unlike most medieval works of that kind, though, it is in English and does not concern what might be called epic material. In some ways, the nearest previous poetic works to it are those poems, though not in English, that deal with outlaw subjects such as Hereward the Wake, Fulk fitz Warren or Eustace the Monk.

It has been shown that at least twelve plots from earlier works in the medieval period have contributed to the narrative in the *Gest*.[38] Holt accepts the use of existing tales and sees the linking passages as 'contrived'.[39] Keen suggested that it might have been the result of joining two separate cycles, works on the Yorkshire outlaw and a separate set on the Nottingham sheriff.[40] This, of course, is purely conjectural and needs to accept that there were such works in existence earlier than the *Gest*. Keen also stressed the likely role of minstrels in the border region between England and Scotland.

What can be argued but not proved is that the *Gest* may consist of several separate known ballads combined to form this work. Many commentators, probably most, have seen the *Gest* as constructed from several separate existing ballads. Stephen

Knight, for example, has suggested that it is probably constructed from several lost ballads.[41] John Bellamy believes it used existing ballads fused into a knightly tale.[42] Many scholars have analysed the *Gest* to identify these separate tales. There may be minor arguments over the number of separate 'ballad' tales involved but it is not difficult to note different strands in the complex plot. We shall shortly examine the stories in the *Gest* in some detail. Among others accepting this concept of compilation have been Child, Clawson, and Fowler.[43] Maddicott also sees the *Gest* as a compilation and argues that the compiler was 'almost certainly a Yorkshireman'.[44]

The editors of the Percy Folio saw the *Gest* as 'strung together and assorted by some editor of Henry VII's time'.[45] One argument in favour of this view is that, although parts sound as if they are for reading aloud, such as 'Lythe and listin, gentilmen', the length and arrangement of the whole poem seems intended rather for private reading.[46] Another possibility is that it was for recitation with a rest between each part or fytte. We know that this was a practice between courses at a dinner. Various analyses accept there is something in this, though not all agree on the number of constituent parts.

The plots certainly show some influence from the earlier outlaw poems but most see the *Gest* as having some sophistication. Peter Coss, for example, considers it to be put together more carefully than a mere joining together — 'a refashioning of earlier tales'.[47] Knight agrees with this view, seeing a reworking of known tales rather than a simple stringing together.[48] As he points out, some of the later ballads are themselves constructed of several separate plots. In the sense that the writer has done more than simply add one existing ballad to another, this is clearly true. There is some awkwardness, though, and obvious signs of not completely sorting out inconsistencies from separate sources, such as the naming of the knight, the appearances of Reynolde Grenelefe and of Gilbert of the White Hand. On the other hand, there is also evidence of literary effort to construct a single work.

The *Gest* is written in sections called fyttes but several of the stories overlap into more than one fytte. It is generally assumed that, given its length, the poem is more likely to have been for reading than for recitation. However, the division into fyttes does not necessarily exclude recitation. Basil Cottle has pointed out that in *Sir Gawain and the Green Knight*, the poet in the story asks for a refill of wine before continuing with the next 'fit'.[49] This suggests that the fytte might be a division to allow for a break in recitation by the minstrel.

There is debate over how the *Gest* has been constructed. Majority opinion, and ours, is that the author relied on several known tales and assembled them deliberately into a single work. Several of these tales, even if only printed later, are known from other sources as individual ballads. It seems most likely that the author of the *Gest* knew a number of early ballads (lost now in the form they then existed) and worked them into his long poem about the activities of Robin Hood. We shall shortly look into the detail of the *Gest* but first let us provide a brief analysis of these separate plots.

The first plot in the *Gest* concerns a poor knight and how Robin helps him repay his debt. The second plot is about a wrestling match seen by the knight.

Then we have the story of a monk forced to dine with the outlaws and then and pay for it. The next story, involving an archery competition, is about Little John and the Sheriff. John has a match with the sheriff's cook and then they go to meet the outlaws. The Sheriff is tempted into the forest and forced to dine and then has to give up his treasure in return for freedom. Following another archery competition, Little John is wounded and Robin saves him. They take refuge with Sir Richard. Sir Richard is captured but rescued by Robin who kills the Sheriff in the process. The king comes to punish the outlaws but has to adopt a disguise in order to find them. He comes to recognise their loyalty and pardons them. Robin goes to court but in the end prefers his old life. The final plot is about Robin's death at the hands of the prioress of Kirklees and Sir Roger.

THE FIRST FYTTE

The *Gest of Robyn Hode* is divided into eight parts called fyttes. Ohlgren makes a reasonable case for the real division of the poem being in four parts rather than eight, each beginning with an appeal to 'lythe and listin, gentilmen'.[50] For our purposes, though, we shall analyse the poem as it stands. Others have suggested that the end of each fytte was intended to allow a break for a further course at a banquet — and dining is mentioned throughout the poem. Let us, at any rate, examine the interwoven plots in more detail as the *Gest* unfolds through its eight fyttes.

In the first fytte we have the story of a poor knight and how Robin helps him pay his debt to the abbot of St Mary's. The poem begins:

> Lythe and listin gentilmen,
> That be of frebore blode;
> I shall tel of a gode yeman,
> His name was Robyn Hode.

The poem is aimed at gentlemen (at least in a polite sense) and is about the yeoman class. The significance of the yeoman class in early Robin Hood works is considerable. We repeat Keen's summary of that class as 'men of independent status and some measure of prosperity, not gentry but certainly a cut about the ordinary peasant husbandman'.[51] Robin is a 'curteyse' outlaw, aiming perhaps at the gentry. The setting is Barnsdale in Yorkshire: 'Robyn stode in Bernesdale'. Little John, 'a gode yeman', is found in Robin's company. Robin is described as a good Christian who hears three masses every day, with a special feeling for the Virgin Mary and care for women in general. Robin promises no harm to good husbandmen who plough or to good yeomen. Nor will he harm any knight or squire who is a good fellow. He is thus no ordinary criminal. He does, however, hold a grudge against bishops and archbishops, and the Sheriff of Nottingham.

So the story begins. Robin tells Little John to take Much and William Scarloke with him and go to 'the Saylis,/ And so to Watlinge Strete' to waylay a wealthy guest and bring him to dine. They encounter a knight and take him back to Robin to dine — the familiar dining plot. The knight says he had been heading for Blythe or Doncaster.[52] In this early part of the poem, the knight is not named. They feed on venison, swan and pheasant. Robin then says the knight must pay for his meal but the knight says he has only 10s. Little John searches him and finds it to be the truth. The knight explains that his son had killed a knight of Lancaster and to save him he has sacrificed his wealth and borrowed from the rich abbot of St Mary's. He will lose his lands if he does not repay £400 by a given date. He says his friends have deserted him and no one will help him out. Robin tells Little John to take £400 from their treasure and they count out rather more than that. John suggests they should do something about the knight's shabby clothes and they provide him with scarlet and green livery. John asks Robin to provide the knight with a horse, so Robin produces a grey courser, a new saddle, as well as a good palfrey. Robin gives him a year to repay the loan and offers Little John to act as the knight's man.

THE SECOND FYTTE

The knight tells Little John he must go next day to St Mary's Abbey in York to pay the abbot the £400 — otherwise he will lose his land. We move on to the monks, discussing the situation while they wait for the knight to repay the loan. The prior expresses some sympathy but the abbot and the cellarer show no lenience. The knight arrives and pretends to the abbot that he has no money. He asks for more time to pay. He is testing the abbot's character. The abbot, the justice and the sheriff refuse to allow any delay. The abbot calls him a 'false knight'. The knight defends himself as having fought in jousts and tournaments and been in danger but, seeing they will not relent, he pays the £400. He goes home to his wife in Verysdale, generally thought to be Wyresdale (or Wyersdale) in Garstang in Lancashire — though some have suggested locations in Yorkshire or Nottinghamshire.[53]

Later, the knight recovers and sets off for Barnsdale to pay off Robin's loan. On the way, he comes across a crowd gathered for a wrestling match. For the sake of Robin Hood, the knight protects the yeoman about to be killed because he is an outsider and gives him money for wine.

THE THIRD FYTTE

The third fytte begins again by appealing to the gentlemen to listen. It launches a new plot centred on Little John. John goes to an archery competition in Nottingham in which he slits the wand three times. The sheriff considers him the best archer he has ever seen. John claims he is Reynolde Grenelef and was born in Holderness (in the East Riding of Yorkshire). The sheriff offers him a place as his man. John agrees but promises to be his 'worst servaunt'. With the sheriff away, John demands a meal from the steward. The butler shuts the door against him but John strikes him, nearly breaking his back, and helps himself to ale, wine and food. The cook confronts John and they fight with swords. John is impressed by the cook's fighting and suggests he join the outlaws. They dine on the sheriff's food and then steal the sheriff's treasure and take it to Robin. John later encounters the sheriff hunting. John asks forgiveness for his actions and tells the sheriff he can show him a fine hart and herd. Instead he leads him to Robin Hood. The sheriff is forced to dine, served from his own stolen silver. Robin has the sheriff's clothes removed except for his breeches and shirt. The sheriff says he cannot bear to stay any longer and promises friendship in return for his freedom. One notes that although the sheriff is the opponent, he is not the violent, wicked sheriff of modern tales.

THE FOURTH FYTTE

> The sheriff dwelled in Notinham;
> He was fayne he was agone;
> And Robyn and his mery men
> Went to wode anone.

Here begins another new tale. The sheriff has returned to Nottingham and the outlaws are in the forest. Robin feels the need to improve his finances. He tells Little John, Much and William Scarlok to 'walke up under the Sayles,/ And to Watlynge strete' and there waylay a traveller. They go to the Sayles but see no one until they reach Barnsdale where they see two Benedictine monks riding towards them. Here is one of the faulty joins, as the poem now refers to only one monk with fifty-two men. They confront the monk and say they wish to take him to their master, Robin Hood. The monk knows that 'stronge thefe' and has heard no good of him. The monk's men clear off leaving only a little page and a groom. The outlaws take him to Robin — interestingly, in a house — to 'the lodge dore'. Robin doffs his hood but the monk does not respond in kind. Robin blows his horn and 140 outlaws appear. They make the monk wash and be seated for dinner. The monk says he is the high cellarer at St Mary's abbey. He swears he knows nothing of the knight's loan. He says he has only 20 marks on him. Robin says if that is true he will not take anything. Little John searches the monk's possessions and finds over £800, which, as he has lied, Robin keeps to pay for the dinner. The monk is sent back to his abbey. The knight then arrives in Barnsdale. He tells Robin he has been delayed by the incident at the wrestling match where he had helped a poor yeoman. He offers Robin £400 to repay the loan plus 20 marks interest as thanks. Robin tells him that the high cellarer has more than repaid him already. He tells the knight that he is welcome any time under his 'trystell tre' — a recognised meeting place for the outlaws. He gives the knight a further £400.

THE FIFTH FYTTE

> Now hath the knight his leve I take,
> And wente hym on his way;
> Robyn Hode and his mery men
> Dwelled styll full many a day.

Another tale now begins about the sheriff who organises an archery competition for 'the best archers of the north'. The prize is an arrow of silver and gold. Robin is informed when under his trystell tree. He takes 140 men to Nottingham. Six are chosen to shoot with him. Robin shoots three times and each time slits the wand but so does Gilbert of the White Hand. John, Scathelike, Little Much and Reynold (now a separate character) also shoot. Robin wins the arrow. At once, horns blow and Robin realises it is a trap. Robin's men shoot so well that the sheriff's men flee. Little John is wounded in the knee and tells Robin to kill him so he will not be captured but Robin takes him on his back and carries him a mile, stopping to shoot as he goes. They come to a castle belonging to Sir Richard at the Lee. Sir Richard thanks Robin for his previous courtesy in the greenwood — so one assumes this is the poor knight of the previous episode. It does suggest two separate ballads joined together and not quite sufficiently adjusted. Sir Richard prepares to defend his castle against the sheriff, shutting the gates and pulling up the drawbridge.

The Sixth Fytte

The sheriff comes to besiege Sir Richard's castle. Finding it defended, he calls the knight a traitor and goes to London to inform the king (not named). The king says he will come to Nottingham. Robin returns to the greenwood. The sheriff waits for Sir Richard to go hawking by the river and then captures him and takes him to Nottingham. Sir Richard's wife rides to tell Robin. Robin heads for Nottingham with 140 men. They meet the sheriff and Robin shoots him with an arrow and cuts off his head with a sword — a far more brutal outcome than the meeting in the forest! The outlaws attack the sheriff's men and release the knight. They take him to the greenwood until they can get pardon from 'Edwarde, our comly kynge' — so the king is now named though not numbered.

The Seventh Fytte

> The kynge came to Notynghame,
> With knyghtes in grete araye,
> For to take that gentyll knight
> And Robin Hode, and yf he may.

The king comes to Nottingham to capture Sir Richard and Robin. He seizes the knight's lands and goes through Lancashire to 'Plomton Parke'.[54] The king promises that anyone who cuts off Sir Richard's head should have his lands. One of his men points out that this will not happen until they first capture Robin Hood. The king remains half a year in Nottingham but has no news of Robin except that he continues to kill the king's deer. Then, a forester suggests that the king should take five of his knights and disguise themselves as monks. He will then lead them to the outlaw. The king dresses as an abbot and Robin confronts the group riding through the greenwood. Robin takes hold of the king's horse and demands money. The king says he has only £40, which Robin takes. The 'abbot' tells Robin that the king wishes to meet him in Nottingham. Robin expresses his loyalty: 'I love no man in all the worlde/ So well as I do my kynge'. He invites the abbot to dine. He blows his horn and 140 men appear. They kneel before Robin. The king thinks they are more obedient to Robin than his own men are to him. They dine on venison, white bread, good red wine and brown ale. They then demonstrate their archery skill. The game is that anyone who misses the target receives a buffet on the head. When Little John and Scathelocke miss Robin gives them a good buffet. Robin hits the target twice but misses at the third attempt. Robin suggests that the abbot should give him the buffet, which the abbot does with such force that Robin is knocked down. At last, Robin and Sir Richard realise that the abbot is really their king and kneel before him, as do all the outlaws. Robin asks pardon, which is granted on condition he goes to court.

THE EIGHT FYTTE

The king asks to buy green cloth from Robin and changes into a Lincoln green garment instead of the monk's habit. They go to Nottingham playing pluck buffet on the way — shooting as they ride, with the king receiving many a buffet from Robin. When the townsmen see the outlaws all in green, they fear that harm has been done to the king, and begin to run off. The king laughs and everyone is relieved. They feast and sing. The king restores his lands to Sir Richard. Robin stays with the king for fifteen months but then decides he has had enough of court. He asks the king if he can return to Barnsdale to the chapel he had built to Mary Magdalene. The king gives him seven days' leave. Robin returns to the greenwood and hears the birds singing. He kills a hart then blows his horn and all the outlaws gather. Robin stays on in the greenwood for twenty-two years. He is then tricked by 'a wicked woman', the prioress of 'Kyrkesly' (Kirklees), who was related to him.[55] She acts out of her love for a knight, Sir Roger of 'Donkesly'.[56] They plan to kill Robin. Robin goes to Kyrkesly to be bled but it is a trick to kill him. This version of Robin's death is very brief and does not even mention that he is actually killed though that is the clear implication. It ends with praise of Robin as 'a good outlawe' who 'dyde pore men moch god'. Perhaps, by this time, the author thought his audience would have had enough poetry.

2: Robin Hood and Guy of Gisborne

There is strong opinion that two other ballads have a medieval origin.[57] We have decided to enter them at this point, but with some hesitation. These are the ballads about Guy of Gisborne and Robin's death. Dobson and Taylor consider the fact that these two works existed 'in some form during the fifteenth century is not of course in dispute'.[58] The existing medieval works show knowledge of the plots in these works but they only exist on paper from a later date. It was necessary to mention these in an earlier chapter since they remained significant in the Stuart period and contributed to the view then developed of Robin's career. Both of these poems have a more violent content than is common in most Robin Hood ballads and some have been convinced that this outlook is one argument for a medieval origin. Hilton, for example, sees the 'harmless' Robin Hood as deriving from post-medieval ballads — in other words, that the medieval Robin was a dangerous and ferocious outlaw capable of cruelty and criminal acts.[59]

There is also a clear link between the plot in *Guy of Gisborne* and that of the surviving play fragment from *c.* 1470. Percy included the ballad in his first edition of the *Reliques* and claimed it was 'never before printed'.[60] He too expressed the opinion that it carried marks 'of much greater antiquity than any of the common popular songs on this subject'.[61] Its language has also been judged to be ancient — that is, medieval.[62] The Percy version also has obvious omissions, perhaps from careless copying. As a result, the ballad, as it stands, seems incomplete.

From the beginning, 'Guy of Gisborne' has a feeling of antiquity in its language. The opening stanza is very like that in the 'Monk' — taking us to the forest with its leaves and the birds singing:

> When shales beene sheene, and shradds full fayre,
> And leeves both large and longe,
> Itt is merry, walking in the fayre fforest,
> To heare the small birds singe.

Robin and Little John come upon a yeoman leaning against a tree. He has a sword and dagger and is wearing a 'capull hyde' — that is, a horse hide. John offers to approach the man first but Robin sends him on his way. John goes on to Barnsdale where he finds that two members of the outlaw band have been killed. One should note in these early works the significance of the Yorkshire and Barnsdale locations. Meanwhile, the sheriff is in pursuit of Scarlet (first name not mentioned). John intervenes and, with his bow, shoots the sheriff's man, William a Trent. The bow is called a yew bow, which 'fell down to his foote' — that is, a longbow.[63] John is captured and tied to a tree. The sheriff promises to hang him.

Meanwhile, Robin has approached the yeoman, who is Sir Guy. Guy says he is looking for the outlaw Robin Hood. Robin does not say who he is. They have an archery competition. They are both good shots, and, with his second arrow, Guy hits the garland but Robin then splits the wand. Robin's opponent says he is called 'Guye of good Gysborne'. Robin says he lives in the wood and his name is 'Robin Hood of Barnesdale' — an interesting link for Robin to a location that suggests more than simply a place where there is an incident.[64] They then fight with swords. Robin trips over a tree root and Guy pierces him in the left side. Robin manages to rise and, with an awkward stroke, kills Guy. He takes his head by the hair and, with an Irish knife, cuts his face so that it is unrecognisable.

Robin changes clothes with the dead Guy, putting on the horse-hide. He takes Guy's horn and blows on it. The sheriff hears it and then sees 'Guy' coming towards him and offers him a reward for killing Robin Hood. Robin says all he wants to do is strike Robin's man, that is, the captive Little John. Instead of which he takes his knife and cuts John free, giving him Guy's bow. The sheriff and his men flee but John shoots and kills the sheriff. Here the poem abruptly ends.

3. Robin Hood and the Potter

The second Robin Hood work to be found in a manuscript of early date is that of the potter. It can just about be called medieval since the manuscript dates from 1500 and the work must be before that. However, Dobson and Taylor have questioned this date and suggest that a sixteenth-century one is more probable.[65] The reference to the proper price of pots at 5d could be a clue to date.

The Potter survives in a second Cambridge manuscript in a collection probably made by a priest.[66] It was previously bound together with a copy of *Prick of Conscience* but has since been separated. It consists of twenty-four leaves, which were rebound in 1875. It is written by six different hands, the main one identified as scribe A. He is considered as possibly a professional scribe, or at least 'semi professional', and possibly a clerk in the Paston household.[67] Matheson, however, having examined the text in detail, believes it to be 'an amateur production'.[68] The conclusion seems to be that the scribe is either a not very skilled professional or else a reasonably competent amateur! The manuscript contains a number of different romantic stories, including item 10 from ff. 14v to 19r, which is 'Robyn Hode and the Potter'.

A reference in the manuscript to meat for the marriage feast of 'my lady Margaret', taking place out of England, may relate to the marriage of Henry VII's daughter, Margaret Tudor, to James IV of Scotland. This happened in 1503 and would support an early sixteenth-century date. For the marriage, a list of food was entered in the manuscript on f. 14r. A more recent and convincing suggestion, however, is that the marriage referred to was in fact that of Edward IV's sister Margaret to Charles, duke of Burgundy.[69] This occurred in 1468 in Bruges and would mean that the manuscript and the poem were about thirty-five years older than previously thought. It would then be dated to *c.* 1468 rather than 1503.[70]

The manuscript probably belonged to Richard Call, a grocer who became bailiff to the Paston family in Norfolk. There is an inscription on the final page suggesting that it belonged to 'Ricardo Calle'. Ohlgren sees the collected items as 'a household miscellany', reflecting the personal interests of Richard Call.[71] Call lived from *c.* 1431 to 1504. He was estate manager to John Paston I and to his two sons — both called John. Call appears in the surviving Paston letters between 1453 and 1503. He was born at Bacton in Norfolk, the son of a grocer. He dealt with the Paston estates, their rents and accounts, among his various responsibilities. His relationship with the family suffered when he married Margery Paston, a union that the family, especially Margery's mother, for a while, did not approve. Margery's brother reckoned that she would now have to sell candles and mustard in the market. Ohlgren suggests this might have led Call to enjoy the potter poem in which Robin Hood, as a lowly potter, wins the favour of the higher social class sheriff's wife. Call had further reason to dislike sheriffs, as he and the family became involved in a case over claims to inheritance. This led to a spat with the sheriff of Norfolk, which resulted in John Paston I being outlawed briefly and he and Call being imprisoned for a spell in 1461. In a letter, Call desired heartily that next year they would have a 'good scheryf'.[72] Call and Margery had three sons before her death by 1482, after which he married a second time and had two further sons. Call was an educated man and knew French and Latin.

This ballad is thought to have been 'recited and not sung' and possibly originally to have been divided in fyttes like the *Gest*.[73] It is not an easy ballad to read since it has a particularly strong dialect element, thought to be from the Midlands.[74] The plot idea of taking on the disguise of a potter is not new with Robin Hood and had appeared earlier in the poems about both Hereward the Wake and Eustace the Monk, as it does with William Wallace.

The introduction of a potter as the central figure alongside Robin is seen as evidence of the developing interest in and by middling men, especially yeomen and urban traders. Richard Tardif has supported Unwin's suggestion that the sense of 'yeoman' in a town was of a journeyman or servingman, and that such as the potter or the butcher was a 'towne yeoman'.[75] Gild livery usually included a hood.[76] The potter ballad seems to be the earliest survivor of this type of plot — to be followed by, for example, the pinder, the butcher, the tanner and the tinker, and, on a more lowly level, the beggar. It is deliberately addressed to good 'yemen'. It is reckoned to be the second oldest Robin Hood ballad, after the monk ballad.[77] The title for it was first given by Joseph Ritson in 1832. It is generally more light-hearted than some other early works, without brutality or killing.

The poem begins with a summer setting in the forest, with blossom on the boughs and birds singing:

> Herkens, god yemen,
> Comley, cortessey, and god,
> On (one) of the best that yever bare bou' (bow),
> Hes name was Roben Hode.

It asks good yeomen to listen to a tale about another yeoman, Robin Hood, who worshipped the Virgin Mary and all women. Robin sees a potter coming towards him whom Little John says he had met at Wentbridge, when the potter had fought him. The location of Wentbridge is interesting since otherwise this poem seems to link more with the urban tradesman and town of Nottingham. Wentbridge, however, is in Yorkshire and near Barnsdale.[78] John wagers that none of the outlaws will be able to make him pay pavage to pass along the road. Robin accepts the bet. He stops the potter's horse and demands pavage. The potter refuses and says 'let go or else'. Robin takes up his sword and they fight. The potter seizes him by the neck and knocks him down. Little John and the outlaws approach, and Robin admits that John has won his bet. Robin then asks the potter if they can change clothes so that he can go to Nottingham in disguise. In the town, he sets up his stall and calls out 'Pots! Pots', which he offers at bargain prices. Wives and widows flock to get their bargain. When only five pots remain, Robin saves them to send to the sheriff's wife. She then invites him to dine.

The sheriff's men talk about a shooting match, which they then go to. The 'potter' boasts about his shooting and they give him a bow. Robin strings it. Robin pulls the string to his ear to shoot, and it is called a yew bow, so, again, we have a longbow. Robin outshoots the others and breaks the mark in three. He tells them that in his cart he has a bow given him by Robin Hood. The sheriff shows interest and the 'potter' promises to take him to Robin Hood the next day. They set out, and Robin bids farewell to the wife, giving her a ring. They go to the forest where Robin blows his horn to summon Little John and the outlaws. Robin takes the sheriff's horse and gear and says the latter must go home on foot. Robin promises to send the wife a white palfrey and says that but for her the sheriff would have suffered worse. The sheriff goes home with the palfrey and is met by his wife. She laughs aloud and says that now her husband has paid for the pots!

4: Robin Hood and the Monk

This ballad is generally recognised as an early work on Robin Hood, possibly the earliest. Maddicott sees it as the 'first surviving ballad'.[79] One argument in favour of its antiquity is the language, which some have thought more ancient than that in the *Gest*. References to yeomen of the Crown, the king's privy seal and the abbot of Westminster give some clue to dating and to a broader interest in the author than some early Robin Hood works. *Robin Hood and the Monk* first appeared in a Cambridge University Library manuscript dated to *c*. 1450, probably just after that.[80] Part of this ballad also survives in a second fifteenth-century manuscript, now in the British Library as Bagford Ballads.[81] *Robin Hood and the Monk* is widely accepted as the first ballad about Robin Hood to be written down and to survive.[82] In this work, we come as close as we can to the nature of the first Robin Hood poetic works.

The first manuscript contains a collection of twenty-eight various comic and moral pieces, often with a religious slant, as well as a short metrical chronicle about Edward I. It is in a small paper quarto of 132 leaves, bound in calf in the seventeenth century.[83] A few pages are lost. There are two main scribes, identified as A and B. It has been badly damaged by attempts to improve it with chemicals, which have stained parts almost to extinction. The scribe is thought to have been an amateur. *Robin Hood and the Monk* appears at the very end of the collection on ff. 128v to 135v. It consists of 358 lines. The religious nature of the material has caused speculation that the collector might have been a priest. If so, given the hostility to abbots and bishops in the contents, it is unlikely he was in a high position. From the poetical nature of the material, Dobson and Taylor suggest the collector was not a priest but a minstrel.[84] This remains a matter of opinion. Given the overall nature

1. Robin Hood fighting Little John, as depicted in *Robin Hood and His Outlaw Band*, Louis Rhead.

2. 1845 engraving of Robin Hood. Mary Evans Picture Library 10067655.

3. Photo of Robin Hood's Bay 1940s. Mary Evans Picture Library 10156004.

Above: 4. Robin Hood statue.

Right: 5. Robin Hood the Teddy at the Nottingham Tourist Centre.

Below: 6. The author's brother dressed as the Sheriff of Nottingham.

7. Errol Flynn from *The
Adventures of Robin Hood*. Mary
Evans Picture Library 10110764.

8. 'Robin and Sir Guy of
Gisbourne'. *Robin Hood and His
Outlaw Band*, Louis Rhead.

Right: 9. '"God-a-mercy, good fellow", Quoth Robin, "Fain would I know thy name"'. *Robin Hood and His Outlaw Band,* Louis Rhead, 1912.

Below: 10. Robin Hood fighting Little John at Sherwood Forest Country Park.

11. Nottingham Canal.

12. The Arboretum, Nottingham.

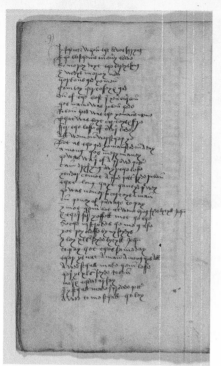

Above: 13. Title page of the early work about Robin Hood, the *Lytell Geste*. Wynkyn de Worde the printer. Cambridge University Library MS Sel 5.18. *c.* 1515.

Left: 14. The text of the early ballad *Robin Hood and the Potter*. Cambridge University Library MS Ee 4.35.f.14v.

15. The entrance to Nottingham Castle.

Above: 16. Nottingham Castle and gardens.

Below: 17. The outlaws.

18. The Friar Tuck statue outside Nottingham Castle.

19. Looking north from Barnsdale Bar.

20. Ye Olde Trip to Jerusalem, the oldest inn in England.

21. The Lacemarket, Nottingham.

22. Sherwood Forest Country Park.

23. An exhibition at Sherwood Forest Country Park.

Above: 24. Sherwood Forest.

Below: 25. The Major Oak in Sherwood Forest.

26. 'The Friar took Robin on his back'. *Robin Hood and His Outlaw Band*, Louis Rhead.

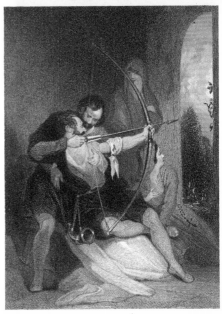

27. 1840 picture of Robin Hood's last minutes. Mary Evans Picture Library 10018534.

28. 'Robin shoots his last shaft.'
Robin Hood and His Outlaw Band,
Louis Rhead.

29. 'With a smile on his face he
reached over and drew forth the
warrant'. *Robin Hood and His
Outlaw Band*, Louis Rhead.

of the collection, the inclusion of the Robin Hood ballad seems more likely to be because it is about the monk than because it is about the outlaw.

Thomas Ohlgren has suggested that the manuscript belonged to one Gilbert Pilkington, ordained at Lichfield in 1465, and that it contained 'a priest's anthology of texts' or 'a clerical miscellany'.[85] This is based on the appearance of an inscription on f. 43r of 'Dominus Gilbertus Pylkyngton', probably the scribe and possibly the author. The collection seems to reflect his interests and to have been for his own personal use. A Yorkshire branch of his family had possessed Kirklees Priory, which was sold to Robert Pilkington in 1548 and owned by the family until 1565. Gilbert had progressed through a clerical career as subdeacon, deacon and priest. He had connections with a nunnery near Lichfield and was ordained as a priest in 1465. The dialect in the manuscript has been identified as West Midlands and, more particularly, from West Derbyshire, probably on the Cheshire/Staffordshire border. The geographical location of Pilkington and his manuscript plus the links with Huntingdon, Kirklees and even Tottenham have some significance, which we shall investigate further at a later stage.

D. C. Fowler has seen *Robin Hood and the Monk* as a piece for recitation rather than singing: 'Thus endys the talking of the munke/ And Robyn Hode', and others have agreed.[86] It consists of ninety verses and is recognised for its quality — 'in many ways the most artistically accomplished of all the Robin Hood ballads'.[87] Its length is also worth comment as it is the longest of those works that may properly be described as ballads (even if for recitation rather than singing).[88] Like the *Gest*, this poem seems to be strongly influenced by older romance tradition.

> In somer, when the shawes be sheyne,
> And leves be large and long,
> Hit is full mery in feyre foreste
> To here the foulys song.

The poem begins with summer in the forest, when the woods are bright, the birds are singing and the deer shelter under the trees. The time is Whitsun and the month is May. Little John finds it a merry morning. Robin responds that only one thing saddens him: that he cannot attend mass or matins. Robin says he intends to go to Nottingham. Much the miller's son advises him to take twelve of his yeomen with him.[89] Robin says he only needs Little John to carry his bow. John answers you carry your own bow and I'll bring mine. Over this, they have a shooting match in which John wins 5s for hose and shoes. They have an argument over it and Robin ends up hitting John. John then pulls out his sword and says if he were not Robin's man he would strike him. He goes off to Sherwood in a huff and leaves Robin to make his way to Nottingham alone.

In the town, Robin enters St Mary's church and kneels before the rood. A monk inside the church recognises Robin, sneaks out of the church and has the gates of the town shut so that Robin will not escape. The monk goes to the sheriff and tells him, explaining that Robin had previously robbed him of £100. The sheriff raises a band and heads for the church. They burst in and Robin now wishes he had not come alone. He takes his two-handed sword and kills twelve of his attackers. He breaks the sword over the sheriff's head and is then without a weapon. There is a damp patch on the manuscript that obscures the following lines but the sense seems to be that Robin is captured.

We return to the forest and John asks the outlaws to help Robin, who has been captured. Much offers to join him. They go to the house of Much's uncle and see a monk riding by with his page. They believe he is going to the king with news of Robin's capture. They confront the monk and ask for news. He says that Robin was captured the previous day and he was the one responsible. They pretend to go with the monk to protect him but John pulls him off his horse, takes up his sword and cuts off his head. Much does to the same to the page in case he tells about the monk's death. John and Much then take the letters on to the king.

Here is another missing patch in the manuscript. They come before the king and hand over the letters. The king asks the whereabouts of the monk who should have delivered them and John says he died on the way. The king gives John and Much money, makes them yeomen of the crown, and sends them back with a message for the sheriff to bring Robin Hood to him. John reaches Nottingham and finds the gate closed. The porter says it is because Robin is in prison. John passes the message to the sheriff, who then asks about the monk. John says the king had made him abbot of Westminster.

When the sheriff has drunk too much and fallen asleep, John and Much head for the gaol. John calls out to the gaoler that Robin has escaped. Then, when he comes out, John kills the gaoler. He takes the keys and releases Robin. The sheriff finds the dead gaoler and raises the alarm but Robin has escaped to Sherwood. Robin wants to reward John and offers to make him master of the outlaws. John refuses and says he only wants to be a fellow. The king hears what has happened. He realises that both he and the sheriff have been tricked and admires John's loyalty to Robin. He decides to take no action.

5: Robin Hood's Death

We conclude this selection of early poems with the ballad called *Robin Hood's Death*. It is difficult to date precisely but some have argued for an early date. As with Guy of Gisborne, so with the death ballad there is a strong likelihood of medieval origin. In this case, the plot of the poem seems to relate closely to the closing part of the *Gest*, which is medieval and may be a much-abbreviated version of the same story. The violence of the plot has convinced some of an early origin and so has the tragic nature of the story — much at odds with the usual more light-hearted Robin Hood ballads of frolics in summertime and dishing the sheriff. Maurice Keen, for example, has noted the similarity of violent action in *Robin Hood and Guy of Gisborne* and this work to the two early poems about Adam Bell and *The Tale of Gamelyn* (fourteenth century).[90] On the other hand, the oldest surviving version of *Robin Hood's Death* is in the Percy Folio, and even that is only fragmentary, with twenty-seven stanzas surviving in a badly damaged manuscript. The complete work is thought to have had over fifty stanzas.[91] The seventeenth-century scribe of the Percy Folio entitled it *Robin Hoode his Death*. Despite the damage with the resulting loss of stanzas, this is still a much fuller version of Robin's demise than in the *Gest*, though the story obviously has a common origin. It is also a fuller version than appeared in later printed ballads. Judging from the number of later surviving copies, the story was more popular in the north than the south, perhaps because of its placement of the site of Robin's final moments and burial.

Robin opens the poem by saying he must go to Church Lees (Kirklees) for his veins to let blood; Will Scarlet says he ought to take fifty archers with him. He warns that there is a threat to Robin's life from some 'good yeoman'. Robin says only Little John need go with him to carry his bow. John says carry you own bow and we will compete at shooting on the way, which they do. They come to black water with a plank to cross it. There kneels an old woman who curses Robin. There follows the first missing section, so we know no more about the curse. Robin approaches Kirklees where the 'dame prior' (prioress) is Robin's aunt's daughter — his cousin. The prioress lets them in and Robin pays her £20 in gold. The prioress brings down a pair of blood irons wrapped in silk. She orders hot water and tells Robin to roll up his sleeve. With the iron, she cuts his vein and blood runs out; it bleeds thick and then thin, until, as he grows weaker, Robin realises he has been tricked. He speaks to John but again we lose the story through a gap. In the missing section, Robin has somehow come to be at the mercy of Red Roger. Robin reaches for his sword but Roger pierces Robin in the side with his sword. Robin is still able to strike Roger between head and shoulders and Robin says the body will be left for the dogs to eat. On hearing of the betrayal, John begs Robin to let him burn Kirklees to the ground. Robin refuses, as he does not wish to harm any widow. He asks John to carry him on his back and bury him with his sword at his head, arrows at his feet and bow by his side. Again, a section is missing and this, sadly, is the end of the poem. In later versions, Robin shoots an arrow and is to be buried where it falls — but we cannot be sure if that story was in the oldest version.

Medieval Plays

We know that Robin Hood was a subject for plays and performances in the Middle Ages. As we have seen, these medieval works inspired new plays in the Tudor and Stuart period. There are a few poetic works on Robin Hood that survive from the medieval period but very little on the content of plays. There is, however, good evidence that many performances occurred. David Wiles has listed the Robin Hood play references up to 1600.[92] The list includes, for example, mentions in Exeter for 1427, Norfolk by 1472, Henley-on-Thames for 1499, Thame in 1474 and 1496, Wells in 1498, and Staffordshire in 1497. One notes that none of the early references to performances are for the North. Because we have evidence of early plays, some historians see the drama evidence as of more importance than the poems. Stephen Knight, for example, has seen the ballads as 'secondary to the plays and games'.[93]

From the Middle Ages, very little survives of the texts for performance. One thing we do have is evidence about the nature of performances in noble households in the fifteenth century and one very brief text for a performance about Robin Hood and the sheriff. There are, of course, texts of plays on other subjects, mostly in the form of interludes or brief plays. These often have a moral tone and were generally performed in noble households. Often, they were intended to instruct and advise young nobles.[94] Young men were seen as likely to be hot headed and in need of guidance for life, models for behaviour and instruction in religion.

The surviving medieval interludes are nothing like the one surviving Robin Hood play text. This work seems more closely linked to rural performances for play-games, which involved entertainment, comedy and athletic competitions. What we are suggesting is that, from our admittedly limited evidence, the dramatic and poetic Robin Hood survivals point to them being for different audiences: the poems for noble and literary households and the country entertainment for a broader audience. This is too strong a division to sustain entirely. The poems include some ballads that were not concerned with matters for the nobility and are concerned with yeomen, urban tradesmen and outlaws. The one surviving play-game text seems pretty rustic in its nature but was probably performed by the noble household of the Paston family. What we are seeing, perhaps, is that already Robin Hood has a wide appeal through different media to both noble and lesser folk.

The Paston Evidence

Let us now examine the one brief play text about Robin Hood that survives and its connection with the Paston family. Like the *Piers Plowman* evidence, it is not direct. Other entertainment for that noble East Anglian family does not survive. The exception is the fragment of dialogue for *Robin Hood and the Sheriff,* from a manuscript that probably originally belonged to the Paston family.[95] This unique survival is enormously important. It gives us clear evidence that plays about Robin Hood were performed in the medieval period and is the only text showing the nature of the content of these plays.

In a letter from John Paston to John Paston II dated 16 April 1473, we hear of the unkindness of servants, including one William Woode, 'God haue hys sowle': 'that iff ye wolde take hym in to be ageyn with me that than he wold never goo fro me; and ther-uppon I haue kepyd hym thys iii yere to pleye Seynt Jorge and Robynhod and the shryff off Notyngham, and now when I wold haue good horse he is goon in-to Bernysdale, and I with-owt a kepere'.[96] William Woode is thought to have been a good archer who had earlier been involved in the military defence of Caister Castle. So here, on the eve of the Tudor age, we have evidence for a fairly high class family being entertained with plays about Robin Hood and employing their own servants to take parts, including that of the sheriff of Nottingham. One assumes that an invited audience, almost certainly including the local population, would come to watch what was clearly intended, with its sporting contests, as an open-air entertainment. It also shows that Barnsdale and Nottingham were well known to be associated with Robin — the reference to Barnsdale here clearly being a joke by Paston upon the well-known phrase that Robin Hood in Barnsdale stood. The mention of three years suggests that a play was performed annually, possibly at May time.

Robin Hood and the Sheriff

The earliest play about our hero to survive is *Robin Hood and the Sheriff* from c. 1475, which survives in a Trinity College manuscript. It had belonged to the Norfolk antiquary Peter Le Neve in the eighteenth century.[97] He had purchased a collection of Paston papers and it is probable that this sheet was included with them. It is written in a hand from the late fifteenth century and the play outline of twenty-one lines takes up only about half of a sheet of paper measuring 8 inches by 10 inches. It has traces of glue on and was probably once bound in a volume with other pieces. On the back of the sheet is a record of money received by a John Sterndalle for 1475-76, during the reign of Edward IV.

The manuscript is believed to have belonged originally to the Pastons. It has been seen as 'one of the most historically significant items in the entire corpus of Robin Hood literature'.[98] It is the first surviving manuscript of a play about Robin and is the only medieval one. It seems to be based on the same plot that we find in the ballad about Guy of Gisborne. It was probably the play performed by William Wood, the servant of the Pastons, who later left them. That play was called *Robyn Hod and the Shryff of Nottyngham*. The entertainment clearly required a good deal of action to go with the dialogue, which consists of a mere twenty-one lines in two brief scenes.

The manuscript play consists simply of dialogue and does not even name the speakers or describe the actions, which have to be inserted. Even the brief summary, which we now give, therefore, has to make some interpretation. An unnamed knight (possibly to be equated with Guy of Gisborne) promises the sheriff that he will catch Robin Hood; this episode certainly suggests that the plot of Guy of Gisborne was known to the playwright. The sheriff replies that he will reward him if he succeeds. The knight goes on to confront Robin and challenges him first to an archery competition. Robin cleaves the wand. Then they compete at stone throwing, which Robin wins. Their next competition is to 'caste the exaltre' — probably meaning to throw the axel tree or axile tree. This was a term for the May pole, so the challenge was probably to toss the caber, though the text does not give the conclusion to this competition.[99] Wiles, however, thinks the exalter competition is wrestling but the wording seems to suggest caber tossing.[100] The rivals do then wrestle and once more Robin is the victor. The knight says he will blow his horn, which again reminds one of Guy of Gisborne using a horn in the ballad. In the ballad, Robin blows the horn and the sheriff recognises it as Guy's and thinks Robin is Guy. In a final fight in the play, the knight is killed. Robin beheads him and puts on his clothes and carries his head in his hood — another similar outcome to that in the Gisborne ballad. We move on to a group of outlaws (unnamed) conferring. One asks for news of Robin and hears that he has been captured by the sheriff. The outlaw threatens to kill the sheriff. Friar Tuck (Frere Tuke) then appears with a bow. The sheriff captures all of the outlaws present and they expect to be taken to prison. Here the excerpt concludes.

One guesses that in the conclusion Robin will rescue his men. The links with ballad plots is clear. Also interesting is the violence with killing and beheading — closer to the early ballads than the later and milder ones. Although not named, the knight in the fragment parallels the role of Guy of Gisborne in the ballad. It adds to the argument that the ballad about Guy was originally early and medieval. This early fragment is also the first known evidence for the appearance of Friar Tuck in connection with Robin Hood — though the name applied to outlaws is found in 1417 as the name given to a Sussex cleric who was outlawed.

Robin Hood and the Sheriff is from *c.* 1475 and is therefore medieval rather than Tudor, but it survives only from the very close of the Middle Ages. The original manuscript has no title and is just a collection of twelve couplets on a single sheet without names for the speakers, except sometimes within the text. As we have suggested above, it was probably the play performed for the Pastons. It is more a series of athletic or sporting competitions than a play and would clearly have taken a good deal longer to perform than it takes simply to read the lines. It has a very clear connection with the play games for public entertainment at certain times of the year. The words simply set each scene for a series of combats or performances. The knight has come to arrest Robin for the sheriff, performing the role of Guy of Gisborne in the relevant ballad. The assumption is that the Robin Hood legend is so well known that it makes a good background for the current actions. Here the rivals go through a series of combats: archery, throwing the stone, throwing the axle-tree (probably like tossing the caber) and wrestling.[101] The knight seems finally to attack Robin with a sword and the final fatal combat occurs. Robin wins and beheads the knight. In the second scene, two men, one of whom is probably Little John, plan to kill the sheriff. The lines do not conclude the action. Friar Tuck is found trying his archery skill — possibly in comic fashion. It is interesting that Friar Tuck appears in this early play before he is named in surviving ballads. The sheriff arrests the outlaws and promises to imprison them. Either the lines are incomplete or else action continued to conclude the performance without words being necessary. Commentators guess that Robin, in the knight's clothes, would come to the rescue.

Clearly, by this late medieval period Robin Hood was a popular subject for local performances, though no other text for these survives. Although we do not have the texts for the contents, there is plenty of evidence for other performances of Robin Hood plays. One took place at Croscombe in Somerset in which Richard Willes played Robin. In 1498, a performance occurred at Wells in Somerset supported by the local authority and supplemented with dancing girls and church ales. In fact, the celebration was even called 'the time of Robin Hood'.[102] Often, these celebrations were accompanied by collections for the benefit of the local church, and they were called 'gatherings' in 1498-99.[103]

Conclusions

We have reached the end of the road in terms of surviving Robin Hood literature — the plays and ballads that provide the earliest evidence of Robin in fiction.

One question we must ask is how different is Robin Hood in the medieval works to Robin in the modern media, with which we opened this book? Given the passing of so much time, there is perhaps a surprising degree of similarity between past and present. Robin's chief outlaws are Little John, Will Scarlet (variously spelled and sometimes with a different surname), Much the miller's son and Friar Tuck. Robin's main enemies are the Sheriff of Nottingham, Guy of Gisborne and Sir Roger of Doncaster, along with some monks, not least the abbot of St Mary's York and Robin's cousin, the prioress of Kirklees. The main plots involve matches, disguise, archery competitions, dine and pay and tricking the enemy.

The main localities are Barnsdale, Sherwood Forest and Nottingham. Holt has argued that 'the nearer Robin gets to Nottingham the less authentic he becomes', yet from these earliest works there seems little to choose between the Nottingham and Yorkshire locations in date of origin or authenticity. Yorkshire and Nottingham, Barnsdale and Sherwood all appear frequently and widely.[104] In most of these early works, *both* locations are introduced.

Given the centuries that separate the medieval poems from the modern media versions, the number of recognisable factors is quite striking. The changes and additions are perfectly understandable and not terribly surprising. The modern media preference is for Nottingham and Sherwood, while Yorkshire is largely ignored. However, Nottingham and Sherwood are as authentic as Yorkshire. We should perhaps conclude that both Yorkshire *and* Nottingham are early settings for Robin Hood stories, and the only modern blip is to ignore the Yorkshire background.

One should note that in medieval English there are no standard spellings.[105] That means that we should not expect precise spellings for names and places but rather be ready to accept considerable variation. Writers, transcribers, printers all attempted to reproduce in their works spellings of the way in which they thought names were said, and, as we know even today, with dialect and regional differences, pronunciation and the sound of a name can vary a good deal. Literature in the English language was something of a novelty in the later Middle Ages and there was little tradition to follow on spellings. Since we only know the medieval pronunciation through the spellings we should not be too quick to condemn them. Sometimes, indeed, it is difficult to identify the places intended.

Our list of characters and localities found in the early works does omit certain elements, which we now take as part of the traditional story. There are a few very familiar outlaws, such as Little John, but few others are named. Many others have joined the outlaw band since — Alan a Dale, Asians from the crusade and so on. One of Robin's major enemies now is Prince John, who does not appear early.

We expect other kinds of plot now that we do not find in the early works. Probably the most common modern plot of this kind is that of romance between Robin and Maid Marian — who does not appear at all in the early medieval works. Indeed, in contrast to modern versions, in the early ballads 'women remain largely on the periphery'.[106]

Nor is there any appearance in the early works of the king one expects to encounter today, Richard I the Lionheart. The only named king is an Edward — without number. This means there are four possible candidates: Edward I, II, III or IV. Each of these kings has some supporter to be our man. If we accept that the king must be placed before the first mention of the rhymes in *Piers Plowman* in 1377 that leaves the choice between the first three Edwards. Edward II is probably the favourite for modern critics, though Ohlgren has plumped for Edward III.[107]

One of the major differences between the medieval poems and the modern media versions is the period in which the tale occurs. The chief clue is in the name of the king. Our modern versions usually have Richard the Lionheart as king. The king named here is Edward. Given that Robin must live before 1377 and the *Piers Plowman* reference, that would mean one of the first three Edwards. In the *Gest,* after Robin has left the king's court and returned to the forest, we find the lines:

> Robyn dwelled in grenë wode
> Twenty yere and two;
> For all drede of Edwarde our kynge,
> Agayne wolde he not goo.

If we take this clue literally then it suggests that the reign of the king continued for at least twenty-two years. That would discount Edward II and leaves us with the choice of either Edward I or Edward III. This clue relating to a real Robin Hood we shall return to in due course.

The attitudes displayed in the early works are of much interest. Why were the Robin Hood ballads written, who for and who by? There has been much modern debate over the intended audience. Maurice Keen initially favoured a lower social group and many have noted the appeal to yeomen. Although he later gave way on this, his point that the Robin Hood works seem aimed at a different audience from the 'chivalrous material' of the earlier French-style romances remains valid.[108] A. J. Pollard has argued that the early poems are about yeomen heroes and that we now see yeomen as a sort of middle class, some indeed with quite high social status.[109] He showed that the term 'yeoman' then could be used for men in various social positions, including those employed at court, and foresters.[110] Many commentators note an urban element in these early works and Ohlgren, for example, sees Robin as 'a mercantile hero to replace the knightly hero of the aristocratic romances'.[111] Holt, later followed by a repentant Keen, argued that the works were really aimed at a courtly audience, the general target for literary works at the time. The argument cannot be resolved with certainty since it can only be argued from the content of the works and not from much evidence about recipients. For what it is worth, it seems, from the content, to be more deliberately aimed at yeomen and the urban populace. These lesser men are generally also the heroes and central figures. In the ballad of the potter, for example, which is a model for many later ballads, there is admiration for the urban trader who proves a good match in fighting. However, it is also true that in the early works we find a good sprinkling of gentlemen, from Sir Richard on the good side to the villainous Sir Roger. Like the potter, Sir Richard is also presented as an admirable character. I am inclined to leave the argument unresolved and repeat the idea that Robin Hood made a good tale for all social levels.

One group the poems do not seem aimed at pleasing was that of clerics and the church. In general, there is an anti-clerical or at least critical attitude. It does not go so far as to allow heresy or proto-Protestantism but was in line with critics of Rome and some of the practices of the traditional Roman Catholic Church. Robin and his men respect Christ and the saints, and particularly the Virgin Mary — there is a clear pro-Christian attitude. But there is also a definite criticism of monks and prelates. The abbot of St Mary's is keen to seize land and to make a profit from loans, which is the sin of usury. The abbot lacks any sympathy for the poor knight who has been forced to borrow from him. Then there is the monk who is forced to dine with the outlaws. He is shown as a liar over what he carries and has treasure with him. The prioress of Kirklees is in cahoots with the treacherous Sir Roger of Doncaster, is probably guilty of sexual misconduct with him and then assists him in killing her own relative, Robin Hood. It is true that Friar Tuck does appear in the early drama survival, though not in the poems. Friar Tuck does become an outlaw and later a popular figure, but in the early plays he is presented as a figure to be ridiculed, a target for those who criticise the church and not living the life that a friar should.

We also note some differences between now and then in the kind of man Robin Hood is. In the earliest works, he is not the kindly and amorous noble of modern film. Robin is violent and lives in a world of violence with his men committing brutal murders. Robin himself kills Guy of Gisborne in a particularly nasty manner. Robin is given a moral position — he is a Christian and he especially favours the Virgin Mary. He does not, however, as now, rob the rich to give to the poor. He does rob the rich clergy and he does help the poor knight, but there is nothing about helping the lowest in society (apart from the outlaws themselves). Robin is a man of violent action rather than peace. He fights. His weapons include a bow and a staff but he seems most often to wield a sword in his combats.

Endnotes

[1] Sargent & Kittredge, p. xiii.

[2] Pollard, p. 13.

[3] Keen, p. 116.

4 Keen, p. 135.

5 Maddicott, *EHR*, pp. 276,280.

6 Percy, *Reliques*, I, pp. 25-6.

7 Knight, *Complete*, p. 45.

8 Dobson & Taylor, p. 18; Knight, *Anthology*, pp. 13-4.

9 Ohlgren, *Early Poems*, p.18.

10 Ohlgren, p. 20.

11 Fowler, p. 5.

12 Fowler, p. 10, for examples, considers these works 'not ballads at all'.

13 Fowler, pp. 66-7.

14 Fowler, p. 67.

15 Fowler, p. 69.

16 Fowler, p. 18.

17 Douglas Gray, 'The Robin Hood Poems', in Knight, *Anthology*, pp. 3-37, p. 23.

18 J. B. Bessinger Jr., *'The Gest of Robin Hood* Revisited', pp. 39-50 in Knight, *Anthology*, p. 39.

19 Sargent & Kittredge, p. 255.

20 Bessinger in Knight, *Anthology*, p. 41.

21 Knight, *Mythic*, p. 22.

22 Lister M. Matheson, appendix, in Ohlgren, p. 210.

23 Holt, p. 110.

24 J.C. Holt, 'The Origins and Audience of the Ballads of Robin Hood', pp. 211-32, in Knight, *Anthology*, p. 228.

25 J.C. Holt, 'Robin Hood: Some Comments', pp. 267-69 in Hilton, p.. 269.

26 J.R. Maddicott, 'The Birth & Setting of the Ballads of Robin Hood', pp. 233-55 in Knight, *Anthology*, p. 234.

27 Pollard, p. 185.

28 Fowler, p. 79; Dobson & Taylor, 71-3..

29 Sargent & Kittredge, p. 254.

30 Ohlgren, p. 25.

31 Bellamy, p. 64.

32 Bellamy, ch.7, 'Other *Personae* of the *Gest'*, pp. 110-28.

33 See Ohlgren, chapter three.

34 Dobson & Taylor, p. 8; Cambridge University Library Ms. Sel. 5.18; Hales & Furnivall, p. 2. date Worde to c.1490 with a Scottish reprint in 1508.

35 Dobson & Taylor, p. 8; Ohlgren, p. 110.

36 Dobson & Taylor, p. 55.

37 Dobson & Taylor, pp. 79-112.

38 J.C. Holt, 'The Origins and Audience of the Ballads of Robin Hood', pp. 236-57 in Hilton, p. 251.

39 Holt, p. 24.

40 Keen, p. xv.

41 Knight, *Mythic*, p. 24.

42 Bellamy, p. 131.

43 See, for example, Knight, *Complete,* p. 48.

44 Maddicott, *EHR,* p. 282.

45 Hales & Furnivall, p. 51.

46 Knight, *Complete,* p. 71.

47 Peter R. Coss, 'Aspects of Cultural Diffusion in Medieval England: Robin Hood', pp. 329-43 in Knight, *Anthology,* pp. 334,337.

48 Knight, *Complete,* p. 75.

49 Cottle, p. 99.

50 Ohlgren, p. 166.

51 Keen, p. xvii.

52 Blith may be Blyth in Nottinghamshire, Dobson & Taylor, p. 81.

53 Dobson & Taylor, p. 88, no. 2; Bellamy, p. 77.

54 Dobson & Taylor, p.105, n. 1, suggest Plumpton Park near Knaresborough in Yorkshire, though Child and others have gone for that in Cumberland.

55 Dobson & Taylor, p. 111, n. 11, suggest Kirklees Priory near Huddersfield.

56 Dobson & Taylor, p. 112, n. 1, alternative 'Donkester' – clearly for Dncaster.

57 Dobson & Taylor, p. 7, consider they derive from 15th-century works.

58 Dobson & Taylor, p. 7.

59 R.H. Hilton, ed., *Peasants, Knights and Heretics,* Cambridge, 1976, p. 227.

60 Percy, *Reliques,* i, p. 115.

61 Dobson & Taylor, pp. 140-45; p. 140.

62 For example Dobson & Taylor, p. 140.

63 Dobson & Taylor, p. 142.

64 Dobson & Taylor, p. 144.

65 Dobson & Taylor, p. 9; Cambridge University Library MS. Ee.4.35, ff. 14v-19r; Holt, p. 15, accepts c. 1503.

66 Ohlgren, p. 20, MS. E.e.4.35.

67 Ohlgren, p. 69

68 Ohlgren, p. 190; appendix by Lister M. Matheson.

69 Ohlgren, pp. 74-5.

70 Ohlgren, p. 21.

71 Ohlgren, p. 22.

72 Ohlgren, p. 82.

73 Fowler, p. 84.

74 Dobson & Taylor, p. 124; Holt, p. 108.

75 Richard Tardif, 'The "Mistery" of Robin Hood: a New Social Context for the Texts' pp. 345-61 in Knight *Anthology,* pp. 348, 350.

76 Tardif in Knight, *Anthology,* p. 359.

77 Dobson & Taylor, pp. 123-32; p. 123 on date.

78 Dobson & Taylor, p. 19.

79 J.R. Maddicott in Knight, *Anthology,* p. 233.

80 Fowler, p. 80; Dobson & Taylor, pp. 113-22; Cambridge University Library, MS. Ff.5.48, ff.128v-135v; Holt, p. 15..

[81] Dobson & Taylor, p. 114, Bagford Ballads. The fragment has stanzas 69-72 and 77-80.

[82] For example by Dobson & Taylor, p. 1.

[83] Ohlgren, p. 29.

[84] Fowler, p. 81.

[85] Ohlgren, pp. 22, 67.

[86] Fowler, p. 82; Dobson & Taylor, p. 9.

[87] Dobson & Taylor, pp. 9,113.

[88] Dobson & Taylor, p. 113 dispute whether it should be called a ballad since it is meant to be recited.

[89] Just possibly the milliner's son as twice it takes the form 'mylner').

[90] Keen, pp.4,78.

[91] Dobson & Taylor, pp. 133-39; p. 133.

[92] Wiles, Appendix 1, pp. 64-6.

[93] Knight, 'Which Way to the Forest?', pp. 111-28 in Hahn *Popular Culture,* p.123.

[94] See Dunlop.

[95] See below, n. 14.

[96] *Paston Letters,* I, pp.460-61, no. 275; John Marshall, 'Playing the Game: Reconstructing Robin Hood and the Sheriff of Nottingham', pp. 161-74 in Hahn, *Popular Culture,* p. 162-66.

[97] Dobson & Taylor, no.19, pp.203-7; Wiles, Appendix 4, p. 71 for the original and pp. 34-5 for a reconstruction; Trinity College, Cambridge, MS.R.2.64.

[98] Dobson & Taylor, p. 203.

[99] J. Matthews, 'The Games of Robin Hood', pp. 393-410 in Knight, *Anthology,* p. 399 gives Axile Tree as the term for the May Pole.

[100] Wiles, p. 34.

[101] John Marshall, 'Playing the Game', pp.161-74, in Hahn, pp. 167,173, offers the suggestion for 'exaltre' in the script as axle-tree (i.e. the wooden bar on which the wheels of a cart are fixed) – a persuasive suggestion.

[102] Dobson & Taylor, p. 39; 'tempus de Robynhode'.

[103] Dobson & Taylor, p. 39.

[104] Holt, p. 75.

[105] Cottle, p. 11.

[106] Sharron Lux, 'And the "Reel" Maid Marian?', pp.151-60, in Hahn, *Popular Culture,* p. 151.

[107] Ohlgren, Outlaws, p. xxi.

[108] Maurice Keen, 'Robin Hood – Peasant or Gentleman?', pp. 258-266 in Hilton, p. 262.

[109] Pollard, p. 30-2.

[110] Pollard, pp. 40-4

[111] Ohlgren, *Outlaws,* p. 219.

6

Heroes and Outlaws in Late Medieval Literature

Introduction

Robin Hood is elusive as a historical figure, a real person. No one has ever found for certain a person in documents who was the original for the ballads and plays about him. There is division among critics and historians over whether he ever existed at all. Perhaps he was always simply an invention, a figure of fiction. I am inclined to side with those who think it most likely there was some original outlaw, however unlike his modern counterpart. If one believes that then it still seems worth searching the records. It is, therefore, inevitable that we first hunt around for any possible clues from any source.

Outlaws were heroes in many medieval works — Robin Hood was only one of many. Outlaw poetry is virtually a genre in its own right. It overlaps with other literature in content and approach but it also has elements that are exclusive to it. There is little doubt that Robin Hood as we know him in modern times was not quite the Robin Hood of history. In the previous chapter we have tried to focus on Robin as he first appears in surviving literature. Assuming there was an original actual Robin Hood, he almost certainly lacked features we commonly associate with him and even more certainly did not take part in most of the episodes with which we are familiar. The figure may have begun as historical but the tales are largely fiction. Too many of the plots are plots that we find in earlier fiction about earlier outlaws. We create Robin, each in our own mind. Just stop and think. How do you see Robin Hood? He may appear to you as most like Errol Flynn or Jonas Armstrong. He is probably associated with Little John, Friar Tuck, and Maid Marion. In your mind, he probably fought against Little John and Friar Tuck. He sometimes took on disguises. Your view of Robin Hood — and mine — is the result of a long process of amalgamation of tales from the earliest medieval poems and plays through the Tudor and Stuart transformation, the eighteenth- and nineteenth-century novelistic fiction and the twentieth-century films and TV. He is now a fictional figure, not a historical one. What has been added to the real Robin is one layer after another of literary embroidery — plots, characters, and situations that have been borrowed from other literary works or simply invented. We have to try and dig back through the layers if we are ever to find a real original. Which factors in the Robin Hood works *are* original?

Early Literature that Contributed to Robin Hood Literature

If plots and characters can be found in other literature that is earlier than the
Robin Hood works then we can probably deduct it from any reality. The Robin
Hood legend has borrowed good and suitable plots and characters. The Robin
Hood literature of the Middle Ages is certainly part of a broader scene. There
can be no doubt that, as we possess it, the Robin Hood material owed much to
other similar works. For a start, it is part of a wider poetic and ballad tradition.
Many of the factors familiar to us from the Robin Hood works are to be found
in other early ballad works — blowing a horn, using bows, archery feats, the
greenwood background, foresters, emphasis on yeoman society, merry men,
Lincoln green and churches dedicated to the Virgin Mary — just to note a few
examples. In other ballads, one even finds other Robins and 'his little man John'.[1]
It is hardly ever certain which idea was borrowed from which other ballad, but it
is clear, however, that certain common topics were in frequent use. Much of the
Robin Hood material is not unique to Robin Hood and hardly likely to reflect a
historical reality. There were other romances with similar themes, and outlawry
was a popular topic.

We shall, in due course, need to consider the influence on the Robin Hood story
from those about such as Hereward the Wake, Fulk fitz Warren and Adam Bell
— all part-fiction and part-history. It is only with the surviving literary works that
we begin to have any details of Robin Hood. It is nearly certain that these works
existed in the Middle Ages from at least the fourteenth century, but we have to
wait some time before any of them survive and often a good deal longer. It is likely
that much of the sixteenth- and seventeenth-century work was closely based on
earlier efforts but it is safer to abide by survival dates than guesswork — as we
have done in previous chapters.

With the country plays there is the problem that few texts survive to give us the
contents; with the ballads, the problem of an oral tradition — how much is preserved
in later versions or how much has been added as the material passes through various
hands? There is no clear answer to these questions in accurate historical terms and we
shall often have to admit that problems cannot at present be resolved. It is likely that
the earliest works on Robin Hood were *not* ballads, but that the ballad development
borrowed from romances and popular forms. The ballad itself may well be only a
late medieval development; in the view of Fowler, its beginnings are in the fifteenth
century, through the merging of traditional songs with a new minstrel form as the
popularity of the older minstrel tradition declined — or at least altered.[2]

Romances and Religious Poems

We may then accept that Robin Hood first appeared in literary form in romances,
the form that popularised Alexander the Great, Charlemagne and, above all, King
Arthur. We know that if there was an original King Arthur then he was a figure

of the late Roman to Dark Age period. But in his literary form he was a medieval hero in a world of knightly heroes, such as Sir Gawain.

We see that there was change in the literary air in the second half of the fourteenth century, when various strands of poetic invention were appearing in parallel. William Langland's poem *Piers Plowman* is hardly like Robin Hood works, but it still presents certain parallels. One notes, for example, the pleasure in nature. 'In a somer seson whan softe was ye sonne' is the opening line — very like many opening verses in Robin Hood ballads. It is the same world, with robbers and minstrels, sinful priests, ploughmen, and cooks crying 'hot pies, hot'. Hoods are worn and there is a miller called 'Munde ye Millere'. It is a world also of knights (including a Sir Waryn) and mesnies, respect for Our Lady and stress on the value of charity. Its sympathies lie more with the poor and helpless than with the rich and powerful. Above all, it is one of the first great poems in the English language — Middle English, that is, rather than Old English. Langland even makes the joke, better known in Chaucer's version, of knowing no French except that of the furthest end of Norfolk. *Piers Plowman* is also surprisingly earthy in its everyday English, with much mention of whores, arses, pissing 'a potel in a paternoster' or drunks whose vomit not even a hungry hound in Hertfordshire would lap up.[7]

The poem *Sir Gawain and the Green Knight* was written in about 1400 and is, therefore, a little later than the first reference to Robin Hood but earlier than any surviving Robin Hood poems. The manuscript of *Sir Gawain and the Green Knight* is in the British Library.[8] It is thought to be in a Midlands dialect. It has been suggested that the Green Chapel of the poem may be Lud's church in Derbyshire. In *Sir Gawain and the Green Knight* the poet promises 'I schal telle hit astit'.[9] His work is divided in fyttes (like the Robin Hood *Gest)* and is even referred to as 'a gest'.[10] It contains the common enjoyment of nature expressed in this period — in spring and summer when 'lively songbirds sing/ From lovely, leafy woods' — though, unlike Robin Hood works, it does feature winter and snow as well as spring and summer.[11]

Sir Gawain and the Green Knight is one of the greatest works in Middle English, universally seen as greater in literary terms than any of the Robin Hood works, 'one of the jewels in the crown of English literature'.[12] It has a tight plot, a compelling narrative, vivid description and remains great poetry in any age. It brilliantly sets the scenes as in Arthur's court or in the countryside. The Robin Hood works may be seen as good but not great and do not compare in quality to such works as *Piers Plowman, Sir Gawain and the Green Knight* or *The Canterbury Tales. Sir Gawain and the Green Knight's* main figures are knightly. The poem continues the use of unrealistic figures, notably the Green Knight, who is a lord transforming into a giant. This approach contrasts with the generally everyday and realistic figures that appear in Robin Hood works. The green man theme of medieval poetry is only too clear in *Sir Gawain and the Green Knight,* where we meet a giant dressed entirely in emerald green, having a green beard and hair, and carrying a green axe and a sprig of holly. When Gawain is invited to behead the giant he does, but the giant simply walks away carrying his head. The forest features in *Sir Gawain and the Green Knight* but there are no outlaws and no lower status heroes.

Romance became a popular form of literature from the twelfth century onwards, especially in France and England. What must be said, though, is that romances did not normally concern themselves with outlaws, the heroes were sometimes figures of legend and sometimes historical figures — though not treated in any very strict sense of historical accuracy. Romance heroes included Charlemagne, Roland and Oliver, King Arthur, Sir Lancelot and Sir Gawain. In the main, these heroes were royal or knightly. Sometimes these heroes found themselves in difficulties and sometimes in forests. Sir Gawain, for example, finds himself 'under the greenwood tree'.[13]

However, the romance heroes were not outlaws. The outlaw element seems to have entered simply in the wake of romances about individuals who happen to have been outlawed, such as Hereward the Wake, Eustace the Monk or Fulk fitz Warren. The poems about these heroes themselves adapted and used material from royal and knightly romances. The romances made a significant contribution to our hero but the form was quite different. Romances were literary, aimed at a courtly and cultured audience. They were lengthy and for a British audience, in Latin or French rather than English. Romances did influence late medieval works in English, notably the poetry of Geoffrey Chaucer, who would use such classic subjects as Troilus and Cressida — and the *Gest* of Robin Hood.

It also soon becomes clear that much of the popular Robin Hood story — most of the well-known episodes indeed — were not original to Robin Hood. This decreases any likelihood that we shall ever know much about a real Robin Hood. The reason for this is the lack of any historical narrative about a historical figure. In the case of Hereward the Wake, Fulk fitz Warren or Eustace the Monk we do at least have some references in historical sources with which to compare what appears in the literary works about them. For Robin Hood, there is hardly anything — perhaps it is truer to say nothing at all. To a degree, this compares with King Arthur. There was long a doubt about the existence of a real King Arthur. It is now generally accepted that he did exist in the period when Britain was disintegrating after its Roman period — but this depends upon a very few brief historical mentions. It is equally certain that the King Arthur of the romances has very little to do with the real king — if he was even a king. It is well to bear this in mind when contemplating a real Robin Hood. If he ever existed, it is almost certain that his life had little connection with the figure he became in the romances and ballads. We may suggest that he would be a forest outlaw. We may feel that there are enough references to give him some geographical location. Beyond that, no historian would be likely to accept as fact, without new evidence, the various tales about him that grew up over the centuries.

It must also be said that the majority of the Robin Hood works are not romances but ballads. Only the *Gest* has any real similarity to romances and even this is not a normal romance work. The preponderance of ballads is probably largely due to the timing of their appearance. Romance as a genre dominated poetic form in the twelfth and thirteenth centuries but gradually became less significant thereafter. The ballad was a new and increasingly important form. As Fowler had suggested, romances 'provided the style and narrative technique' that formed the early ballads.[14] It was natural that materials used in late romances would also be used in early ballads. Robin Hood was the topic that most inspired the ballads.

To start filling in the basis of the tales, let us see what similarities there are between the earlier heroes and Robin Hood. Outlaw tales were certainly not new with Robin. Clawson, in 1909, considered there were a dozen outlaw stories before Robin Hood appeared.[15] As Keen has pointed out, however, one should note that 'outlaw' can have different connotations. Some of our earlier medieval 'outlaws' were, in effect, exiles rather than 'outlaws' in the Robin Hood sense. In other words, we tend now to see an outlaw as someone hiding from the law in his own land rather than as a political exile.

Outlaws in Earlier Poetic Works

HEREWARD THE WAKE

Hereward the Wake was one such early outcast, though his career saw him at different stages as first an exile abroad and then an outlaw at home after returning to England in 1068 and for a second time after a visit to Flanders. He was an historic figure but we know little about the real Hereward. His life was filled out in epics and it is almost impossible now to disentangle the real life from the fictional. In particular, the *Gesta Herewardi* or *De Gestis Herwardi Saxonis* is probably a twelfth-century work about this eleventh-century hero found in a thirteenth-century collection of legal documents. The collection belonged to Robert of Swaffham, the cellarer of Peterborough Abbey. The manuscript is now in Cambridge University library.[16] The poem contains more fiction than fact. This is true of all our heroes of medieval myth and legend. Most are actual people whom we know a little about but who had a wealth of fictional achievements woven around their exploits.

Hereward was not a great lord, only a dispossessed squire from Lincolnshire, and this is an obvious reason for lack of historical evidence about him (as with Robin Hood). Hereward opposed the Normans and was exiled. He later returned to become an outlaw who was active against the conquerors. He used the Isle of Ely as a base for his operations. The E version of the *Anglo-Saxon Chronicle* refers to the event in 1070 and speaks of 'Hereward and his gang' (genge) and calls them 'outlaws'.[17] When William the Conqueror attacked and took over the Isle of Ely the revolt collapsed, but Hereward escaped. What happened to the historic Hereward then is unknown — there is no further historical evidence.

There are certainly points of comparison between Hereward and Robin Hood. One is the frequent use of disguise by the hero. On occasion, Hereward dyes his blonde hair black and his beard red to look like a foreigner! Hereward, like Robin, on one occasion disguised himself as a potter, taking shelter with a widow. He then pretends to be a potter, calling 'Pots, pots, good pots and jars'. On his return to England, Hereward gathers his men in the forest. Later, he once more shelters in the forest. One notes that most outlaw heroes, like Robin, are skilled archers. Hereward uses his bow and on one occasion his shot hits an earl, the arrow rebounding from his mail but with force sufficient to knock him from his horse. Hereward is not always respectful to prelates, capturing one abbot whom he then ransoms.

EUSTACE THE MONK

Eustace the Monk is another historical person who figured in poetic literature. 'Li Romans de Wistasse li Moine' is a Norman-French poem dating from the later thirteenth century. It survives in a mansuscript of *c.* 1284, which is now in the Bibliothèque Nationale.[18] Its origins may be some fifty years earlier. Eustace was the son of Baldwin Busquet, a lord of the Boulonnais, born at Course near Boulogne in *c.* 1170. He probably had experience of sea-going before becoming a Benedictine monk at St-Samer near Boulogne. He left the monastery to avenge his murdered father. Eustace became seneschal to Renaud de Dammartin, count of Boulogne, but antagonised the powerful count in 1203 and was forced into outlawry. After acting as a pirate, Eustace offered himself as a mercenary to King John of England by 1205 and received lands from him in Norfolk. He led naval forces for John and returned to piracy, seizing Sark in the Channel Islands. When John made an alliance with Count Renaud, Eustace was forced to change his allegiance. He went over to the king of France, Philip Augustus, and served his son, Prince Louis. Eustace became a notable naval commander for the French, participating in Prince Louis' invasion of England in 1217. Eustace's downfall came with the defeat of the French fleet at Sandwich in that year, when he was captured and beheaded on board his own ship.

The poem about Eustace shows him as a forest outlaw at one stage. He collects a band of men around him. He also frequently assumes disguises (on 17 occasions), for example, as a prostitute who offers sex to a sergeant, a peasant, a leper, a potter, a merchant, a pilgrim and a charcoal burner in a black hood. His great enemy is the count of Boulogne (the real life Renaud de Dammartin) who figures in the poem much as the sheriff does in the Robin Hood works. Eustace, like Robin, questions those he captures and robs those who are untruthful. The Eustace poem also has a hostile abbot, in this case the abbot of Jumièges. As in Robin Hood tales, the abbot lies about how much wealth he carries — and loses it as a result. At one point, Eustace also wears a hood.

Much of the poem is clearly fictional. It also has more of the magical qualities found in knightly literature, such as 'Gawain'. Eustace possesses magical powers and uses them for somewhat non-knightly purposes, such as making monks fart in the cloister or causing an innkeeper's wife and other ladies to strip to the waist! An anti-monastic attitude is also continued in a spell to make monks curse when they are supposed to be reciting the office. Nor is Eustace a hero in Robin Hood mould. Apart from his magical and often unpleasant tricks, he is described in the poem as 'bold and cruel', and at his execution, the comment is that 'no man who spends his days doing evil can live a long life'.[19]

Fulk fitz Warren

Fulk fitz Warren was another historical person who became a literary hero. He was born during the reign of Henry II of an established knightly family and claimed to inherit the barony of Whittington in Shropshire though he failed to gain it. He was outlawed at the very beginning of the thirteenth century for opposing King John. Fulk headed a band of outlaws and was probably based in Shropshire, though he was active elsewhere, including in Wiltshire. He was pardoned in 1203 along with thirty-eight others who seem to have made up his band. He finally gained his barony and survived into the reign of Henry III. During his final years he became blind.

There was an original poem about Fulk fitz Warren but it has not survived. The *Gesta Fulconi* about Fulk fitz Warren survives as *Fouke le Fitz Waryn* in an Anglo-Norman prose version. It formed part of a collection made in *c.* 1330 in Herefordshire, probably by a canon of Hereford, and is now a British Library manuscript. The origins of the work itself are thought to be earlier and probably thirteenth-century.[20] It seems to be taken from a lost poem in Middle English. Leland apparently read that version, 'an old Englisch boke yn ryme'.[21]

Like the works on Robin Hood, it is not always easy to disentangle truth from fiction in *Fouke*, though some of it is clearly based on folklore and magical tales; the story of the old hag's seven sons who ravish seven girls is unlikely to be fact (the girls are rescued by Fulk)! Fulk also fights serpents and beasts in Sweden, a dragon belching smoke in Iberia and a giant described a 12 feet taller than men in Ireland.

There is a hint of connection to 'Sir Gawain and the Green Knight' when we meet Fulk's father 'clad all in green with ivy leaves'. His son, our hero, was known as Fulk le Brun, or the Brown, from the colour of his eyes. 'Fouke le Fitz Waryn' is a knightly work. It has much on knightly apparel, tournaments, standards and so on. Fulk is given the training of a knight. The tale is full of knightly romance. A lady called Marion de la Bruere lowers a cord to aid entry to the castle at Dynan and loves Ernalt. (We note the name Marion). When she finds he has tricked her she kills him and then herself — not the sort of tragedy one finds in Robin Hood. The knightly aspects of the poem include Fulk's participation in tournaments in France — compared to the more plebeian combats of Robin Hood. Peasants here are seen as robbers and justifiably killed by Fulk and his men, though he does rescue captured damsels.

Fulk belongs to the Plantagenet period, the time of John and Richard the Lionheart. He plays chess with John and they fight over it. John hits Fulk with the board and he responds by kicking the prince. Somewhat unfairly, John is then punished with a whipping and thereafter bore a grudge against Fulk. John is presented as a villain, 'who all his life, was wicked, contrary and spiteful'.[22] He is 'lustful' and 'without conscience, wicked, cross and hated by all good people'.[23] As king, John confiscates Fulk's lands. He then renounces his homage to the king. Fulk becomes a rebel, going to Brittany and then returning to England. He takes refuge 'in woods and moors' and 'a forest called Babbing', later moving to 'the forest of Bradene' (Braydon).[24] Fulk's brother John waylays ten merchants who are brought into the forest and attacked by Fulk. Fulk moves on to another forest in Kent. Three of his men are brothers who are noted crossbowmen and another of his men is called Alan.

At one point, Fulk goes in disguise as a monk, with 'a belly big enough to hold two gallons of cabbage', to misdirect pursuers.[25] He then fights with a staff and, later, disguises himself as a merchant. He cuts off the head of one enemy. He has a fight at a ford. Fulk takes on an alias as Amys del Boys (Wood). Later Fulk goes to the forest of Windsor. He changes clothes with a charcoal burner and thus disguises himself. He meets King John who carries 'un molt bel arke' (a very fair bow) and encourages him to shoot at a stag that he leads the king towards.[26] It is a trap, and the king is forced to pardon Fulk in return for his own freedom — though, in true King John style, he later ignores his promise as given under duress. Rondulf (Randulf/Ranulf), earl of Chester, is then sent against Fulk. Again, one notes a significant name and remembers the first ever comment on Robin Hood made by William Langland in *Piers Plowman* on rhymes of Robin Hood and 'Randolf Erl of Chestre'. In the New Forest, Fulk is pardoned by the king. He later founds a priory, himself becoming a monk and dying in *c.* 1256.

From the poem, Fulk, then, is another archer outlaw hero, though probably with crossbow rather than longbow. Fulk also frequently takes to disguise, for example as a monk and a charcoal burner. A major opponent of Fulk is Ranulf, earl of Chester, which reminds one of the first references we have to Robin Hood literature. In *Piers Plowman*, the warning is against reading the works of Robin Hood and Ranulf earl of Chester. In the works about both Fulk and Eustace, King John appears as a villain. This is actually *not* the case with the original Robin Hood. It is only in modern re-workings that Prince John becomes a figure let alone a major villain. A similar case concerns Marion, Marion de la Bruere (or 'of the Heath'). She is a figure in the Fulk work but only a late addition with regard to Robin Hood. In the Fulk poem, there is even a second Marion, or rather Maryn (the name taken by the king's sister Isorie when Fulk is in exile), who comforts him. She calls herself Maryn le Perdu (the Lost) of France.

We have, then, noted certain factors that remind us of Robin Hood in the *Fouke* poem, including an outlaw tale, a heroine called Marion and a Ranulf, earl of Chester. There are greenwood locations and a link to the mythological greenwood of the past. At one tournament, Garyn goes to the tournament dressed in 'ivy leaves all green out of the forest'.[27] There is also a poor knight (as in Robin Hood) who is brought into the hall, though poorly clothed, and given food. One also notes the link between the fitz Warren family and that of Hodnet. Baldwin de Hodnet was a companion of Fulk. Hodnet, and variations of it, were sometimes confused with names for Hood. It is probable that some of the material in the early Robin Hood works were borrowed from the tale of Fulk fitz Warren.

The Song of Trailbaston

The Song of Trailbaston also predates the known Robin Hood literature and deals with outlawry. The manuscript work in Anglo-Norman French is dated *c.* 1341 and was probably written in Ludlow in Shropshire. The surviving copy may have been made for Sir John Talbot and is now in the British Library.[28] However, the poem itself is thought to originate from the early fourteenth century, perhaps 1305-7.[29] The poem criticises the royal commissions of trailbaston, in which royal judges attempted to deal with armed criminals committing robbery and assault in the localities. The trouble was that those appointed to enforce the new law used their power corruptly to make personal profit. This practice began in 1304 and the poem was composed probably soon after that. The sheriff who 'comes round for his payoff' was one object of its attack.[30] The anonymous author himself claims to be an outlaw as well as an archer. The outlaws take refuge in the Forest of Belregard, otherwise 'the green wood of Beauregard'.[31] In the forest, there is no treachery or twisting of the law, so 'it's better to come and live in the woods'.[32] The outlaw band is made up of companions who know how to shoot bows and they are also referred to as 'hoods'.[33]

Outlaws in Poems Contemporary with Robin Hood Works

One point of considerable importance in the early Robin Hood works is the language in which they are written. They are all in English, the form which we now call Middle English. We tend to take this for granted, but it was, in effect, a new development of its age. Rhymes in English only reappeared from about 1200, and the revival of English as a literary language is generally dated to about 1350.[34] Between those periods, the languages of literature in England had been French and Latin. *Piers Plowman,* in which we find the first mention of Robin Hood rhymes, was itself an important part of this revival. The border country between England and Scotland was also significant in this development, and the dialect of many works from the period, as well as their content, reflects this. Border battles, such as Otterburn (1388); border raids, in both directions; and men of the border — all are common in this period of English poetry.

In order to set the Robin Hood literature in its correct place, we need to compare it with other roughly contemporary works as well as with the earlier outlaw poetry. They have many subjects and themes and plots in common. It is unlikely that they all borrowed from Robin Hood where there are similarities. It is more likely they all borrowed from earlier works and from each other. It is probable that the earliest Robin Hood works followed the tradition of romances and epics, mainly concentrating on the achievements of an outlaw hero. The ballads come later in time.

GANDELYN OR GAMELYN

Probably the earliest of the new type of ballads was 'Robyn and Gandelyn', seen as the first outlaw legend turned into a ballad in English.[35] It undoubtedly contributed elements to the Robin Hood ballads (or just possibly borrowed from them), though this Robyn is *not* Robin Hood — despite being a good bowman who shoots at deer. The poem has such lines as 'Robyn lyth in grene wode bowndyn' and 'Robyn bent his joly bowe'[36]. The story also introduces a sheriff. The poem appears in a manuscript, dated *c.* 1450, and is thought to be 'the first extant popular English ballad'.[37]

Apart from the name Robin, there is much use of Gandelyn, Gamwell or Gamelyn, or similar versions of the name. The poem of 'the Tale of Gamelyn' may date from as early as *c.* 1360 and deals with outlaws. There is much swearing by St Richard, believed to be St Richard of Chichester who died in 1253. The poem seems to have been collected by Chaucer, perhaps for his own use. It begins with the familiar 'Litheth, and Listneth'.[38] Probably the best of the surviving twenty-five versions is in the Petworth manuscript, which was used by Knight and Ohlgren.[39] Its form seems transitional between romance, epic and ballad — not unlike the *Gest* of Robin Hood.

Gamelyn is a younger brother, who is forced into exile and who takes up with outlaws in the forest. The 'master' or 'king' of his outlaw band is pardoned and Gamelyn then takes over as the leader of the remaining band. With the aid of his men, he finally recovers his proper inheritance. It has been suggested that the outlaw 'king' could have been Robin Hood.[40] Gamelyn becomes involved in a match — at wrestling. Even without the direct links, it is quite likely that the Robin Hood works owe something to this poem, dating only about twenty years before the first mention of Robin Hood poems in *Piers Plowman*. There is a similar contempt for certain abbots. Gamelyn curses anyone 'who ever does a prior or abbot good'.[41] Adam replies that Gamelyn should respect their tonsures — and break their legs and arms! When going to court, Gamelyn removes his hood and confronts the 'broken-back sheriff'.[42]

As we have seen, there were soon poems about Robin amd Gandelyn — undoubtedly using the Gamelyn character, though the Robin is not named as Robin Hood. Indeed, in one work, this Robin is killed by an arrow, which is shot by the boy, Wrennock. A further confusion is that the unusual name Wrennock was also one of the enemies of Fulk fitz Warren. The name Gamwell also turns up as a relative, an uncle, of Robin Hood himself in the later ballad *Robin Hood's Birth*. The interconnections between the early outlaw works are confusing but also intriguing and surely not without some significance. We can be fairly certain that the authors of these closely dated works knew of each others' compositions and borrowed, without embarrassment, names, characters, plots and situations.

Adam Bell

A well-known work that has parallels with the Robin Hood tales is called *Adam Bell, Clim of the Clough, and William of Cloudesly* — 'these noble archares all thre'.[43] Like the origins of Robin Hood, this work probably appears only later than its first writing. Apart from Robin Hood works, it was the first outlaw poem to be printed. It is not as long as the *Gest* but is longer than the ballads. It is another outlaw work, and in length bears perhaps the nearest comparison to the *Gest*. In the Tudor period, like Robin Hood, it became a subject for popular drama. From our uncertainty over origins, it is impossible to claim that one work influenced the other, but the similarities are certainly notable. *Adam Bell, Clim of the Clough, and William of Cloudesly* is about 'Yemen of the north countrey'.[44] It is set in

Inglewood Forest. Its opening could easily be the start of a Robin Hood work:

Mery it was in grene forest/
Amonge the leves grene.

The men have bows and it contains the familiar: 'now lith and listen, gentylmen'. William of Cloudesly is an archer 'good ynough' and has been 'outlawed for venyson'. They are all 'outlawes of the forest'.[45] Their enemies are again the sheriff and the justice, who lead the attack on William's house. They set fire to the house, despite the fact that William's wife and three children are inside. William gets the children out but he is taken and imprisoned. They plan to hang him in Carlisle. At the end of the first part we are told: 'Her is a fyt of Cloudesli', with another to come — so the division of the poem is in fyttes like the *Gest*. Adam and Clym then set out to rescue William. They claim at the gate to be from the king. They wring the porter's neck and take his keys. As William is brought out for his execution, they shoot arrows and hit the sheriff and the justice. They release William and, after a fight and much killing, they escape to the greenwood. Part two explains it is the end of this 'fet'. William is reunited with his wife and children. The three leaders then all go to the king and ask a pardon. The king says he has heard of them and will hang them, and he has them arrested. The queen, who has come from another land, then asks, as a boon, that the three be handed over to her. She releases them. Then news reaches the king of the earlier events in Carlisle, including the killing of the sheriff and the justice. He now sends archers to catch them but agrees to let William demonstrate his ability with the bow. As promised, William cleaves the wand in two. He then says he can shoot an apple off his son's head — shades, or perhaps previews, of William Tell. The king says that if he fails he will be hanged. The son is tied to a stake and an apple set on his head. They measure 120 paces. With a longbow, William cleaves the apple in two. The king then promises to take him on as his man, pay him 18*d* a day and make him his chief rider in the north. Other gifts are made by the royal pair, with promises for the future of his wife and children. So, the 'good yemen' live happily ever after.

Other Works

There are various other ballad works of about this period. Several of them have either outlaws or events reminiscent of Robin Hood tales. Another border country outlaw of fiction was Johnnie Cock. A ballad about him appeared in the Percy Folio. He wore Lincoln green and killed deer, though he himself was killed by foresters

One problem in literary comparisons is the great uncertainty about the date of Robin Hood's existence — if he did exist — or of the date of the actual writing of the earliest literature about him. It must be before 1377. Otherwise, the dating is conjectural since none of it survives. Thus, it is unclear if some literature about outlaws could have affected the Robin Hood literature or vice versa. This is true of the Scottish material on such as William Wallace and Robert Bruce, both of whom spent some time as outlaws and became heroes in literature. There are certainly some points of comparison. Wallace, for example, wears a hood and claims 'I'm aye a woman's friend'.[46] He also disguises himself as a woman, and once as a beggar.

It is also probable that much of the material in the popular ballads and plays of the early modern period did not originally derive from Robin Hood works but had their own standing and were then drawn into association with the popular hero. This is probably true of most of the well-known figures in modern Robin Hood dramas, including the sheriff, Friar Tuck and Maid Marian. Marian does not appear in the early Robin Hood stories. But there are other Marians of popular literature, the one associated with Gandelyn and the one from French literature — the pastourelles — who was partner of the shepherd Robin, who is *not* Robin Hood. This Marian appeared in French country games much as Robin did in English ones. It was common for her to be the sexual target of knights.

Foreign Outlaws

There are medieval outlaws other than our familiar English heroes. Some of the poems about them may pre-date Robin Hood, while others are roughly contemporary. One such is Án Bow-Bender, who appears in a fifteenth-century saga but also figured in a twelfth-century Latin version in Saxo Grammaticus. It is suggested that the actual saga originates in the fourteenth century.[47] Like the *Gest* of Robin Hood, it is divided into eight fyttes and is of similar length. Án is no handsome hero. He is large (too big to get his shoulders through a doorway), ugly, scruffy and not too bright — though he is powerful. Án is outlawed by the king of Norway and takes to the forest. He is a master archer and can also wrestle. When outlawed he became leader of the men around him.

Another such figure is Marsk Stig, who, like Robin, became a hero of ballads, but in Denmark. He, like most of our English heroes, was also a historical figure from East Jutland — indeed he was High Constable of Denmark from 1283-86 for Erik V. He was exiled to Norway and was an outlaw from 1290, dying in 1293.[48] Several commentators have pointed to similarities between Scandinavian works and those about Robin Hood, not least in the interest in outlaws.

The one famous outlaw who bears comparison to Robin Hood in terms of the difficulty of locating an historical origin is surely William Tell. The latter seems to originate in Icelandic sagas.[49] In any case, there is little in the William Tell story that relates closely to Robin. The shooting at the apple only appears in the Adam Bell story with William of Cloudesly and not in Robin Hood.

The Debt of Robin Hood to Other Works

It is clear that before the Robin Hood ballads appeared there was already a considerable outlaw literature. It is also clear that when Robin Hood works did appear they were not alone in looking at other works with outlaw activities. Although these works were not all of the same nature — some in romance form, some as ballads, some in Latin or French or Scandinavian languages as well as in English — they do share some factors in common. There is a tradition of outlaw works into which Robin Hood is absorbed. Some common factors can easily be noted. There is the greenwood and forest background. There are the tales of disguise, partly necessary because an outlaw was always in danger of discovery. There are the warrior matches such as wrestling, sword or archery fights, bouts or competitions. What we conclude is that most of the popular Robin Hood tales are not original to our hero and are unlikely, therefore, to be a true representation of an historical Robin Hood.

One question we do need to consider is what elements in the Robin Hood tales *were* original. If we can detect any such factors we may be getting closer to a real and original Robin Hood. One such factor is the location evidence. Other outlaws lurk in various forests but none has the same connection with Barnsdale, Yorkshire, Nottingham and Sherwood. Other tales have clerics figuring in them but few are as hostile to the Church as the Robin Hood tales are with regard to grasping abbots and high churchmen.

Outlaw Works that are or may be Later than Robin Hood

Since we cannot securely date either the lifetime of a real Robin Hood, or the date of origin of works about Robin Hood, it is impossible to be sure what works pre-date Robin and which are slightly later. We therefore need to take into consideration later medieval outlaw works, which may still have either influenced Robin Hood works or have been influenced by them.

William Wallace

As with Hereward, Fulk fitz Warren and Eustace the Monk, there are later actual historical heroes who figure in later medieval literature. One of these is William Wallace. A fifteenth-century work by a monk refers to Wallace as 'the Scottish Robin Hood'.[50] 'The Acts and Deeds of William Wallace' appeared in a manuscript now in the National Library of Scotland in Edinburgh dated to 1488.[51] The first printed version was issued in 1508. It was attributed to Blind Hary, a minstrel born in c. 1440. He was a soldier and apparently became blind after the poem had been written.

Wallace was not a great lord but he came of a family with some status, small landholders — who might have been seen as yeomen. He led opponents of the English under Edward I. He killed the unpopular English sheriff of Lanark, Thomas Hazelrigg. He led a band of thirty men and assembled his army in Selkirk

Forest. He won a great victory against English forces under Earl Warenne at Stirling Bridge in 1297. Wallace was defeated by Edward I at Falkirk in 1298 but managed to escape. He spent some time seeking support abroad. On his return, he was outside the law, a hunted man. He took refuge in forests, including that of Clyde. The chronicler Peter Langtoft wrote about Wallace in his verse chronicle as an outlaw and 'master of thieves'.[52] Eventually, Wallace was betrayed, taken to England and executed in brutal fashion in London.

Scyr William Wallace by Blind Harry is one of the best-known works that come into the category of later medieval literature about actual historical figures. The work is dated to the later fifteenth century. Wallace is a larger than life hero — 7 feet tall to be precise — broad, strong, brown-haired, bright-eyed and scarred. The poem is clearly told from the Scottish viewpoint, and Edward I is 'that false king', while Wallace becomes a 'martyr'.[53] He is a 'master of thieves', possessing a bow so strong that 'no man could draw Wallace's bow'.[54] He also fights with a staff and a sword. He leads a band of archers. He also disguises himself, twice as a woman. At one time, in particularly unlikely manner, Wallace disguises himself in women's clothes while spinning. On other occasions, he disguises himself as a priest and a potter. Wallace also came into conflict with an unpopular sheriff in Hazelrig — that 'cursed knight', 'cruel and fierce' — and his love was called Marion (Marion Bradfute).[55]

ROBERT THE BRUCE

The importance of the English-Scottish border as a source of medieval outlaw works, including ballads, has already been noted. It is therefore no surprise to find that Scottish as well as English heroes figure in the literature. Living as a contemporary of Wallace, Robert the Bruce was also a subject of verse, notably in the long poem by John Barbour called 'The Bruce'.[56] Barbour lived in the fourteenth century, dying in *c.* 1395. This poem, therefore, was written at almost exactly the same time that we have our first knowledge of Robin Hood rhymes. 'The Bruce' is dated to *c.* 1375.[57] Two manuscripts of the poem survive from the later fifteenth century. The first printed version, of 1571, was from a now lost manuscript.[58] The author describes the work as a 'romance'.[59]

Barbour was the archdeacon of Aberdeen but his language is northern English. He also spent time in England and France. He probably wrote the poem for its hero's grandson, Robert II. An unusual element in the poem is the role given to Sir James Douglas, whose career is given almost equal emphasis to that of the Bruce, perhaps partly because Barbour had access to a manuscript work on Douglas by his herald.[60]

Like most of the outlaw verse, this work rejoices in nature: as the month of May 'Quen byrdis syngis in ilk spray' (when birds sing on ever branch) and there are blossoms and flowers.[61] Robert the Bruce spent part of his life being hunted and taking shelter in forests. When in trouble he leads a mesnie (menye/meynhe).[62] He hunts with three archers and catches deer to eat. He blows a horn to summon his men. He defends a ford. A Randolph appears, in the form of Sir Thomas Randolph. Bruce's men 'stud than rangyt all on a raw' (stood then all ranged in a row), just as Robin's men do.[63] The famous spider story is probably a late addition. The Bruce is chivalrous to women, declaring that all men would have pity on a woman.[64]

BORDER BALLADS

There is a large body of balladry, mainly from the Scottish border region, which incorporates outlaws — not necessarily as the heroes. Many of these ballads are as difficult to date in origin as the Robin Hood works — often appearing first in relatively late collections. We need only mention a few that have an obvious link to our hero.

The B version of the poem, *Erlinton*, has its hero walking with his love in the greenwood, when 'up start fifteen of the bravest outlaws'. The hero kills all except the eldest who is allowed to carry the tidings home.[65] There are several similarities in subject matter. Many ballads, apart from those about Robin Hood, have bands of merry men as, for example, *Dives and Lazarus, The Carnal and the Crane,* or *Fair Annie and Sweet Willie*.[66] Another common factor is a church dedicated to the Virgin Mary, as Mary's kirk in *Fair Janet, Lord Ingram and Chiel Wyet* or *Lord Thomas and Fair Annet*.[67] There is an oddly familiar ring about the hero's associate in *Child Noryce*, referred to as 'his little man John'.[68]

There are other late ballads that reflect aspects of the Robin Hood works. Some, for example, refer to characters that we associate with Robin. Maid Marian and Friar Tuck sometimes appear. Occasionally, we find Much the miller's son, as in *Jock o the Side:* 'And fare thou well, Much, Millers sonne!/ Much, Millars sonne, I say'.[69] In this work, Much's comrades are John o the Side and Hobby Noble. We note that Hob is an alternative for Rob or Robin. In another associated poem, 'Archie o Cawfield', Hobie Noble with his bow is banished to Liddisdale and is compared as a hero with William Wallace.[70]

Other late ballads have points of comparison, possibly because they borrowed from Robin Hood works — but the parallels are still of interest. One example is 'King Edward the Fourth and a Tanner of Tamworth'. The appearance of a tanner is one point. Another is the similarity of minor points from the very start, 'In summer time, when leaves grew green,/ And birds were singing on every tree', to blowing a horn to call for support. In this case, the king blew 'And five hundred lords and knights/ Came riding over a hill'. This work also mentions Plumpton (Plompton) Park. One notes that in the earliest Robin Hood work the king was the comely 'Edward'.[71]

Some very late works seem clearly to borrow from Robin Hood works. One such ballad is 'The Outlaw Murray' set in Ettrick Forest. The hero is an outlaw with a band of 500 men. His 'merie men' dress in Lincoln green. Mention of Birkendale seems to hint at Barnsdale though the noble king in this work is in Edinburgh. It features archers and the king grants a pardon. Another such work is 'Jock the Leg and the Merry Merchant'. In this ballad, we have mention of Barnsdale (Barnisdale) and a fight in the greenwood. A blast on the horn brings twenty-four archers.[72]

POLITICAL SONGS

It is also worth looking at works that are not exactly outlaw poems but do have a link. These are poems about political events and situations, several of which were written in the later Middle Ages. For the most part, these are tougher works than the outlaw poems and less focused on individual heroes. Nevertheless, there are links in material that has parallels with the outlaw works. Thomas Wright made a useful collection of political songs that was published in 1839. These poems include works in Latin, Anglo-Norman French and English. They parallel the development that produced the Robin Hood ballads in English. The earliest political songs date from the time of King John but most come from the later thirteenth century onwards. Even from King John's period, we have a familiar thread of pleasure from nature — 'when 'leaf and flower appear'.[73] This continues in the later works — 'when the rose will open, when the seasons will be fair, and the nightingale sing'.[74]

An interesting point about these songs is that the majority seem critical of government, and there is a distinct lack of material from our period with this slant. One notes the generally hostile attitude of the Robin Hood works to sheriffs and prelates. From King John's reign, comes an attack on three bishops who supported the king and are compared to leeches. A Henry III song is also aimed against bishops. From the reign of Edward I, one poem attacks monks and nuns, visualising a double house but with no ditch or wall to separate the sexes. The Benedictines are described as liking their drink. The friars preach poverty but always lodge with rich men.[75]

From the reign of Henry III, we have an interesting group of poems supporting Simon de Montfort and his rebels. 'Right good men were the barons', while Simon 'loves right and hates wrong'.[76] Edward I is criticised and warned that every king 'is a servant of God'.[77] After Simon's death at Evesham in 1265, some of his supporters became outlaws. One theory about Robin Hood places him in this group, though the evidence is thin. The language of these songs often compares with that of the Robin Hood works, including the by now familiar form of address in a poem on the evil times of Edward II, ye 'that wolen abide, listneth'.[78]

One rather odd poem, 'A Song on the Times', is aimed against four persons who have not been identified. They are given the names of four brothers — Robert, Richard, Gilbert and the illegitimate Geoffrey. The poem says 'by Robert is very sufficiently indicated a robber'; Robert 'fleeces, extorts and threatens'.[79] This sounds historical but no one has found who they are. Could the Robert possibly be our Robin?

Connections and Conclusions

The point in looking at this tradition of outlaw literature is to find links with Robin Hood. The survey gives some aid in dating the Robin Hood material. It also provides comparisons in themes and contents. The Robin Hood stories are unique in part but in various other ways they do not stand alone. The unique character is the hero and his location. In examining other literature, it becomes clear that the Robin Hood plots are rarely original. Tales of disguises and matches and so on are so common that we must see them as a tradition of outlaw poems. It is almost certain that the poets who composed the Robin Hood works borrowed most of their plots from this traditional material. The plots clearly then do not give an account of the historical life of Robin Hood. That is not to say that no incident in the poems ever actually occurred, only that we cannot trust the material as historical evidence. If there was a real Robin Hood, we have to find him by examining the uncommon or unique material and what that tells us.

We have attempted to look at the Robin Hood poems in previous chapters and so far as possible disentangle the early contents from later accretions. In this chapter, we have examined the literary works most akin to Robin Hood poems in other medieval outlaw literature. This helps to eliminate non-original aspects and to extricate whatever in the Robin Hood poems is, or at least *may be*, about Robin Hood himself rather than simply borrowed literary material.

To sum up, what can we conclude? The most noticeable distinguishing facts about the material on our hero seem to be the following. Firstly, that Robin is of the yeoman class and not knightly. Heroes of this kind were not common before the fourteenth century. The Robin Hood works are also by and large not upper class literature, though the *Gest* was obviously aimed at the small literate class. On the whole, however, the works seem to be not by the courtly poets.

Some critics do indeed see the Robin Hood works as 'popular literature', 'sub-literary material' and 'not particularly distinguished', even the *Gest* is viewed as 'a minor work'.[80] We are not altogether happy with this. The Robin Hood works have their own distinction even though they are not perhaps the elite works of their day.

Secondly, Robin seems to be associated with particular geographical regions. Nottingham and Sherwood, and perhaps even more distinctive — Barnsdale and Yorkshire — seem the best regional connections.

Thirdly, the king mentioned first in connection with Robin is not Richard I or John but Edward. Since we know the origin precedes 1377, this gives us the first three Edwards after the Norman Conquest: Edward I, Edward II and Edward III. They reigned consecutively from 1272 to 1377.

Fourthly, almost all other outlaw literature is about historical figures. This does not prove that Robin was not a fictional creation but it leaves the likelihood that there was an historical Robin Hood even if he has not been and may never be identified for certain.

As one moves further on in time from the original Robin Hood, the outlaw element reduces in reality. We move from violent deaths, robbery and atrocities to the peaceful greenwood, and humorous and harmless activities. The outlaw element is clearly one of the major initial forces behind the early poems and the degree of its closeness to real outlaw life is in itself a clue to the dating.

Endnotes

1   Sargent & Kittredge, p. 11, in *Child Noryce*.
2   Fowler, p. 7.
3   Kane & Donaldson, *Piers Plowman: the B Version*, p. 227.
4   Kane & Donaldson, *Piers Plowman: the B Version*, p. 240.
5   Kane & Donaldson, *Piers Plowman: the B Version*, p. 261.
6   Kane & Donaldson, *Piers Plowman: the B Version*, p. 320.
7   Kane & Donaldson, *Piers Plowman: the B Version*, p. 327-28.
8   Armitage, *Sir Gawain,* p. v, BL MS Cotton Nero A.x.
9   Robert W. Hanning, 'Sir Gawain and the Red Herring', pp. 5-23 in Carruthers and Kirk, p. 10.
10 Ibid, p. 20.
11 Armitage, *Sir Gawain,* p. 29.
12 Armitage, *Sir Gawain,* p. v.
13 Fowler, p. 140.
14 Fowler, p. 182.
15 J.C.Holt, 'The Origins and Audience of the Ballads of Robin Hood', in Hilton pp. 236-57, from *Past & Present,* 18, 1960.
16 Peterborough Cathedral Manuscript I, ff. 320-39; see Ohlgren, p. 13-4.
17 *Anglo-Saxon Chronicle* ed. Whitelock, pp. 151-2; *Peterborough Chronicle,* p2; Keen, p. 12.
18 BN Fonds Française 1553 ff. 325v-38v; see Ohlgren, p. 61.
19 Ohlgren, pp. 97-8.
20 Ohlgren, p. 106; BL Royal Ms 12.c.xii.
21 *Gesta Fulconis,* p. xxiii; W.F. Prideaux, 'Who was Robin Hood', pp. 51-7 in Knight, *Anthology,* p. 52.
22 Ohlgren, p. 130.
23 Ohlgren, p. 142.
24 *Gesta Fulconis,* p.330-3
25 *Gesta Fulconis,* p. 340.
26 *Gesta Fulconis,* p. 388.
27 *Gesta Fulconis,* p. 292.
28 Ohlgren, p. 101; BL Harley MS 2253.
29 Ohlgren, p. 99.
30 Ohlgren, p. 103.
31 Coss, *Political Songs,* p.234, 'Al vert bois de Belregard'.
32 Ohlgren, p. 104.
33 Ohlgren, p. 105.
34 Cottle, pp. 42-3.
35 Keen, p. 88.
36 Sargent & Kittredge, p. 244.
37 Dobson & Taylor, p. 7.
38 Keen, p. 80.

[39] Ohlgren, pp. 168,362.

[40] Knight, *Biography*, p. 75.

[41] Ohlgren, p. 180.

[42] Ohlgren, p. 183.

[43] Dobson & Taylor, pp. 258-73; quote p. 268.

[44] Holt, p. 69.

[45] Sargent & Kittredge, pp. 245,251.

[46] Sargent & Kittredge, p. 376 in *Gude Wallace*.

[47] Ohlgren, p. 187.

[48] Dobson & Taylor, pp. 274-77.

[49] Holt, p. 71.

[50] Keen, p. 65.

[51] Ohlgren, p. 253; MS Advocates 19.2.2.

[52] *Political Songs*, p. 321, 'mestre de larouns'.

[53] Ohlgren, pp. 258,285.

[54] Ohlgren, p. 264.

[55] Ohlgren, pp. 266,269.

[56] Bruce, ed. Duncan.

[57] Bruce, p. 1.

[58] Bruce, p. 32.

[59] Bruce, p. 69, 'The romanys now begynnys her'.

[60] Bruce, p. 27.

[61] Bruce, p. 583.

[62] Bruce, p. 89.

[63] Bruce, p. 427.

[64] Bruce, pp. 593-5, 'thar is no man/That he will rew a woman than'.

[65] Sargent & Kittredge, p. 16.

[66] Sargent & Kittredge, pp. 101,102,156.

[67] Sargent & Kittredge, pp. 127,132,153.

[68] Sargetn & Kittredge, p. 177.

[69] Sargent & Kittredge, p. 457.

[70] Sargent & Kittredge, p. 466.

[71] Sargent & Kittredge, pp. 595-97.

[72] Sargent & Kittredge, pp. 607-9.

[73] *Political Songs*, p. 3, 'E pareis la fueill' e la flors.

[74] *Political Songs*, p. 63'que ce ros panirra,/Que ce tens serra beles roxinol chanterra'.

[75] *Political Songs*, pp. 137-48.

[76] *Political Songs*, pp.60-1, 'mout furent bons les barons'; 'Il eime dreit, et het le tort'.

[77] *Political Songs*, pp. 94,107.

[78] *Political Songs*, p. 324.

[79] *Political Songs*, pp.49-50, 'Competenter per Robert, robbur designatur'; 'Robertus excoriate, extorquet, et minatur'.

[80] Douglas Gray, 'The Robin Hood Poems', pp. 3-37 in Knight, Anthology, pp. 4-5; J. B. Bessinger Jr., 'The Gest of Robin Hood Revisited', pp. 39-50 in Knight Anthology, p. 39.

7

Where to Look for Robin Hood

We have already looked at some of the evidence relating to the location of Robin Hood in the poems about him. It is now time to examine this matter in more detail. The point of this chapter is to examine where we should search for the origins of Robin Hood, in fiction and perhaps in reality. We are therefore reviewing the earliest records and the earliest poems to see what clues they offer.

Locations in the Early Poems

As we now know, the record evidence found to date does not identify an original Robin Hood. We must therefore first turn to the poetic evidence for hints and beginnings for any real locations that might exist. The major difficulty here is that an original poem may be entirely fictional and certainly the poems included borrowing from other heroes and inventions. A second problem is that the poets of the earliest works are all unknown. It is a custom with fiction to use one's own, that is, the author's own, locations because that familiarity allows for greater conviction in the work. In medieval works, poets often also had in mind the background of their audience or readers who would appreciate settings with which they were familiar. In other words, although we must examine the locations mentioned in the poems, and hope for clues to reality, we must beware of thinking that even the earliest works provide cast-iron evidence.

A) YORKSHIRE

We have already noted what we think are the earliest poems. We shall keep to that short select list for this chapter, that is, the *Gest, Robin Hood and Guy of Gisborne, Robin Hood and the Potter, Robin Hood and the Monk*, and *Robin Hood's Death*. We suggest that the locations that are mentioned in the earliest works are likely to be the most authentic.

In examining the *Gest* and the early poems we have also noted the limited number of basic locations. Let us briefly review this material. Our first location is Yorkshire. 'Robin Hood in Barnsdale stood' is one of the most familiar and oft repeated lines about our hero. In the *Gest* it appears in the third verse: 'Robyn stode in Bernesdale'.[1] At the end of the *Gest*, when Robin tires of life at court he desires to return home and says 'I made a chapel in Bernysdale' dedicated to Mary Magdalene and 'longeth sore' to return.[2]

Barnsdale Bar is a real location. It is just north of Doncaster in the West Riding of Yorkshire near the old Roman road. The saying may have become popular from the poems about Robin or it might even have been a popular saying that was taken up by the poems. In any case, it is certainly one of the very earliest clues. Yorkshire locations are common in the early poems but Barnsdale is one of the most interesting since it is a relatively unknown place. One should, however, note that there is also a Barnsdale nearer to Nottingham, by the River Leen and in Sherwood Forest.[3] Most historians have favoured the Yorkshire location but, as always, we must keep our options open.

Barnsdale in Yorkshire is not an especially famous place. This has been pointed out by those who also noted the appearance of the place-name 'The Sayles' in the *Gest*. This is an even less known place-name, but also a real one. The area *was* known as one where travellers needed to protect themselves from highway robberies in the Middle Ages. It had been the scene of an actual highway robbery in 1329.[4] As we know, many Robin Hood stories depend upon way-laying travellers. In the poems, Robin may sometimes return what is taken, he may use it for good ends, but basically he is carrying out highway robbery.

The *Gest* has further Yorkshire place-names in its tale. The knight in the poem owes £400 to the abbot of St Mary's Abbey, York. When Robin leaves court to return to the forest, it is to Barnsdale that he goes for his last years. After a period at court, Robin tells the king that he wishes to return north to where he 'made a chapel in Bernysdale'.[5] This reference has not always been given the attention it deserves. It is one of the few e.arly references providing Robin with a local base. Why should he found a chapel? Why in Barnsdale? It does suggest a man of some local standing and that this is his home area. The only problem is that there is no known chapel or ecclesiastical building of any kind in Barnsdale. The only name that seems at all similar is that of Baysdale Priory in Yorkshire, a house of Cistercian nuns (as was Kirklees), and near Guisborough (sometimes then called Gisborne). But there is no direct evidence to link Baysdale to Robin Hood. Walker suggested that the chapel might be that at Skelbrook, which had the arms of Monk Bretton priory over its door. Again, with Walker this is conjecture; there is no real evidence.[6] Nevertheless, the foundation of a chapel is not a normal outlaw activity and it may relate to some real action of a real Robin Hood.

In the *Gest*, Robin finally meets his end at Kirklees Priory (Kyrkesly), which was a real priory located between Huddersfield and Barnsley. The prioress who plans his death is described also as 'nye was of hys kynne'.[7] This also seems important. Why should the prioress be there and related to Robin unless he were a local man from a local family, and one of some standing? Kirklees Priory existed. It was a house of Cistercian nuns founded in *c.* 1138 by Reiner le Fleming and dedicated to St Mary and St James. One notes the St Mary in particular, given Robin's favour of Christ's mother.[8] A reconstructed gatehouse put up in the fourteenth century still stands on the spot.[9]

When Little John impresses the sheriff with his archery he lies about his name and says he is 'Reynaud Grenelefe' who was born in 'Holdernes'.[10] Holderness is a Yorkshire site near Kingston-upon-Hull and more easterly than most of the other Robin Hood locations. The villain who plots Robin's death with his mistress, the prioress, is Sir Roger of 'Donkesly'. In the *Gest*, he is then called 'of Donkestere' so there seems little doubt that it is of Doncaster, which is also not far from Barnsdale in Yorkshire.[11] No record has been found of the historical Sir Roger, though some historians have argued that he might have been a cleric or an ordinary layman, who could still be called 'sir' rather than a knight. They have put forward possible candidates called Roger — but they are mostly unconvincing suggestions. P. Valentine Harris did find, in the record of Wakefield court, a Roger, son of William of Doncaster, which showed that it was a local name. Another reference, probably to the same individual, refers to him as a chaplain. Harris was then convinced that this was 'the very man'. However, there is no real evidence that he should have been known as 'Sir Roger' or any other link except location.[12]

Arguably the most significant location in all the poems is the *Gest's* mention of 'the Saylis'. Robin instructs Little John to waylay a 'guest (gest)' there — in other words, to commit highway robbery. From the Sayles, they look east and then west and 'loked in to Bernysdale'.[13] Robin tells John to 'walke up to the Saylis, and so to Watlinge Strete' and wait for a traveller.[14] The same instruction is repeated later in the poem: 'walke up under the Sayles,/ And to Watlynge strete'.[15] Again, they climb 'up to the Sayles' and this time, as they look towards Barnsdale, they see two monks approaching. The monks are taken to Robin in a nearby 'lodge'. Watling Street is clearly the old Roman road that passes by Barnsdale on its way to Pontefract. It was sometimes so called, though it should more correctly be known as Ermine Street. Joseph Hunter identified the Sayles as a small tenancy of the manor of Pontefract. A terrier of 1688 lists an acre in 'Sailes' under Kirk Smeaton.[16] Later, this is called 'Sailes Close'. The location is near to Wentbridge and in Barnsdale. The site is on a rise and made a good lookout point for highway robbers.

Lee is a common name, and one would love to know the location of origin of Sir Richard at the Lee. Most have suggested he had a Lancashire base but Yorkshire is also possible and the Yorkshire Feet of Fines for 1314-15 mention one Richard de Lee in Aston.[17] Bellamy has given especial attention to trying to identify Sir Richard and settled on a family related to Gower. He attached importance to the lines in a Robin Hood poem:

Sir Richard Lee,
Thou art a knight full good;
For I do know by thy pedigree
Thou springst from Goweres blood. [18]

However, this comes from *Robin Hood and Queen Katherine,* a late poem, and may well relate to a contemporary of Henry VIII — as John Bellamy suggests. Less certain is that this leads us back to the Sir Richard of the *Gest.* The fourteenth-century Lee that Bellamy notes seems more of a model for the sheriff than the good knight of the poem. Nor does Bellamy find a 'Richard' Lee to fit. The nearest Richard he could discover did have debts — but he was a cleric, parson of Bletchingley in Surrey, and not a knight. Another (I think another) Sir Richard atte Lee is recorded in Edward III's reign and was actually outlawed — but this would fit Robin's life rather than that of the Sir Richard of the poem![19] One cannot but agree with Thomas Ohlgren that it is pointless to expect to be able to match all the figures in the poems with actual historical personages.[20] Despite that, he goes on to suggest that the poem's character of the knight links with the Richard Lee who was lord mayor of London in the fifteenth century — though he clearly could not be the original. If there were any connection at all, it would surely be that the existing character in the story provoked interest in the coincidental name of the mayor.

All that we can conclude about the identity of Sir Richard in the *Gest* is that there were quite a few Sir Richards and Richards of Lee through the relevant centuries, whose names would fit. However, there is no evidence to pin down any one of them as the man of the poem. Bellamy, in the end, plumped for the Richard who became parson of Arksey, but we find it difficult to accept the conclusion without some further evidence of confirmation.[21] Harris plumps for a Yorkshire Richard of the Lee in the Wakefield rolls, but he was not a knight. As with Sir Roger, Harris is content to argue that he could have been so-called. In our view, none of the Sir Richards, or Richards, completely fit the picture, whether in Yorkshire or Lancashire. Sir Richard cannot be identified and neither can the location of Lee — except to conclude it was probably either in Lancashire or Yorkshire.

In *Robin Hood and Guy of Gisborne* we get mention not simply of 'Barnesdale/Barnsdale' but of Barnsdale as a forest — which it was not. Little John goes there to find that the outlaw band has been attacked by the sheriff and two of them left dead.[22] Barnsdale here seems to be enclosed and has entry 'gates', which sounds like a park rather than a forest.[23] Dobson and Taylor suggest that the 'gates' merely mean ways through, but the traditional meaning of the word is possible. In this piece, Robin even introduces himself by saying 'My name is Robin Hood of Barnesdale'.[24] Gisborne is a Yorkshire place-name, though other regions may be the possible origin. The Yorkshire Feet of Fines for 1314-15, in the reign of Edward II, mention a 'William de Gisburn'.[25] Again, no suitable Guy of Gisborne has been found.

In *Robin Hood and the Potter*, when the outlaws see the tradesman Little John says he met him at Wentbridge (Went breg), which is at a road crossing of the River Went and close to Barnsdale.[26] The potter is on a horse and cart and they demand that he pay pavage, a tax for passing. Travellers from the north would go through Wentbridge as they approached Barnsdale.

In *Robin Hood's Death*, the location of the final scene is again the priory of Kirklees. In the two versions of the poem printed by Dobson and Taylor, there are various spellings of the name but all clearly of the same place — Church Lees, Churchlees, Churchlee, Kirkley and Kirkleys.[27] In the B version, as printed by Dobson and Taylor, the priory is referred to as the 'hall'. Only in *Robin Hood and the Monk* of these early poems is there no Yorkshire site mentioned.

B) NOTTINGHAM AND SHERWOOD

Our second major location is Nottingham with Sherwood Forest. Many commentators have seen the Yorkshire and Sherwood elements of the poems as coming originally from separate traditions, yet the *Gest* itself not only uses the same locations but mentions them in the same breath. The knight says that his purpose is to dine in 'Blith or Dancastere' (Blyth or Doncaster) and that is in either Nottinghamshire or Yorkshire.[28] The Nottingham Blyth is en route from the north for Nottingham. The monk from St Mary's similarly says he could have dined in 'Blythe or in Dankestere', and one might note that the two towns are only 10 miles apart.

When a town appears in the early poems it is usually Nottingham, especially if it has a significant part in the story. In the *Gest*, Nottingham, like Barnsdale, appears early — in this case in verse 15. This is in reference to the 'hye sheriff of Notyingham', later called the sheriff, who 'dwelled in Notingham'.[29] Little John joins an archery competition, which is watched watched by the sheriff of Nottingham, who thinks him the best archer he has ever seen. Robin goes to Nottingham for another archery competition arranged by the sheriff, to win a gold and silver arrow. Robin leads his men to Nottingham to deal with the sheriff, whom the king has ordered to take him. When the king comes to try and capture Robin it is in Nottingham that he stays for six months. After Robin has been pardoned, he returns with the king to Nottingham.

In *Robin Hood and Guy of Gisborne* the main location is Barnsdale and Yorkshire. There is no action in Nottingham and no mention of Sherwood but there is an appearance by 'the sheriffe of Nottingham'.[30] And at the end of the poem the sheriff flees 'Towards his house in Nottingham'.[31] We also meet a sheriff's man called William a Trent — the Trent being Nottingham's river.

In *Robin Hood and the Potter* the main focus of the story is when Robin takes over the potter's wares and goes to sell them in 'Notynggam'.[32] He sets up by the sheriff's gate. It is there that he meets the sheriff's wife, and, through her, the sheriff, when invited to dine in their hall. They return to the forest, but it is not named. Sherwood is not mentioned.

Robin Hood and the Monk places Robin in 'mery Scherwode' but the focus of the poem is the town of Nottingham, which is presented as a very real location. Geographically, Nottingham and Sherwood must clearly be linked, and both appear regularly in the early evidence. At the beginning of *Robin Hood and the Monk* Robin says he will go to Nottingham, and he chooses to go with only Little John to support him.[33] Later, the two quarrel and Robin goes on to Nottingham alone, while John returns to 'mery Scherwode', along paths of which he knew every one.[34] Robin goes into St Mary's church. He is recognised and all the gates of the town are barred against to stop him escaping. John goes to Nottingham with Much to rescue Robin. On the way, they enter the house of Much's uncle near the highway. They find the town gates barred but manage to locate Robin in the town prison and release him. The sheriff searches the streets and alleys of Nottingham but Robin has escaped to 'mery Scherwode'.[35] It is again to Nottingham that the sheriff takes the captured Sir Richard. Robin comes to his rescue and kills the sheriff in the town. The king then arrives in Nottingham and, after a search around the north, staying in the town for six months and more. The poem *Robin Hood's Death* is set entirely in Yorkshire, with mentions of Barnsdale as well as Kirklees. There is no reference at all to Nottingham or Sherwood.

The examination of the five poems, widely accepted as the earliest, does have some significant results. It becomes clear that Yorkshire figures more broadly than elsewhere in that more towns and sites are mentioned in the region; Sherwood and Nottingham, though, with fewer surrounding places brought in, receive virtually equal attention.

c) OTHER LOCATIONS

Yorkshire and Nottingham are the two key locations in early evidence, but they are not the only places to appear in the poems. Other northern sites are mentioned, which perhaps only underline the two main locations. Thus, several Lancashire names appear. In the *Gest*, we have Verysdale named as the home of the knight.[36] This is generally taken to be Wyresdale (Wyersdale) in Garstang hundred in Lancashire. In that hundred is also a village called Lee.[37] John Bellamy has argued that Wyresdale is by no means a certain solution and thinks that 'Wyresdale in Lancashire is unlikely'.[38] He points to a number of other possibilities, including Wiresdale in Yorkshire.[39] He argues that the 'W' beginning is not likely for a place beginning with 'V' and suggests other possible names, such as Iverishagh near Nottingham, which is near a Robin Hood Hill and with a Walter de la Lee mentioned there is 1314. Another suggestion of his is Irewysdale as the valley of the River Erewash (then called Yrewys). This valley is between Nottinghamshire and Derbyshire. Bellamy points out that there are several castles in the vicinity and, in particular, Annesley castle near Nottingham.[40] One also should perhaps remember that the relevant sheriff of Nottingham was also sheriff of Derbyshire. Bellamy suggests other possibilities but they seem increasingly unlikely. Going even further afield, Thomas Ohlgren has tried to connect the place with his Richard Lee (a fifteenth-century mayor of London) and suggests it could be in Worcestershire — but this does not take us closer to Robin Hood.[41]

Holt links together various possible Lancashire references to Edward II and local families and, for once, seems to overemphasise the possible connections. His suggestion is that the localities represent different phases in the building of the legend — first Yorkshire, then Nottingham, then Lancashire.[42] This is by no means impossible, as we have no idea of the progress of the tales before the survival of the earliest works, none of which can date from the time of origin — whenever it was. This sounds an attractive and possible explantion of how the story might have built up over time but, again, is little more than conjecture.

The poor knight in the *Gest* says that his son has slain 'a knight of Lancaster'.[43] There must be a question over whether this means a knight from Lancaster or a follower of the noble earl of Lancaster — if the latter it could be an important clue to dating. A reference in the *Gest* that is not easy to explain is at the wrestling attended by the knight when we are told that the best yeomen 'of all the west countree' were present.[44] When the king comes north he goes through 'Lancasshyre' until he comes to 'Plomton Parke'.[45] This is generally thought to be Plumpton Park in Cumberland, though a Yorkshire location has also been suggested near Knaresborough.[46] The York Feet of Fines for 1318-19 mentions a Robert de Plomtom, whose lands included the manor of Plompton.[47] This Plompton is in Yorkshire, just east of Harrogate and right next to a Loxley Farm. The same source mentions a Robert Fraunk of Plumpton under 1323-24, a William of Plumpton with 20 acres of wood in Plumpton under 1325-26, as well as a Marmaduke de Plumpton.[48]

The knight in the *Gest,* when he reappears in the fifth fytte, is named as 'Syr Rychard at the Lee'. The location of Lee, a common name, is uncertain. Lancashire is a possibility. The castle, presumably at Lee, where the outlaws shelter with the wounded Little John, is described in the *Gest* as being within the wood, surrounded by a double ditch and a wall, and having gates and a drawbridge. London comes into the *Gest* twice as the place the monk and the sheriff go to inform the king — but it does not come into the story directly. Another possible Lancashire site is the place from which Guy of Gisborne originated. Again, it is uncertain but may have been Gisburn in Lancashire.

Therefore, we see that Yorkshire and Nottingham with Sherwood both figure largely in the earliest surviving Robin Hood poems. Yorkshire has a greater variety of place-names and seems to be a fundamental location for Robin's life. Of the earliest poems only one, *Robin Hood and the Monk*, has no mention of any Yorkshire site. Nottingham appears as frequently as the town of any action and only fails to get a mention in the *Robin Hood's Death*. Sherwood is less common and does not appear in *Robin Hood and Guy of Gisborne, Robin Hood and the Potter* or *Robin Hood's Death*. We must conclude, therefore, that Yorkshire is the main region and Nottingham the main town but Sherwood more incidental. In general, northern sites predominate in the early poems.

Although Yorkshire and Nottingham figure largely in the texts of the early poems, there is another way of looking at this particular evidence. R. B. Dobson and others have examined the language of the poems and come to the conclusion that they seem to be written in an East Midlands dialect rather than a Yorkshire or northern one, which would fit better with Nottingham than Yorkshire — at least for the anonymous authors.[49] The examination of this question by Lister M. Matheson, perhaps the most detailed to date, has mixed conclusions. This study concludes that the early poem of *Robin Hood and the Potter* is written in an East

Anglian dialect, more likely Norfolk than Suffolk, *Robin Hood and the Monk* in dialect from the North West Midlands around West Derbyshire, and the *Gest* was certainly in a northern dialect, possibly that of Yorkshire.[50] One general point that seems worth making is that all the early poems are in English and in local dialect in a period when Latin was still the language of educated literature. It seems some evidence that the Robin Hood story was spread by and for ordinary English folk rather than the highly educated nobility.[51]

Locations in the Early Plays and Play Games

Several historians, such as Stephen Knight, now believe that the plays may have been produced before the poems.[52] Knight, indeed, sees the ballads as 'secondary to the plays and games'. Unfortunately, only a very limited amount of written script survives for medieval play versions. There is evidence that performances occurred in the medieval period but there is only one surviving example of what the performances contained.

One of the most interesting facts about the early Robin Hood plays is how many are mentioned before 1600, being no less than 260.[53] Unfortunately, virtually none of the texts for these early plays and play games survive. Locations for Robin are not mentioned. But interest remains in the locations of the actual performances — which were widespread. Mention is made of places in Scotland, such as Aberdeen, and widely through England, from the West Country to Reading, Wolverhampton and Norfolk. The earliest reference to a play is at Exeter in 1426-27. Other medieval mentions of Robin Hood play games come from Somerset, Devon, Reading, Willenhall, Kingston-upon-Thames, Henley-on-Thames and Edinburgh. Oddly, there is no mention of play games in northern English sites. In fact, all the early references with regard to England are to places south of Nottingham.[54] This is especially odd, as practically all the early poem locations direct us to the other side of this geographical line — that is, to the north.[55] It is difficult to explain this contradiction. Presumably, the plays and games were more popular in southern regions — but it does seem a striking contrast.

The scraps of dialogue that survive from medieval performances come next in our list of sources to examine for locations. The earliest surviving play, generally known as *Robin Hood and the Sheriff,* from *c.* 1475, does indeed have the sheriff as a participant. He is, however, only referred to as the sheriff and not the sheriff of anywhere in particular. There is, in fact, no location of any kind in this fragment. There are no other known play scripts surviving until the latter part of the sixteenth century.

There is virtually no evidence for Robin Hood locations in historical records since none of the Robin Hoods listed in records has yet been identified as *the* Robin. Only if we knew this could we conclude anything much concerning his location. About the only evidence we can quote here is an oddity. It comes from an historical record that probably relates to the earliest surviving Robin Hood play text. This is a single reference in the Paston Letters to and from various members of that East Anglian family. A letter to John Paston II, dated 16 April 1473, complains about one of the Paston servants leaving the family. This servant had played Robin Hood and the sheriff of Nottingham in performances for Sir John and has now, jokes Sir John, 'goon in-to Bernysdale'.[56] This clearly refers to the whereabouts of the hero in the play rather than to the actual destination of the servant and shows that 'Robin Hood in Barnsdale' was a well-known phrase.

Locations in Early Histories

Locations given by early historians — that is, by those writing a deliberate 'history' of events in England — are also of considerable interest. We often do not know the reasons behind their statements but we presume, in this case, they were not usually invented. Sometimes, no doubt, the information was simply taken from the poems. Sometimes, it may have been from poems now lost. But it may also be that some traditions and information has been handed on, and we do notice that some locations are not the same as those mentioned in the poems. We must at least look at this separate evidence.

With this evidence, it makes sense to start with what is likely to be the least significant — that is, the later works — and move back through time to the few early histories that mention Robin Hood.

WILLIAM STUKELEY

William Stukeley was a parson, doctor, archivist and antiquarian from Stamford in Lincolnshire. He was a respected fellow of the Royal Society and of the Society of Antiquaries. He produced an account of Robin Hood in 1746, including a pedigree. If Dr Stukeley's statements sound impressively serious, one might take into account a contemporary's view of him as full of 'simplicity, drollery, absurdity, ingenuity, superstition'.[57]

Stukeley seems to have garnered some information from Dugdale's *Baronage* but then to have distorted it further.[58] Stukeley's information in his *Palaeographia Britannica* has been largely dismissed since. It traced Robin Hood's lineage back to the earls of Huntingdon and the Anglo-Saxon Earl Waltheof. It listed Robin as son of William Fitzooth — Robert 'commonly called Robin Hood, pretended earl of Huntington' — and gives a date of death as 1247. No other reference to a family with the name Fitzooth is known.

Like many of the early efforts at a life of Robin Hood, this one is dismissed by modern historians as invention. Stephen Knight, for example, refers to 'this ludicrous family tree', while Holt sees it as a 'spurious pedigree', much of which is 'fictitious'.[59] But, again, like many early accounts, we have no idea where the unusual part of the information came from or how much of it was invented. It is wise, until we have answers, not to dismiss any early account. The pedigree is mainly of a family with a Lincolnshire background and connects to the earldom of Huntingdon. Stukeley does call Robin the 'pretended' earl, which is interesting.

THOMAS GALE

Stukely referred to the epitaph for Robin Hood found among Dr Gale's papers. Thomas Gale was dean of York from 1697-1702. The epitaph begins 'Hear undernead dis laitl stean/ Laiz robert earl of Huntingtun'.[60] It deserves little serious attention. It is in false antique language and clearly based on the earlier epitaph provided by Martin Parker. Maurice Keen is surely right to dismiss it as 'clearly spurious'.[61] Gale also gave a date for Robin's death as the 24 Kalends of December 1247.[62] There is no such date in the Roman system, which Gale almost certainly knew, and this adds to the likelihood that the whole thing is a hoax or joke invention. This does not invalidate the existence of a grave of some kind at Kirklees, which is well attested elsewhere.

ROGER DODSWORTH

In the seventeenth century, Roger Dodsworth had attempted a brief biography of Robin Hood. He says Robin was born at Bradfield in Hallamshire — that is, south Yorkshire. Robin committed murder and fled, meeting Little John at Clifton upon Calder. He says Little John was buried at 'Hathershead' in Derbyshire where there was a tombstone. For Hathershead we should probably read Hathersage, which is in Derbyshire and not far from southern Yorkshire. This is an interesting account because it suggests different locations to those found elsewhere. Dodsworth, like Stukeley, was an antiquarian and it is a pity we have no idea of the source of his information. The supposed grave at Hathersage was examined in 1784 when a thighbone of 29½ inches in length was found. It was later stolen by Sir George Strickland and then lost.[63] Another burial claimed to be that of Little John was in Scotland where the body was said to have been 14 feet long!

RICHARD GRAFTON AND WILLIAM CAMDEN

In the Tudor and Stuart period, two historians noted that Robin Hood's grave was at Kirklees. These were Richard Grafton in 1569 and William Camden in 1607. Grafton was royal printer for Edward VI and claimed to have information from 'an olde and auncient Pamphlet', though few have believed him. As Bellamy points out, Grafton's summary of this pamphlet suggests nobility and Tudor times rather than any great antiquity.[64] Grafton does not locate the outlaw activities of Robin but does detail his death at a nunnery in Yorkshire 'called Bircklies'.[65] This, presumably, should be taken to be Kirklees. Grafton described the gravestone, saying that the name William of Goldesborough was on it. The noted and serious historian William Camden also mentioned this gravestone in the fifth edition of his *Britannia,* published in 1607.[66]

NATHANIEL JOHNSTON

In 1669, a drawing, clearly of this same Kirklees grave, was made by Nathaniel
Johnston, a Yorkshire doctor. It was published in *Sepulchral Monuments of Great
Britain* by Richard Gough in 1786.[67] It certainly looks real enough and there is no
real reason to doubt its authenticity. The question is rather of its interpretation.
To my mind, the Robert Hude name looks as if it has been added to the stone,
and its positioning is certainly peculiar if it had been the original inscription. We
suggest therefore that it was someone else's gravestone, which was given an added
inscription in the hope of supporting the place as Robin's burial site. The stone
seems to have disappeared by the end of the eighteenth century.

MARTIN PARKER

It is not entirely clear where Martin Parker should stand in the study of Robin
Hood, whether as an historian, a believer in myth or simply a writer of fiction.
He was a professional poet. Since he produced one of the first real attempts at a
life of Robin Hood we have decided to count him also as an historian. His work
was, however, in verse form and not to modern minds 'historical'. Parker's work
appeared in 1632 as *A True Tale of Robin Hood*. He also provided an epitaph:
'Robert Earle of Huntington/ Lies under this little stone'.[68] The verse underlined
Robin's area of activity as 'these northerne parts he vexed sore'.[69] Parker says that
there was also a note of the date of death as 4 December 1198, in the reign of
Richard I.[70]

THE SLOANE MANUSCRIPT

There is an earlier anonymous attempt at a *Life of Robin Hood* preserved
in a Sloane Manuscript in the British Library.[71] It seems mainly to base its
information on ballads and especially on the *Gest*. It claims that Robin was born
in Locksley, which the author claims was the Locksley 'in Yorkshire or after
others, in Nottinghamsh'.[72] It is not altogether clear if he means that Locklsey
might be in Nottinghamshire or simply that others believe Robin was born in
Nottinghamshire. Most have presumed that Locksley or Loxley in question is that
in Yorkshire near Sheffield.

JOHN LELAND

John Leland was an important historian of the sixteenth century, royal antiquary
to Henry VIII and probably responsible for that monarch's interest in Robin
Hood. Leland has been called 'perhaps the first genuine antiquarian'.[73] He tells
us that Robin was buried at Kirklees, and that information was accepted by
Stukeley and Ritson following him. Gutch gave the same information for a burial
in 1247.[74] Thus, the Yorkshire background was broadly accepted early on. What

is new is the ennobling of Robin, who was now associated with the earldom of Huntingdon.

John Maior

John Maior (otherwise Mair or Major) wrote at about the turn of the fourteenth to fifteenth century. He was the last of a little group of Scottish historians who took an interest in Robin Hood. He had been educated at Haddington, Cambridge and Paris, where he became a professor of theology. He was a serious scholar. His historical work was the *Historia Majoris Britanniae* (History of Greater Britain), originally in Latin and later translated. For reasons unknown to us, he had some innovations in his view of the outlaw hero. Firstly, he placed Robin in the Plantagenet era — the start of a long acceptance of this as the prime period for Robin. Secondly, Maior also seems responsible for the idea that Robin robbed the rich to aid the poor. He does not provide any location and only seems to know of Robin from the stories 'told in song all over Britain'.[75] But the very fact that the three earliest historians to mention Robin were all Scots is itself of interest.

Walter Bower

The second of the Scottish historians to tackle Robin Hood was Walter Bower. He became abbot of Incholm on the Firth of Forth. He was born at Haddington, where Maior went to school. Bower was an historian who, in the first half of the fifteenth century, mentioned Robin Hood in a straightforward historical setting when he continued the chronicle of John of Fordun. The additions made by Bower were once mistakenly attributed to Fordun, but it is now clear that the section in which we are interested was his work. He tells of Robin Hood and Little John 'in Barnesdale' and Robin 'once when in Barnisdale' among 'woodland briars and thorns'.[76] Bower places the sheriff in Barnsdale as well, which is interesting. Bower does not suggest that Robin lived in Barnsdale, saying only that once he was there. Some historians suggest that Bower's account of Robin probably depended at least partly on knowledge of ballads and perhaps of one that has not survived in its early form, concerning Robin being attacked in a chapel — possibly a variation of *Robin Hood and the Monk*.[77]

The English Monk

Thanks to some very recent research by Dr Julian Luxford of St Andrews University, we have an extra historian to add to the early list.[78] Luxford has noted an important annotation to Eton College MS 213, which contains a Polychronicon from *c.* 1420, at which point the main text finishes. It has a number of additional marginal notes added after that date. The significant one for us occurs on f234r. It is made by the person already identified as the 'principal annotator' by Neil Ker. We follow Luxford in accepting our reference as being in this hand, though it is in a darker ink than most of the other entries by him. It consists simply of twenty-three words in Latin about 'a certain outlaw named Robyn hode'. It has a more critical attitude to Robin than some accounts and says that he and his men 'infested shirwode and other law-abiding areas of England with continuous robberies'. Luxford suggests that information might have been taken from the monk ballad, but the short note retains importance for us. It is clearly meant as a serious historical point. It places Robin in the years 1294-99 because the addition is made at the section of the manuscript covering this period. Interestingly, this is very close to the date given by the very earliest historian to deal with Robin. In terms of this chapter, it is an early historical record placing Robin in Sherwood, though not necessarily only or permanently in Sherwood since it adds 'other areas'. The fact that the earliest three writers on Robin before this discovery were all Scots now needs a little modification too. Luxford believes that the chief annotator was operating at the monastery where the manuscript was placed in 1460, that is at Witham in Somerset in the diocese of Bath and Wells. As we have pointed out, the location of writers on Robin and interest in him has its own significance.

Andrew Wyntoun

Andrew Wyntoun was the first serious historical author to tell us anything about Robin Hood. He wrote, in the early fifteenth century, the *Orygynale Cronykil*, dating from *c.* 1420. He was an Augustinian canon at St Sers Inch by Loch Leven in Scotland.[79] Wyntoun placed Robin and Little John 'in Inglewood and Barnsdale' (Yngil-wode and Barnysdaile) in 1283, during the reign of Edward I.[80] It is the mention of Inglewood that is of particular interest here, being an unusual location for Robin Hood. It is in Cumberland between Carlisle and Penrith. Inglewood was a genuine forest area near another major ancient roadway and was another haunt of actual medieval outlaws. It was also the stamping ground of another medieval ballad hero and outlaw, Adam Bell, and his comrades.

Wyntoun also mentioned a different person called Hood, which it would be unwise of us to ignore. The later 'Hwde' attacked Roxburgh in Scotland in 1342. He was called Hood 'of Edname'. Knight thought this site was not known but it is surely Ednam, which is just north of Kelso on the Scottish border. It is very close to Roxburgh, then an important stronghold on the border. As noted before, Wyntoun cannot have believed that this Hood was our Robin, given his previous comment, but no information can be ignored in this intriguing, if ultimately unsatisfying, search.

One point we must not ignore in this discussion is the location of the historians themselves. Of special interest is the fact that the three earliest historians to make any mention of Robin Hood as an historical figure (Wyntoun, Bower and Maior) were all Scots. To all of them he was an English outlaw. Partly the fact of the three Scots' interest was due to interaction between those historians but it does suggest an interest in our hero in that region. It possibly connects to the significance of the border country for songs and poems. It may also be some sort of pointer to the origins of Robin himself. If nothing else, it must link with the Tudor and Stuart connection between Robin Hood and the Bruce family.

THE EARLY HISTORIANS: A GENERAL COMMENT

One important reservation about the evidence from these early Scottish historians is the source of the information, which we do not know. Most modern commentators have seen at least an element of the information having come not from historical sources but from folklore traditions and the ballads.[81] They may therefore not be reflecting any historical evidence that is not from and in the ballad and poetic sources — though, given their dates, they may have had access to works now lost. As with nearly all evidence about Robin Hood's origins, we are left with uncertainty and puzzles that cannot easily be solved.

We also now have the brief note on the fifteenth-century English manuscript. This is not exactly by an historian but is clearly by someone with some knowledge of and interest in history. We do not know the background of this annotator but Julian Luxford has argued that the addition was made in the writer's Somerset monastery. As the Scottish interest ties in with the border poems, so the Somerset interest ties in with our knowledge of the play game performances in that geographical region of England.

Locations in Historical Records

There are few if any certain locations related to Robin Hood to be found in ordinary local or national records from the Middle Ages. This is because we cannot be sure when and where to look. At present, it is possible to know or find vital records without being able to know their true significance. Only when the real Robin Hood is found will that be possible.

There are a few examples, however, which are certainly worth consideration. For a start, the famous, perhaps most famous, line about Robin is 'Robin Hood in Barnsdale stood'. It appears in poems. Its appearance in records probably has nothing to do with the real Robin Hood but seems to refer always to the literary hero. Thus, the first recorded example, 'Robin Hode en Barnesdale stode', actually appeared in a legal record from the Court of Common Pleas of 1429.[82] Ten years later, a parliamentary petition likened the criminal Piers Venables to 'Robyn Hode and his meynee'.[83]

Confusingly, there is an early record of the famous line about Sherwood on where Robin stood: 'Robin Hood in Sherwood stood'. This survived first in a few lines scribbled in a manuscript kept in Lincoln cathedral dated to about 1425. It should perhaps, strictly in this chapter, have been listed among the poems, as it seems to be a fragment of verse — but it nicely balances our legal Barnsdale example. This piece begins: 'Robyn hod in scherewod stod'.[84]

Incidentally, one notes that Lincoln and its surrounding area is one of the regions that every now and then crops up as showing an interest in Robin Hood. So we find that even that famous line is used for both of the major locations. The *Gest* has much about Yorkshire locations but it equally has a good deal about Nottingham, the base for the sheriff. It might also be worth remembering that as early as 1432 a clerk wrote in the Wiltshire parliamentary roll: 'Robyn Hode Inne Greenwode Stode'. One has a sneaking suspicion that this unlocated line might be the ancestor of both the other two![85]

Locations of Real Robin Hoods

There were many people in the records of the Middle Ages whose surnames were either Hood or Robinhood. It seems worthwhile just briefly to summarise the geographical location of these people. Summerson found another ten Robehod (or Robinhood) surnames between 1265 and 1322.[86] They came from Lancashire, Kent and London. Some historians argue that the very appearance of 'Robinhood' as a surname proves that Robin Hood was known before the date that this surname was used. According to Bellamy, for example, the appearance of the surname Robinhood shows that Robin was 'a legend already extant in the 13th century'.[87] We do not necessarily concur but, certainly, it is worth noting the name. Thus, two of the first three people found who were named Robinhood came from Sussex. Historians have argued that the name could have been transferred from the north — but this is conjecture and it is odd that the earliest examples come from the south. Holt has argued that the Robinhood surname is significant because it shows that the legend existed before this name could have emerged.[88] However, his discussion itself rather contradicts the conclusion, noting that one Katherine Robynhod was the daughter of Robert Hood, a councillor in London, who died in 1318. This suggests that the surname could simply be used for a descendant of a Robert Hood.

Several of the people named Hood or Robinhood were linked with forest regions. This includes the 1354 Robin Hood, who was imprisoned for activity in Rockingham Forest in Northamptonshire. Knight, in particular, sees this as a significant reference.[89] It is certainly a rare example of a real Robin Hood known to have been in prison.

The earliest known Robin Hood (Robert Hod) was found in 1226 and the record comes from York assizes, when his goods, worth 32s 6d, were confiscated and he had become a fugitive.[90] He owed the money to St Peter's in York. In the following year, he is called 'Hobbehod'. He is the only known early Robin Hood to be an outlaw, but there is no additional evidence about him. He remains one of the best candidates to be the real Robin so far found. Another Robin Hood is to be found in the Pipe Roll of 1241-42, this one 'Robertus Hod de Linton'.[91]

The Robin Hood found by Joseph Hunter and linked with King Edward II's court appears to have left the royal service in York.[92] He is another major candidate to be the real man. Though we do not know if any of the individuals were *the* Robin Hood one cannot fail to note how many have been found in early records in the Yorkshire area, which certainly adds to the Barnsdale-Kirklees-Sayles material from the poems. Thus, following Hunter, J. W. Walker found further Hoods, including one Robert married to Matilda at Wrengate in the Wakefield muster records for 1316 and 1317. He was amerced 3*d.* Another was named at Bitchhill (Bichill) in Wakefield in the 1350s.[93]

Walker argued that these references referred to the same man. He thought the first Robert was the one who failed to attend military service in 1316. Walker saw this Robert as a follower of Lancaster. He linked all this to the Edward II Robert at court. However, though this is possible it is rather tenuous conjecture than established fact. Walker's records may relate to two or probably even three different Robert Hoods. Holt saw Walker's construction as 'a tissue of errors' and this process of linking historical records without historical evidence as 'guesswork inspired by wishful thinking'.[94] Holt goes on to suggest that the reason the 1316-17 Hood does not appear thereafter is likely that he had died. Bellamy points out that there were five Robin Hoods in the Wakefield manor court records for the period of Edward II and early Edward III.[95] Two of these came from Sowerby, one from Newton, one from Wakefield and one not located. It was presumably the Wakefield Robin Hood who was behind the Hunter, Walker and Harris arguments.[96]

The Feet of Fines from York mentions several names of interest for Robin Hood studies, including Gisburn, Lee and Plompton, but perhaps the most exciting is the record of a Thomas, son of 'Robert Hode of Houeden', under 1320-21. He held four and a half acres of land there. The place mentioned is probably Howden. There are several Howdens in Yorkshire including the Howden Moor region west of Sheffield. This Thomas Hood was the first party in two disputes over lands and rents in Howden.[97]

Probably the favourite candidate to be the real Robin Hood, the one who was a valet in the chamber of Edward II, does not have a location — unless one makes the jump of associating him with one of the Robin Hoods in other records. The valet appears in the wardrobe accounts for 1323 and 1324, when he was paid off as 'no longer able to work', but the fact is he could have come from anywhere. There just is no evidence to place him.[98] Several historians seem satisfied that this is the same man (or one of them) found in the Wakefield records and therefore place Robin in the reign of Edward II and in Wakefield manor — but we find this connection too great an assumption without further evidence. We agree with Holt that the main conclusion from all this is *not* that we should link various Hood references together to make a life for one Robin, but we should simply note that in and around Wakefield were several Hood families with a number of individuals given the name Robert.

It therefore remains likely that Robin's origins could well belong in the Yorkshire setting even if we are unable to identify one individual as the hero figure.[99] Hood families lived in this region near Barnsdale throughout the thirteenth and fourteenth centuries.

Some historians have tried to get to Robin by finding real persons for other characters in the poems. There are, for example, several John Littles and Will Scarlets (or similar surnames).[100] If we cannot identify the real Robin Hood then there seems little profit to be got from examining possible candidates for other associated characters. The major problem, as always, is to know which period to search.

Robin Hood Place-Names and Monuments

The evidence for any location for a real Robin Hood is not strong in its own right. In general, we are sent back to the early poems. As we have seen, they mostly suggest a northern and especially a Yorkshire and Nottinghamshire background. The areas where the songs and plays of Robin Hood originated or were popular might give some clue. The areas that most stand out in this respect are first the border country between England and Scotland and second the English West Country.

Another kind of evidence that might give a clue is that of place-names connected to Robin Hood — Robin Hood's Bay and so on. They might be in areas actually connected with Robin. On the other hand, the names are found in so many areas: from Berkshire to Cumberland, from Bournemouth to London — virtually everywhere in England. Lord Raglan's slant is that Robin 'owns hills, rocks, caves, and wells in Lancashire, Derbyshire, Shropshire, Gloucestershire and Somerset'.[101] This spread of names most probably reflects Robin's later popularity for plays and minstrels rather than any link with an outlaw who lived in a given region. There are many place-names that suggest Robin Hood links and some of them are referred to in the medieval period. We cannot really know if Robin Hood place-names are in honour of a real person or a celebration of the famous poems. In some cases, place-names seem to have been altered because an association, real or imagined, was seen with Robin Hood. The places named in the poems are significant and no one can ignore Barnsdale or Sherwood, for example. Maddicott thought the author of the *Gest* was 'almost certainly a Yorkshireman' — but this may throw light upon the places in a different way.[102] They may be names familiar to the writer rather than the real origins of Robin Hood. Unless we know more about a real Robin this will always be a possibility.

It is worthwhile giving some time to looking at the earliest recorded place-names. Of course, it may be that some names were only recorded well after their date of origin but it seems a reasonable way to limit our effort. The early recorded names will at least give some indications about areas that either saw Robin as a significant figure for their locality or believed that he had at one time lived in or visited the place concerned.

The Yorkshire names seem to lead the way and we have several times referred to Barnsdale, the Sayles and the other Yorkshire names in the early poems. Knight has suggested that Barnsdale might be the forest in Rutland near Stamford rather than the Yorkshire site, but he has not won much support.[103] Barnsdale in Yorkshire is in the West Riding north of Doncaster. John Leland, who died in 1552, called it a 'famose forest' in his *Itinerary*, though few others have considered it ever to have been a forest. Wentbridge and the Sayles, mentioned in the early poems, are places that exist near Barnsdale. Hunter first identified the actual site of the Sayles from the *Gest*. It had been a small tenancy of one tenth of a knight's fee in the manor of Pontefract.[104] The road passing by Barnsdale was the old Roman road, which in the later Middle Ages was known as Watling Street.

The earliest known Hood name in Yorkshire, and indeed many of the others, may or may not have anything to do with our Robin Hood. The earliest is a place called La Hode in 1264, which John de Eyvill was given the right to crenellate.[105] One of the towers in York's city walls was called Robin Hood Tower in 1622 though it was known as Bawing Tower in 1370 and Frost Tower in 1485.[106] Richmond Castle in Yorkshire also has a Robin Hood's Tower, so named in the fifteenth century. There is a village in the North Riding of Yorkshire called Robin Hood, which is on the old Great North Road, and another village with the same name near Leeds — this type of name is interesting because probably ancient.

Robin Hood's Bay near Whitby was so called in at least the first half of the sixteenth century. There is a reference to this particular place as early as the first half of the fourteenth century when it was named as 'Robin Oeds Bay' in a letter, though whether we can take that as being Robin Hood must be uncertain. The letter giving this name was from Louis I count of Flanders and most probably written in the 1320s under Edward II.[107] It remains probably the earliest Robin Hood place-name and opens several lines of possible interest. However, one must say that a bay seems an unlikely place to be named after the original outlaw hero — only late works relate any of his exploits to the sea. It therefore seems probable that the 'Oeds' in the early name had no connection with the outlaw and that the name was later changed after the outlaw had become a literary hero.

There are, not surprisingly, many Robin Hood names in Nottingham and Nottinghamshire but only a handful are recorded early. One of the most interesting, Robin Hood's Close (Robynhode Closse), is in the town. It was recorded in the city's chamberlain's accounts in 1485, 1486 and 1500.[108] Another early record exists for Robin Hood's Well near Nottingham, first mentioned in 1500 and probably the same place referred to in 1548 as Robyn Wood's Well. The well was also referred to in the sixteenth century as St Anne's Well. There can be no doubt that many Robin Hood names began with a different name. Wood was often exchanged for Hood in place-names, for example, a place called Robin Wood could be changed to become a Robin Hood name.

Robin Hood place-names beyond Yorkshire and Nottingham are not often recorded before the seventeenth century. Some may be of interest, including Robin Hood in Lancashire near Wigan which is the name of a village. A Robin Hood's

Cross is nearby. There is a Plumpton Park also in Lancashire. Some historians, from Hunter on, have been impressed by the argument that of the three Edwards, Edward II is the only one to have definitely made a tour through Lancashire. This was in 1323 when the crown was dealing with corruption by officials.[109] The evidence seems to suggest that the number of Robin Hood names has multiplied through time, especially from the seventeenth century onwards. The later names are not likely to have much importance concerning the origin of the story but, of course, sometimes the surviving names may have been used before we have evidence of them.

Other related names are worth a mention. The association between Robin and the name Loxley dates back to the Tudor period. There are, in fact, two candidates for the possible origin, if it came from a place-name. These are Loxley in Warwickshire not far from Stratford-upon-Avon, but more likely is the Loxley in Yorkshire just west of Sheffield. Here are also Loxley Chase and Loxley Common.

Another group of sites that provide evidence in some form is that claiming to possess, or once to have possessed, monuments to Robin and his men. Mostly here we are dealing with burial sites. One interesting use of the name was for a ship in 1438 at Aberdeen.[110] This is clearly a new naming with the use of a well-known hero and may be the method behind some or even all of the place-names.

Yorkshire, with the Barnsdale connection, is, of course, a leading area for sites with Robin Hood names. A charter in the Monk Bretton Cartulary for 1422 records a 'stone of Robert Hode'.[111] This is an early date to record such a place-name. Monk Bretton is in Barnsley and its priory was dedicated to St Mary Magdalene.[112] Some historians have hastened to associate these names directly with our hero though the evidence, as always, is interesting but not conclusive. The location is Shelbrook in the West Riding. Some have thought this may be the same site as that for a Robin Hood's Well. Holt has argued persuasively that the stone and the well must have been on different sites, on different sides of the Great North Road, though not far apart.[113] Whether there was originally both a stone and a well or whether the stone and well refer to a single monument matters little.

There is a Robin Hood's Well in the middle of Barnsdale. Given the obscurity of Barnsdale and even more of the Sayles, it is significant that nearby stood a Robin Hood's Well. In the eighteenth century the site was covered by a dome. The obscurity of the place and the early date of the recorded well and stone are suggestive of this site as the best claimant to a connection with any real Robin Hood.

The association between Robin Hood and Kirklees in the poems is, of course, as the site of Robin's betrayal and death. The treacherous prioress in the poems is said to be a close relative of Robin's. Kirklees is believed to be the site between Huddersfield and Barnsley though Scotland has also been suggested for the place.[114] The Yorkshire site has been known since as Kirklees Estate. There are still to be found two now separate tracks each called Kirklees Way. In the Middle

Ages, this was the site of a Cistercian nunnery. The gatehouse of the nunnery still survives. In fourteenth-century records there are references to priory holdings in the manor of Wakefield.[115]

It was claimed in the sixteenth century that here was the site of Robin's burial though there remains confusion over the authenticity of stones claimed to have been part of it. Richard Grafton in his *Chronicle at Large* in 1569 described Robin's death at the nunnery, which he called 'Bircklies'. We must take this as being Kirklees and Grafton specifically says that the nunnery was 'in Yorkshire'. He also described in detail the grave, which is depicted in a seventeenth-century drawing. Grafton says that at either end of the tomb there was a cross of stone 'which is to be seene there at this present'. He says that on the gravestone were the names of 'Robert Hood, William of Goldesborough, and others'.[116] We earlier commented on these names. There clearly was a grave and at some time the Hude name was inscribed upon it but we retain serious doubts as to whether it was originally Robin's monument.

It seems to be a second tomb, which is described by later writers. Gough, in the eighteenth century, mentions a stone with a cross 'fleuree', 'broken and much defaced', and apparently not the same as the Goldesborough one. This was the one to be excavated in the eighteenth century by Sir Samuel Armitage, the owner of Kirklees Park, and it is no great surprise that the dig produced nothing of interest.[117] There seemed to be no burial at all beneath the stone.

There are also place-names relating to other members of the outlaw band. Wakefield Museum possessed a bow said to come from Hathersage Church. There it was claimed was the tomb of Little John and a yew bow with its ends broken, said to be 7 feet long and having belonged to John. This legend seems to originate at least from the seventeenth century. Near Hathersage is also a Little John's Well and several Robin Hood place-names including an inn, a cave, a stoop and a croft as well as a Robin Hood Cross. This latter was a medieval wayside cross whose base still survives.[118] It was mentioned as 'Robin Crosse' in 1316 and in the seventeenth century as 'The Robin Crosse'. Also near Hathersage is Robin Hood's Stoop, which, like the cross, might have originated as a boundary mark in the Middle Ages. Hathersage is in Derbyshire but not far from Sheffield and Yorkshire.

Historians' Views on this Evidence

So what have modern historians made of this naming evidence — the place-names and the monument sites? Dobson and Taylor seemed convinced concerning Robin Hood that 'in the later middle ages he was more often associated with Barnsdale than Sherwood'.[119] Holt has suggested Yorkshire and Sherwood were linked with separate poetic creations that in time became joined and also favoured Yorkshire as the original location. Others have been confused by the different locations in the literary works. Helen Phillips has pointed out that in different works we are given different locations, which she thinks cannot all be correct. She examined the likely location for Robin Hood's forest and notes that some say Sherwood, some Barnsdale and others Inglewood. Her conclusion is that we cannot trust the place-names on any definite historical original location for Robin.[120] We would not press the point, but it has been also noted of real outlaws and criminals on the run in the middle ages that they did actually did tend to move around a good deal.[121]

Other historians have been persuaded that none of the locations is real and that Robin Hood is an entirely fictional creation. Pollard, for example, sees Robin as 'essentially a fictional creation' and the location, whether Sherwood or not, 'only an imagined forest'.[122] He points out that the medieval forest was not what we think of as a forest – it was not always woodland. He adds that 'forest' was a legal concept rather than the description of a natural scene and included arable areas and settlements. Nevertheless, he sees the North as the setting for such tales as Robin Hood because it was conceived as the wild region, with Nottingham as 'the gateway' to the North.[123] Some have argued that the origin of the Robin Hood stories was, in fact, from stories developed for the entertainment of London companies and that the northern background was chosen as suitable rather than as a factual and historical truth. We appreciate how open all these questions are but we persist in seeing Yorkshire, Nottingham and Sherwood as the probable real background for Robin Hood.

Conclusions

We need now to see if we can reach any conclusions over this evidence for a real location for Robin Hood. The spread of the evidence over all is broad and takes us to unexpected regions, such as the south, the west and Scotland. Why is this so? Obviously, if there was a real Robin Hood he can not have been active in all these regions. The answer is surely that the naming often, and perhaps virtually always, does not come from the presence there of Robin Hood. One major explanation is the popularity of the poems and perhaps even more of the plays about Robin. We agree with Holt that the probable explanation of the widespread use of Robin Hood place-names connects with the geographical spread of the popularity of the story.[124]

Nevertheless, the various pieces of evidence lead to inevitable conclusions. The first is that Yorkshire is one of the two most popular and common locations in the earliest works. The second is that Nottingham is the most popular and common town, indeed virtually the only town, for actual Robin Hood activity in the early evidence. But this does not place Robin securely in any single historical location.

The Yorkshire setting has some unresolved problems. Barnsdale in the early works seems to be treated as a forest but the Yorkshire Barnsdale was not a forest. There was a Barnsdale Forest but that was in Rutland — some 25 miles from Nottingham. Stephen Knight has pointed out the possible significance of this place-name and noted that the Great North Road also runs near to it and also nearby is a Robin Hood's Field and a Robin Hood's Cave.[125] He also suggested that the Paston servant may have gone off to this Barnsdale. Knight further pointed out that the Rutland Barnsdale was held by the earls of Huntingdon. However, if this was the Barnsdale of the poems then what about the Sayles – clearly established as being near the Yorkshire Barnsdale?

Some historians have thought Yorkshire was the original location and Nottingham and Sherwood only a later addition. They have come to the conclusion that there were two separate original threads to the Robin Hood literature: the Yorkshire element and a separate Nottingham one. There is broad support for the view of Holt that 'the nearer Robin get to Nottingham the less authentic he becomes'.[126] We cannot accept this conclusion. So far as we can see, there is nothing to choose between Yorkshire and Nottingham from the earliest evidence of all kinds. Unless we can identify the original real Robin Hood we cannot satisfactorily settle on a definite location for him. The balance between Yorkshire and Nottingham in the earliest poems is nearly even. In the present situation of the evidence it seems wisest to keep that balance and continue to look for Robin in both regions. We cannot yet be at all sure that Robin was not in both areas; Nottingham and Sherwood, after all, are not that far south of Barnsdale and Kirklees. As we have seen, the two sites are often brought together into the same poems. We know that actual outlaws usually moved from one region to another and Robin Hood may have done the same. Nevertheless, uncertainty remains about any true location for Robin Hood.

Real Robin Hoods and Robin Hood place-names are to be found in a variety of regions north, south, east and west. There may be special interest in certain virtually lone mentions of such places as say Inglewood or Rockingham forests or towns and villages from Wentbridge to Hathersage. The place-names across Britain often seem to come from the later popularity of Robin, especially in plays and games, rather than from his actual presence. An open mind is wise to keep even the secondary place-names in mind as possibilities. The place-names, like the literary locations, are not conclusive in placing Robin. They give clues and inspire possibilities but they all depend on finding Robin first.

Endnotes

1   Dobson & Taylor, p. 79.
2   Dobson & Taylor, p. 111.
3   Rutherford-Moore, p. 149.
4   Maddicott, ''Birth', p. 293.
5   Dobson & Taylor, p. 111.
6   Bellamy, p. 17.
7   Dobson & Taylor, p. 111.
8   Midmer, p. 184
9   Ohlgren, *Poems*, p. 123.

[10] Dobson & Taylor, p. 90.

[11] Dobson & Taylor, p. 112 and n. 1; other versions of the poem have 'Donkester'.

[12] Harris, pp. 73-4.

[13] Dobson & Taylor, p. 80.

[14] Dobson & Taylor, p. 80.

[15] Dobson & Taylor, p. 94.

[16] Dobson & Taylor, p. 22.

[17] Roper, *Feet of Fines,* p. 24.

[18] Bellamy, pp. 84-109

[19] Bellamy, p. 103.

[20] Ohlgren, *Poems,* p. 169.

[21] Bellamy, p. 105.

[22] Dobson & Taylor, pp. 142,144.

[23] Dobson & Taylor, p. 142.

[24] Dobson & Taylor, p. 144.

[25] Roper, *Feet of Fines,* p. 22.

[26] Dobson & Taylor, p. 126.

[27] Dobson & Taylor, pp. 134-39, A and B versions.

[28] Dobson & Taylor, pp. 81,98.

[29] Dobson & Taylor, pp. 80,94.

[30] Dobson & Taylor, p. 144.

[31] Dobson & Taylor, p. 145.

[32] Dobson & Taylor, p. 127.

[33] Dobson & Taylor, pp. 115-16.

[34] Dobson & Taylor, p. 116.

[35] Dobson & Taylor, p. 121.

[36] Dobson & Taylor, p. 88 & n.2.

[37] Bellamy, p. 77.

[38] Bellamy, p. 80.

[39] Bellamy, p. 78.

[40] Bellamy, p. 80.

[41] Ohlgren, *Poems,* p. 170.

[42] Holt, p. 105

[43] Dobson & Taylor, p. 82.

[44] Dobson & Taylor, p. 88.

[45] Dobson & Taylor, p. 105.

[46] Dobson & Taylor, p. 105 and n. 1.

[47] Roper, *Feet of Fines,* p. 48.

[48] Roper, *Feet of Fines,* pp. 93, 107.

[49] Dobson, 'Robin Hood: the Genesis of a Popular Hero', pp. 61-77 in Hahn, p. 65.

[50] Lister M. Matheson, 'The Dialects and Language of Selected Robin Hood Poems', pp. 189-210, in Ohlgren, *Poems.*

[51] A.A. MacDonald, 'Early Modern Scottish Literature and the Parameters of Culture', pp. 77-100 in Mapstone and Wood, on p. 91 makes the point of Latin and educated attitudes to the vernacular.

[52] Knight, 'Which way to the Forest? Directions in Robin Hood Studies', pp. 111-28 in Hahn, p. 123.

[53] Knight, *Complete,* p. 100.

[54] Wiles, p. 3.

[55] Knight, *Complete,* p. 103

[56] *Paston Letters,* ed. Davis, no. 275, p. 460-61.

[57] Bellamy, p. 3.

[58] Holt, p. 42.

[59] Knight, *Mythic,* p. 86; Holt, p. 42.

[60] Keen, p. 179.

[61] Keen, p. 180.

[62] Holt, from Ritson, p. 42. 'Obiit 24 kal dekembris 1247'

[63] Keen, p. 182

[64] Bellamy, p. 3.

[65] Knight, *Complete,* p. 40.

[66] Holt, p. 41.

[67] Holt, p. 41.

[68] Knight, *Complete,* p. 17.

[69] Knight, *Complete,* p. 21.

[70] Keen, p. 181.

[71] Knight, *Complete,* p. 17; BL Sloane MS, 780.

[72] Harris, p. 32.

[73] R.B. Dobson, 'Robin Hood: the Genesis of a Popular Hero', pp. 61-77 in Hahn, p. 63.

[74] Gutch, pp. ii, 8.

[75] Knight, *Complete,* p. 37.

[76] Bower ed. Watt, v, pp. 355, 357.

[77] E.g. Pollard, p. 3; Keen, p. 177.

[78] Luxford, the whole of this paragraph uses this article.

[79] Ohlgren, *Early Poems,* p. 17.

[80] Wyntoun, *Cronykil,* p. 263.

[81] See for example comments by Juliette Wood, 'Folkloric Patterns in Scottish Chronicles', pp. 116-35, in Mapstone and Wood, e.g. p. 119.

[82] Dobson & Taylor, p. 3.

[83] Dobson & Taylor, p. 4.

[84] Dobson & Taylor, p. 18; Maddicott, 'Birth', p. 277.

[85] Knight, *Mythic,* p. 8.

[86] R.B. Dobson, 'Genesis', in Hahn, p. 74.

[87] Bellamy, p. 31.

[88] Holt, p.52; Crook, *Sheriff,* p. 59.

[89] Knight, *Complete,* p. 28.

90   Knight, *Complete,* p. 24.
91   PR, 20th Year of Henry III, p. 98.
92   Knight, *Complete,* p. 23.
93   Bellamy, p. 17; Harris, p. 66.
94   Holt, pp. 48-9.
95   Bellamy, p. 114.
96   Bellamy, p. 115.
97   Roper, *Feet of Fines,* pp. 420, 524.
98   Harris, p. 64: 'qil ne poait plus travailler'.
99   Holt, pp. 50-1.
100 See, e.g., Bellamy, p. 123.
101 Lord Raglan, 'Robin Hood', pp. 385-91 in Knight, *Anthology,* p. 387.
102 Maddicott, p. 282.
103 Knight, *Complete,* p. 29; Knight, *Mythic,* p. 5.
104 Bellamy, p. 8.
105 Patent Rolls, Henry III, 342.
106 Dobson & Taylor, p. 305.
107 Ohlgren, *Poems,* p. 123 and n. 60. The research was done by David Crook.
108 Dobson & Taylor, p. 301.
109 Bellamy, p. 9.
110 Knight, *Complete,* p. 27.
111 Dobson & Taylor, p. 23, state that the correct date is 1422 though 1322
     appeared on the document. Bellamy, p. 119.
112 Bellamy, p. 119.
113 Holt, p. 107.
114 Lord Raglan in Knight, *Anthology,* p. 387.
115 Bellamy, p. 119.
116 Knight, *Complete,* p. 40.
117 Keen, p. 181.
118 Dobson & Taylor, p. 296.
119 Dobson & Taylor, p.18.
120 Helen Phillips, 'Forest, Town, and Road: the Significance of Places and Names
     in Some Robin Hood Texts', pp. 197-214 in Hahn, pp. 202,205
121 Bellamy, *Crime.*
122 Pollard, pp. 15,58.
123 Pollard, p. 67.
124 Holt, p. 106.
125 Knight, *Complete,* p. 29.
126 Holt, pp. 74-5

8

Real Robin Hoods

Introduction

Some people believe Robin Hood never existed, that he was a fictional creation possibly based on some kind of mythical spirit. As J. C. Holt has written, 'it is easy to invent Robin Hoods'.[1] Holt thought him 'a legend rather than a man'.[2] Stephen Knight concluded that 'it seems highly improbable, or at least unprovable, that a Mr. R. Hood ever existed'.[3]

Probably rather more historians and commentators believe that he did exist as a real outlaw. Dobson and Taylor point out that the outlaw heroes of literature tend to be based on real people and would expect Robin Hood to follow the pattern. They do, however, agree that research has simply unearthed 'a bewildering variety' of Robin Hoods without establishing a clear original for the hero.[4] If Robin did exist he has never been identified from historical records, or at least he has been 'identified' several times certainly by several historians, but not in a manner that satisfies most other historians. Usually few beside the historian making the definite identification are convinced that his candidate is the correct one. The comment of Sir Sidney Lee that 'the arguments in favour of Robin Hood's historical existence, although very voluminous, will not bear scholarly examination', still largely holds good.[5]

The problem for any searcher after a real Robin Hood is twofold. First there is no clear historical record in any contemporary or near contemporary annal or chronicle that tells us about Robin Hood in the way that we find accounts of other medieval outlaws of literature, such as Hereward the Wake, Fulk fitz Warren or Eustace the Monk. Each of those figures became the hero of poems but they also figured in straightforward historical records so that we know they existed even if we do not believe all the details of the poetic versions of their lives.

The second problem is that Hood was quite a common surname and too many Hoods have been found, even some called Robert or Robin, as well as others with Robinhood as a surname, who we shall consider later.[6] The surname Hood might reflect (in origin) the employment of the person as one who made hoods (a hooder), or a nickname for one who wore a hood (compare the modern 'hoodie'). One must also note the variety in spelling that could be Hood — from Hude, Hode, Hod, Hwd or Hoode. There are many Hoods but none of them quite satisfies the historian and none can be accepted as *the* Robin Hood with any degree of certainty.

In this chapter we are not able to identify the original Robin Hood but we shall look at scholars' attempts to do so through chronicles and historical records of various kinds. Only in this way can we see the difficulty in identification and have some idea of how and where to search, even if we never find the answer.

Robin Hood in Chronicles and Prose Accounts

Since there is no agreement over when Robin Hood lived it is difficult to know in which period to search for relevant historical records. We shall now look at works other than the ballads and poems that mention Robin Hood. Some are attempts at an historical account; some are attempts at a biography. Others offer some sort of material about Robin's life and activities. They are all at least pretending to be 'historical' though the historical value is often difficult to assess.

We begin with the handful of early chronicles by historians rather than literary poetic works that actually mention Robin Hood. Even these chronicles do not provide secure evidence. For a start they are all too late in time. They present their material as if it is historical fact but it is possible that their information came from poems or was invented. Nor do even these few historians agree in their information, even on the period for Robin Hood.

Three major chroniclers and one annotator provide the earliest information of this kind on Robin Hood. We have used them in the previous chapter for their information on location but we now need to use their information in a broader way. Oddly, the three historians were all Scottish — Andrew Wyntoun, Walter Bower and John Maior (otherwise Major). The reason for them all being Scottish has never been satisfactorily explained though some historians have suggested they were well placed to know border ballads and that that was the source of their information. They certainly influenced later serious historians, such as Richard Grafton and John Stowe, as well as several playwrights in the Tudor and Stuart period, such as Anthony Munday and Ben Jonson.

Andrew Wyntoun

The earliest chronicle reference to Robin Hood as an historical figure appears in the work of Andrew Wyntoun. He was an Augustinian canon of St Andrew's priory. He became prior of the daughter house of St Sers Inch at Loch Leven. He wrote a verse chronicle in couplets for his patron, Sir John of Wemyss, in *c.* 1420.[7] By this time, he was an old man and therefore had lived not long after the period in which he places Robin.[8]

Wyntoun's *Orygynale Cronykil* places Robin in Inglewood and Barnsdale in the thirteenth century under the date 1283. This is the earliest attempt at an historical account of Robin and is a date that no one else has used or even really examined.

The fact that 1283 does not tie up with any obvious historical event (such as the efforts of the Montfort rebels in 1266) has made it difficult for commentators to tie it in to known facts. On the other hand, it perhaps gives greater credibility to a unique and early dating. Unfortunately, Wyntoun provides no further clue as to what evidence he based the date on. Wyntoun's comment on Robin Hood is brief. It is in rather crude verse that runs as follows:

> Lytill Jhon and Robyne Hude
> Wayte-men ware commendyd gud.
> In Yngil-wode and Barnysdale
> Thai oysyd all this tyme thare trawale.[9]
> [Little John and Robin Hood were outlaws who were thought good men; in Inglewood and Barnsdale they continued all this time their efforts.]

There is a second interesting passage in Wyntoun. Given the previous quotation, one must think that the second Hood could not have been seen by Wyntoun himself as the famous outlaw. Nevertheless, it is a passage worth examining. Under 1342 Wyntoun wrote:

> Throwch covyne off ane, that to name
> Hwde wes hatyne the Edname,
> Come to Roxburch, quen it wes myrk,
> And with his menyhé thare gert he wyrk
> Wyth helpe off Hwde, that his men all,
> Wyth leddris clame wp oure the wall.
> Downe oure the wall syne ar thai gane,
> And with fors has the Castelle tane.
> Of all the folk, war tham agayne,
> Sum hawe thay tane, sum hawe thai slayne.
> Thai tuk the gud all that thai fand.
> Seltown wes that tyme in Ingland,
> Tharfore ethchapyd he the dede.

To summarise the meaning of this passage from Wyntoun: this Hood (not given a Christian name) came from Ednam; in 1342, Hood came to Roxburgh at dusk with his mesnie; with the help of Hood and his men the attackers climbed the wall on ladders and took the castle; they captured some of the garrison and killed others; they took the possessions they found; because of the problems in England at the time Hood got away with the act. Although we must repeat the reminder that Wyntoun himself had identified Robin Hood the outlaw in 1283, this 1342 Hood must remain a candidate for the outlaw — though most have ignored him.

Walter Bower

Walter Bower is the second in time of our three early historians. He compiled
a work of history in the 1440s. The manuscript of this is now in the library of
Corpus Christi College, Cambridge.[10] It was not printed until the mid-eighteenth
century. It was largely based on the earlier work of John de Fordun to which
Bower made some changes and additions, including the material on Robin Hood.
Bower lived from 1385 to 1449.[11] He was born at Haddington in East Lothian.
He became an Augustinian canon at St Andrews and attended the new university
there. The earlier Robin Hood chronicler, Wyntoun, had also been at St Andrews
and Bower, therefore probably knew of his work. Bower gained degrees in canon
law and theology and then became abbot of the new Augustinian monastery at
Inchcolm on the northern shore of the Firth of Forth. He spent the rest of his life
there until his death. He had experience of the political world since he attended
royal councils and parliaments. He wrote his additions to Fordun towards the
end of his life.

The chronicle by John de Fordun had been written in the 1360s. Fordun wrote
a history of the Scots from their origins up to 1153. After that he added a few
random passages. Much of it Bower copied but he also altered parts, inserted
some passages and then added new material taking the account up to 1437. As
Bower's recent editor has pointed out: 'It is not always easy to distinguish in his
account historical fact from comment and literary embellishment'.[12]

Bower's attitude was very pro-Scottish and anti-English as indicated by his
choice of title for the work as 'Scotichronicon'. He claimed 'He is not a Scot
who is not pleased with this book'.[13] In an interesting switch of the name usually
given to Edward I, William Wallace becomes 'the hammer of the English'.[14] Thus
Wallace is seen as 'the noble William' while Edward I is 'that tyrant'.[15] Bower was
always ready to praise the Scots and deride the English. He heartily criticised the
Englishman John de Strivelyn, who was made sheriff of Perth. Thus one begins to
see the attraction of Robin Hood to Bower — the opponent of the English king
who invaded Scotland and the enemy of an English sheriff.

Earlier historians once thought that the Robin Hood material in the chronicle
came from Fordun but it is now accepted as one of Bower's additions. The length
of his work is clear from the fact that the best modern edition, published from
1989 to 1993, is in nine volumes.[16] Walter Bower placed Robin Hood in the
thirteenth century as one of the Disinherited, a follower of Simon de Montfort
opposed to King Henry III and his son Prince Edward, later Edward I. To Bower,
Robin was one of those followers of De Montfort who continued to oppose the
monarch even after their leader's death in 1265.

Had Roger Godberd been called Robert he would have been one of the best
historical fits for our man. Godberd was a follower of Simon de Montfort who
became an outlaw in Sherwood forest. The constable of Nottingham Castle,
Reynold de Grey, was offered no less than 100 marks to capture Godberd.
Nevertheless, whatever his sources, Bower clearly distinguished Godberd from

Robin Hood and placed the latter as an outlaw in the period after the Battle of Evesham of 1265.

Bower wrote (in Latin and here translated) of Simon de Montfort's supporters after their leader's death. Robin Hood to Bower is therefore one of the dissidents, 'a famous cut-throat' (*siccarius*).[17] Bower says 'at this time... Robert Hood with Little John' (*Robertus Hode cum Litiljohn*) were among the rebels. He continues with a story which strongly suggests a ballad source. In it, Robin is saying mass in the forest in a 'secluded woodland spot' when attacked by the sheriff's men. Robin refuses to break off his worship. Knight suggests Bower may have had play-games as a source, since he speaks of comedy and a foolish audience.[18] He places Robin in Yorkshire, in 'Barnesdale'. He repeats his placing of Robin under 1266, naming Roger Mortimer in the Welsh Marches and John d'Eyville in Ely along with Robin Hood 'an outlaw amongst the woodland briars and thorns'.[19] Interestingly, when Bower tells of Robin being 'once in Barnsdale' he is said to be 'avoiding the anger of the king and the threats of the prince'.[20] Like Wyntoun therefore, Bower mentions Robin in Barnsdale but does not confine him to that location. Given that this is in the 1260s during the reign of Henry III, it brings in Prince Edward (the later Edward I) who after Evesham was almost beginning his own rule on his father's behalf, and who could tie-in to Edward the 'comely king' of the poems.

As Knight points out, this version of the Robin Hood story is earlier than any known ballad.[21] Nevertheless, it seems likely that Bower was aware of ballads that we do not know. He tells us that the Robin Hood stories were known by the 'foolish common folk [who] eagerly celebrate the deeds of these men with gawping enthusiasm in comedies and tragedies, and take pleasure in hearing jesters and bards singing [of them] more than in other romances'.[22]

The material on Robin Hood by Bower is important but also very brief. He writes:

> At this time there arose from among the disinherited and outlaws (exheredatis et bannitis) and raised his head that most famous armed robber Robert Hood along with Little John and their accomplices. The foolish common folk eagerly celebrate the deeds of these men with gawping enthusiasm in comedies and tragedies, and their pleasure in hearing jesters and bards singing [of them] more than in other romances.

He continues, with what sounds very like ballad material as a source, that once when Robin was in Barnsdale he was 'hearing mass most devoutly as was his habit'.[23] This mass was in the forest and is interrupted by the viscount, presumably equivalent to the sheriff. Robin refuses to flee. The outlaws face their attackers and beat them, enriching themselves from the proceeds. Finally, Bower adds that 'Robin Hood was an outlaw amongst the woodland briars and thorns'.[24]

This last comment of Bower's is placed under 1266. He therefore sees Robin Hood as belonging to the period of Henry III and Simon de Montfort. Bower writes of Robin suffering the anger of the king and prince, clearly Henry III and the Lord Edward. After the Robin Hood episode Bower writes of Edward 'the king's son' going to Alnwick to meet the King of Scots at Roxburgh. Bower's placing of Robin in period is, therefore, quite clear and straightforward. The question is whether or not we should accept it. The mass story sounds suspiciously as if it derives from a ballad, but where did the De Montfort period idea come from?

Bower's comment on foolish common folk is reminiscent of Langland's *Piers Plowman* and may follow from reading that work. The passage itself makes it clear that Bower knew of plays, tragedies and comedies about Robin Hood, and also of the poems from jesters and bards. Bower was not a straightforward chronicler. He borrowed from and indeed simply copied a number of earlier writers, not always acknowledging his source. We know that he claimed only to be following John de Fordun but he often used other sources, such as Vincent de Beauvais on French history. Like many medieval 'historians', Bower was as interested in moral teaching as in history. He was often prepared to use dubious historical material in order to make a moral point and the Robin Hood material could be seen in this way. Nevertheless, unlike some of his other tales, Bower does seem to believe that his version of Robin Hood is historical.

To summarise the Bower version: according to him Robin Hood and Little John were followers of Simon de Montfort, outlawed as a result of their attachment to that leader and to be numbered among the 'disinherited'.

JOHN MAIOR

John Maior (otherwise Mair or Major) gave an influential account of Robin as an historical figure. He is the third and last of the three major early commentators on Robin writing in the context of an historical account. There is a link between all the three early Scottish chroniclers who wrote of Robin: Andrew Wyntoun, Walter Bower and John Maior. Wyntoun and Bower were both Augustinian monks and were both at one time resident at St Andrews priory. John Maior went to school in Haddington, where Bower had been born.[25] Maior went on to Cambridge University and then to Paris where he taught theology. He returned to Glasgow University in 1500.

One of the oddities about our three Scottish historians who made early mention of Robin Hood is that each of them placed him in a different period. Not the least of Maior's influences was he chose to place the outlaw in 1196, in the age of the Plantagenets, the time of Richard the Lionheart and Prince John. Maior wrote that Robert Hood was active 'about the time of King Richard I, according to my estimate'.[26] The phrase 'according to my estimate' suggests that he is going on some simple information, possibly a supposed date of death for Robin. One would love to know what guided him to make this estimate. Antony Munday the playwright and Walter Scott the novelist followed Maior in this respect and thus shaped the modern version of the Robin Hood story. Maior, though, is the

latest of our three early historians and the furthest of them in time from any real
Robin Hood. His *History of Greater Britain* was not issued until 1521. Its role
in influencing the future legend is, therefore, enormous but its claim to historical
accuracy not strong.

According to Maior in the Angevin period there 'flourished those most famous
robbers Robert Hood an Englishman, and Little John, who lay in wait in the
woods, but spoiled of their goods only those that were wealthy'.[27] They robbed
abbots but in order to aid the poor. To Maior, Robin is the good outlaw who
took no life unless under attack, did not treat women unjustly and helped the
poor. Maior says that 'of all robbers he was the humanist and the chief'. He had
a band of 100 good archers. Maior notes that Robin's exploits were 'told in song
all over Britain'.[28]

THE ANNOTAROR

We noted in the previous chapter the discovery by Dr Luxford of a note about
Robin Hood added to an Eton College MS of a Polychronicon. The Polychronicon
dated from *c.* 1420 and the note was probably added by the 'principal annotator'
who Luxford suggests was a monk at the Somerset charterhouse of Witham. The
note was probably added soon after 1460. It was attached to the manuscript against
the period 1294-99 and thus places Robin Hood during the reign of Edward I.
The note consists of a mere twenty-three words in Latin, here translated.
'Around this time, according to popular opinion, a certain outlaw named Robyn
hode, with his accomplices, infested shirwode and other law-abiding areas of
England with continuous robberies.'[29]

Again, we have no clue as to why this monk thought Robin Hood belonged to
the time he has given. It does match closely to Wyntoun's 1283 and strengthens
the claim for this period. The writer is clearly no fan of Robin who he refers
to baldly as an outlaw who 'infested' Sherwood with his accomplices with his
'continuous robberies'. Perhaps the monk was put off by the anti-monastic tone
of the Robin Hood stories — if he knew them. This seems likely since he is writing
quite a time after Langland's comment against the rhymes of Robin Hood. It may
well also be, though, that many nearer to Robin's time simply saw him as a real
outlaw and robber whose activities deserved to be condemned rather than praised.
That smacks more of a belief in him as an historical figure than a fictional hero.

RICHARD GRAFTON

As Stephen Knight suggests, the mention of Robin Hood in Richard Grafton's
Chronicle at Large of 1569 seems to be a summary of the account in Maior, but
its repetition did help to further the accepted change of date for Robin's life to
the Plantagenet period.[30] Grafton was a printer and 'a fanciful chronicler'.[31] He
does, however, also add one rather mysterious comment. He says that he found 'in
an olde and auncient Pamphlet' that Robert Hood, though 'of a base stocke and

linage', had become an earl.[32] If this document existed it has not survived. Maurice
Keen has suggested it might have been the source both for the Sloane manuscript
and for Grafton.[33]

According to Grafton Robin was outlawed because he failed to answer suits
against him. He then collected a following of 'Roysters and Cutters'. They lived
in the forests and 'wilde Countries' and lived by robbing. He adds the story of
Robin's death at a priory, which he calls 'Birklies' (rather than Kirklees) — which
seems to be simply an error. He adds that Robin was buried there by the roadside
where he had carried out highway robbery. He mentions the grave that also had
on it the names of 'William Goldesborough and others'. He says at the end of
the tomb was erected a stone cross 'which is to be seene there at this present'.
One suspects the origin of this material as Maior's work and the *Gest,* but the
reference to the earldom remains interesting coming at about the same time as its
appearance in drama.

THE SLOANE MANUSCRIPT

Earlier than Dodsworth, the anonymous prose work contained in the Sloane
Manuscript is the earliest attempt to give an account of the whole life of Robin
Hood.[34] The account is known thus because it appears on three folios of British
Library Sloane Manuscript 780. It was discovered by the historian Joseph Ritson
who used it for his work on Robin Hood published in 1795. The item in the
Sloane Manuscript is written in Secretary Hand dated to *c.* 1600 and is thought
to be a copy of some lost work. The spellings are inaccurate and a second person
who seems to have known the original has filled in some omissions. Dobson and
Taylor thought the entry 'of little value as an independent historical authority'.
Most of it seems to be simply a prose version of the *Gest* with some reference to
a handful of other ballads. Yet the author places Robin in the Plantagenet period
of Richard the Lionheart though, again, he may have simply been following John
Maior's chronicle. Even so, the gathering number of people who place Robin in
this period has influenced all consequent views on the subject.

ROGER DODSWORTH

Let us go on a little further. Apart from the ballads and poems there developed
an interest in prose accounts of the great hero, gradually forming into the life
with which we are nowadays familiar in films. One attempt was made by Roger
Dodsworth, a seventeenth-century antiquarian.[35] Although this is a late and
derivative effort it is worth a brief examination since some of its statements are
not of the usual 'facts'. Dodsworth, for example, calls Robin 'Robert Locksley',
and says he was born in Bradfield parish in Hallamshire (southern Yorkshire).
He says that Robin was first outlawed for killing his stepfather when ploughing.
His mother gave him aid while he was hiding in the woods. He met Little John
at Clifton upon Calder. Dodsworth believed that John was buried in a very long

grave at Hathershead (Hathersage?) in Derbyshire and that John rather than Robin was earl of Huntingdon. We have no way of knowing whether the unique material was from some unknown source or simply invented. It remains an interesting, unconventional account.

MARTIN PARKER

In 1632, Martin Parker published a ballad about Robin Hood. He also sought to make a life of Robin as a real person. Parker's effort deserves consideration at least for its impact on later views about the outlaw. His account has been seen by historians as a 'biography'.[36] He called it *The True Tale of Robin Hood* and claimed to present 'truth purged from falsehood'.[37] He probably gained some of his material from Grafton and the playwright Munday.

Parker claimed that Robin died during the reign of Richard the Lionheart. He wrote of 'Robert Earle of Huntington vulgarly called Robin Hood who lived and died in AD 1198'.[38] We see in this period the crystallising of the tale of Robin belonging to the Plantagenet period. Parker repeats the familiar tale of Robin's death through the prioress but adds that Robin was also depressed by the recent betrayal of his men. Another interesting addition in Parker is the comment that some of Robin's men fled to Scotland shortly before their leader's death.

Parker wrote an epitaph that he claimed to have seen on Robin Hood's gravestone. It read:

> Robert Earle of Huntington
> Lies under this little stone.
> No archer was like him so good:
> His wildnesse named him Robbin Hood.
> Ful thirteene years, and something more,
> These northerne parts he vexed sore.
> Such out-lawes as he and his men
> May England never know agen.[39]

Knight suggests that Parker himself made this up, which seems quite likely.

The Kirklees Tomb

We have seen that several people writing of a real Robin Hood have mentioned the tomb at Kirklees, some from having seen it. We now need to investigate the significance of this item in more detail. In 1669, Nathaniel Johnston, a Yorkshire scholar and antiquary, made a drawing of this famous tomb in which he claimed Robin Hood was buried.[40] The tomb had earlier been written about by both Richard Grafton (1507-73) and William Camden (1551-1623). The physical tomb (as portrayed) remains something of a puzzle. Three names are carved on the stone. They seem to be 'robard hude', 'Willm Goldburgh' and 'Thoms' (Thomas). Why there should be the three names has never been explained. Knight has suggested that it was a different Robert Hood.[41] One cannot but wonder, given the odd positioning of the inscription, if the original name on it was simply William Goldburgh Thomas, which takes the major position along the top. The Robard is carved up one side with Hude at right angles to it. It is not impossible that someone added the Robin Hood part of the inscription at a later date. There is no other known connection between Robin Hood and anyone called either Goldburgh or Thomas. No one knows the answers to the puzzles. The inscription was described as illegible by the eighteenth century.[42]

As well as names there was supposed to be an epitaph on the tomb — if it was the same one. There is some confusion over the tomb epitaph and the one recorded in written works. It is by no means certain that either was genuine or that they were the same as each other. The drawing of the tomb does not include an epitaph. Descriptions of the tomb are not all compatible and may not all be of the same tomb. According to Knight the tomb drawn by Johnston was lost or broken up in the eighteenth century and then a replacement was carved with the 'epitaph' originating with Parker and generally seen as 'spurious' added to it.[43]

The site of the tomb was examined in the eighteenth century on the orders of Sir Samuel Armitage who owned Kirklees Park. The supposed area was excavated to a depth of 6 feet but nothing was found beneath the position of the stone.[44] One account suggests the epitaph stone was removed to a knight's house — but, if so, no one knows where and it has never resurfaced.[45]

William Stukeley's Pedigree For Robin Hood

An even more dubious 'historical' account is an attempt at giving Robin Hood an historical lineage. One of the best-known attempts of this kind was made by William Stukeley, an eighteenth-century antiquarian from Stamford who was both a doctor and a cleric. In 1746, in his *Palaeographia Britannica* he provided what he claimed was an authentic pedigree for Robin and his descent going back ten generations.[46] John Bellamy sees this as the genealogy of the family of Ghent or Gant from Lincolnshire into which Stukeley has simply inserted the presumably fictional Fitzooth branch. No one has found any further evidence for this added line.[47] Its importance lies in the fact that it was accepted at face value by Joseph Ritson, whose contribution to the Robin Hood story is well known, and that it includes the claim of a link between Robin Hood and the earldom of Huntingdon.

The added family line begins with Ralph Fitzooth, Norman lord of Kyme. Stukeley's Robin is Ralph Fitzooth's descendant Robert Fitzooth 'pretended earl of Huntingdon... commonly called Robin Hood' who died in 1247 or 1274.[48] He is the son of William Fitzooth and the line traces right back, through marriage, to the Anglo-Saxon Waltheof earl of Northumberland and Huntingdon. The tree gives a further connection to the line of the earls, again through marriage, to Simon de Senlis III. Few historians give much credence to this pedigree. It remains a mystery where the information came from, possibly simply invented by Stukeley, as Holt and Knight believe.[49] Knight ridicules Stukeley's genealogy as a 'ludicrous family tree'.[50] We cannot do otherwise than agree with Holt's conclusion that it is 'a spurious pedigree'.[51]

Robinhoods

As we have pointed out earlier, there were also people from the thirteenth century who were surnamed not Hood but Robinhood. Some historians believe this proves they were descended from Robin Hood, though this seems uncertain. It certainly does not prove at all that they had to be aware of a famous and real Robin Hood as some argue.

Since the surname first surfaced in modern times, further examples of Robinhood surnames continue to be found. An early and interesting example of the Robinhood name was found by David Crook in a record made in 1262, though it is not quite a Robin Hood find. The man who was declared a fugitive was William Robehod, son of Robert Le Fevre (the smith). William came from Enborne in Berkshire. He had fled from justice in 1261. He was suspected of 'many larcenies and of harbouring thieves'. A second reference in the following year to the same man names him William Robehod 'outlaw', though why this should be so is not known. He probably had a gang of at least five men, one of whom was called John de Len (suggesting Little John) and two of whom were female (neither called Marian). They failed to appear in response to a summons on five occasions and hence were all outlawed. It is another interesting find but without any confirmatory evidence that we have *the* Robin Hood. If anything the fact that he was descended from Robert the smith argues for a use of the name Robinhood for someone who was *not* descended from any Robin Hood let alone *the* Robin. After all, the outlaw is not Robert or Robin but William, and his father, so far as we know, was a law-abiding smith.

Holt, Crook and Dobson see the name Robinhood as a reference to *the* Robin Hood but why, in the case just quoted, it is the father rather than the son who is so-called is not clear.[52] Holt and Crook see the reference as significant because they believe it shows that *the* outlaw Robin Hood must have been well known by 1261.[53] Dobson argues that it probably suggests a twelfth- rather than thirteenth-century origin.[54]

Perhaps unexpectedly, not only is Hood a common surname but so too is Robinhood. No less than ten examples of that name have emerged from records for the period from 1265-1322.[55] Equally unexpectedly perhaps, none of these examples come from either Yorkshire or Nottinghamshire. Summerson, who unearthed several examples, has argued that they suggest criminals were taking on the alias of a known figure but, again, it is simply surmise.

Several Robinhood surnames have been found from before the time of *Piers Plowman* — the first clear reference to works about our hero in 1377.[56] The earliest Robinhood surname was that just discussed from 1261-62 related to the 'fugitive' William Robehod.[57] In 1272, there is a John Rabunhod at Fareham in Hampshire who killed John, son of Simon, in the inn at Charford, so another criminal. In 1286, there is a Gilbert Robehod in Suffolk. In 1294, we find one Robert Robehod at Winchester, who was born at Sutton Scotney and was charged with sheep stealing — another criminal. There is another William Robynhod from Tilbrook in Huntingdonshire under 1295. We also have a Gilbert Robynhod in a subsidy roll for Fletching in Sussex in 1296 and a Robert Robinhood at West Harting in the same county for 1322. We find a woman called Katherine Robynhod in London in 1325, the daughter of a common councillor called Robert Hod. The number of Robinhoods known before 1377 is increasing all the time.

Some historians are convinced that the use of Robinhood as a surname depended upon the legend, which must have been known by then.[58] This seems a possibility, that people with the name of Hood or Robert Hood were labelled after a well-known outlaw. If we accept that argument then Robin must either have lived before 1262 or the tale about him must have been known by then. Some historians have been convinced that this is the case. David Crook considers that the discovery of the Robinhood names 'has put an effective end to interpretations attempting to show that the legend of Robin Hood began only during the fourteenth century'.[59]

One could perhaps even accept another possibility: the real Robin Hood was actually someone surnamed Robinhood. In any case, the existence of a Robinhood surname does not prove that it must have derived from the famous outlaw. If he was of that early origin it is odd that there is absolutely no evidence of his fame until the later fourteenth century.

Hoods In Historical Records

The information about Robin Hood from chronicle, tomb and pedigree is all rather questionable as being either direct or accurate. There is another kind of record that we have not yet examined. This is the genuine historical record of various kinds that mentions a person called Robin Hood or a related name. There is no question that this is genuine historical material, the problem is to know if it concerns our original outlaw hero or some other person altogether. We might as well confess before we begin that no single item of this is truly acceptable as being definitely about our man. On the other hand it is quite possible that we have the real information without being able to confirm its importance.

As with the chronicle accounts, so with some the other historical material we have so far examined, there remains the problem that most if not all of them might derive from knowledge of the poems rather than of a real man. Thus we should read repeated popular sayings, such as 'Robin Hood in Barnsdale (or

Sherwood) stood' or 'he speaks of Robin Hood though he never shot his bow'. At least such remarks give us a date when the hero was known. Thus 'Robyn Hode in Barnesdale stode' first appeared in a 1429 lawsuit.[60] But we must now turn to records that do not have this problem.

There are historical records, often with little information beyond the name, of many men actually called Robert (or Robin) Hood as well as even more with the surname Hood. Let us repeat some examples dating from before the *Piers Plowman* mention of the rhymes in 1377. We take that date for the end since if there was a real Robin Hood the outlaw hero, he must have lived some time before that. We learn little more for certain from this evidence than the fact that there were several men called Robert Hood in the likely period of the outlaw's life but we must look at rather than ignore it.

One Robert Hood has been found who served the abbot of Cirencester and killed Ralph of Cirencester at the end of the reign of King John (between 1213 and 1216) — about the only reference that would fit with the modern placing of Robin in Plantagenet times.[61] There is little more to say about him but he is called Robin Hood and he has committed a crime. He therefore remains one possible candidate to be our man.

Several modern historians have preferred a thirteenth-century origin for Robin Hood, and they also have some real Robin Hoods to point out. The pipe roll for the twentieth year of the reign of Henry III (1241-42), notes 30s against 'Robertus Hod de Linton'.[62] Another Robin Hood, discovered by L.D.V. Owen, appeared in the pipe roll account of the sheriff of Yorkshire. The sum of 32s 6d was recorded in 1226 for the previous year as the value of the chattels of Robert Hod 'fugitivus' (fugitive).[63] He owed money to St Peter's in York. This is another rare case of a medieval Hood who was an actual outlaw and this one lived in Yorkshire. Apparently the same man was named in the pipe roll as 'Hobbehod' during the years 1228-30.[64] Presumably this was the same man who appears in ten successive pipe roll records from 1225 to 1234.[65] That would make his name Robert and hence Robin. Some historians (who favour a thirteenth-century Robin) have seen this individual as the 'best candidate' to be the original Robin Hood.[66] David Crook thinks him 'the only realistic candidate already in the field'.[67] Maurice Keen also considers the case of Hobbehod 'probably the strongest'.[68] James Holt points out that the same Robert is 'the only possible original of Robin Hood, so far discovered, who is known to have been an outlaw'.[69]

Some have tried to look around Robin Hood candidates in this period to see if other characters associated with him can be found. David Crook investigated the career of the sheriff of Yorkshire, Eustace of Lowdham, who was a contemporary of the Robert Hood of 1225. Eustace had also held the office of deputy sheriff for Nottinghamshire and Derbyshire and was later again to be temporary sheriff of those linked shires.[70] Crook equates this Robert with the outlaw Robert of Wetherby but I think has not been followed in this, though it is a possibility. In 1225, the king allowed money for the sheriff of Yorkshire to 'seek and take and behead Robert of Wetherby, outlaw and evildoer of our land'.[71] This Robert was probably subsequently captured. One is inclined to agree with Richard Gorski that the stories in the poems do not really tie up the connection between Robin and any sheriff. Gorski asks a pertinent question: why should the sheriff of Nottingham play cat and mouse games with the outlaw, and especially with an outlaw from Yorkshire?[72] Gorski, probably rightly, suggests that the point of the sheriff in the poem is that he represents authority and corruption.

The other major period that historians have searched for the real Robin is the fourteenth century before 1377. One of the mentions of a Robert Hood which has received much attention comes from the time of Edward II. This 'Robyn Hode' was the valet de chambre of that king in 1324, discovered by Joseph Hunter in the records. He was paid as a valet in 1324 and left the court in York 'because he can no longer work'.[73] Some historians, such as Hunter and Walker, have built from that record the possibility of this Hood being the original and have then suggested that the Wakefield Hood and the chamber Hood were one and the same — with no evidence to connect them apart from the name. Some have suggested further (without evidence) that this same man was in trouble as a follower of the earl of Lancaster and was outlawed after the earl's rebellion.[74] Thomas of Lancaster rebelled against Edward II. He was defeated at the battle of Boroughbridge in 1422 and executed as a result. The case for the valet being Robin Hood has been given some support by, for example, Holt, Harris and Bellamy, but there is, in fact, no further definite evidence of the valet's actual career.[75] The evidence that he was paid off rather suggests that the most likely cause was old age and does not encourage much belief in a subsequent outlaw career. Even so, he remains one of the strongest candidates so far found to be the real Robin — albeit that all candidates are unlikely or at best unproven.

There are many other Hoods, often called Robert or Robin, in the records. No less than five appear in the Wakefield records alone: one at the manor court, two at Sowerby and one referred to without further location in the pleas.[76] Another Robert Hood is named in the court roll for 1328 and again when he, or possibly his son, died in 1341-42.[77] One Hood was charged with trespass of vert and venison and imprisoned in 1354 — though this was in the Northamptonshire forest of Rockingham.[78] Not quite a Robin Hood reference but nevertheless one to note occurred in 1331 when an act of parliament referred to 'people called Roberdesmen' who committed crimes.[79] It could read as 'Robert's men'. It may have no connection to Robin Hood whatever but it is a possibility and may also help to explain the name's meaning to people then.

Robin Hoods

There are also quite a few Robin Hood names for the period after 1377. Clearly, they cannot be the outlaw hero, and examining these records will not find the real Robin directly but it may still give some clues to his identity. After the key date of *Piers Plowman,* 1377, we find people using the pseudonym 'Robin Hood', or that of one of his band such as Little John or Friar Tuck. Clearly these people did know the Robin Hood stories and saw themselves as in some ways like the outlaw hero or one of his men. In other examples a late medieval writer compared living individuals to Robin Hood or members of his band, and the same arguments apply.

As Holt has pointed out, there are several such aliases from Robin and his band used by later outlaws and criminals, or given to them. As he also notes, the very name Robin Hood the outlaw may in origin itself have been an alias.[80] A thirteenth-century medieval political song makes it clear that the name Robert could be interpreted as that of a robber: 'by Robert is very sufficiently indicated a robber'.[81] That is 'Robin Hood' may not necessarily have been the real name of the original outlaw. Until the real Robin is identified, if ever, we cannot know.

Let us briefly consider some of these men with other names but referred to by the more famous alias. In the south, leading a band in Surrey and Sussex in 1417, we find Robert Stafford who called himself Friar Tuck.[82] Of those whom others compared to Robin, one must include the notorious Piers Venable. Venables was a gentleman from Aston. He was recorded in Tutbury in Staffordshire in 1439 leading a gang of 'misdoers' whom he dressed in 'his clothing like it hadde be Robyn Hode and his meynee'.[83] A late medieval action in 1497 was taken in Star Chamber against one Roger Marchall of Wednesbury in Staffordshire who had called himself 'Robin Hood' and led a gang of some hundred men.[84] In the same period, a manuscript mentions 'men of Combur', presumably Cumberland, who knew of 'Reynall and Robyn Hood'. This seems to be Reynold Greenleaf and Robin Hood, and Cumberland is mentioned in connection with the outlaw on several occasions but this particular reference does not clearly maintain that Robin was actually connected with the area — though it hints as much. Unlike the Robinhood names, these late examples clearly do prove that Robin Hood and his men were well known by this later medieval period. It suggests that Robin Hood and his band were already the most famous of all English outlaws.

The Period To Search For Robin Hood

The information from chronicles and records, if anything, makes the search for a real Robin more difficult. We still do not know for certain even in which century to search or under which monarch. It all depends on which records we most trust or which interpretation we favour.

Which period is most likely? Is it the twelfth century (Richard the Lionheart and King John), the thirteenth century (Henry III and Simon de Montfort plus the early reign of Edward I) or the fourteenth century (the three Edwards — I, II and III)? Although the modern fictional view of Robin places him almost always in the Plantagenet period — late twelfth and early thirteenth century — virtually no modern historians favour this period.

THE THIRTEENTH CENTURY

Several historians followed the period put forward by the medieval chronicler Walter Bower and have placed Robin Hood in the thirteenth century. Many have also followed Bower in making Robin a follower of Simon de Montfort in the mid-thirteenth century. In 1847, J. M. Gutch rejected the popular Plantagenet background and accepted this thirteenth-century period. He was followed by the highly respected modern historian F.M. Powicke who thought 'it would be rash to maintain that the legend of Robin Hood originated in this period' but believed that it fitted well.[85] Gutch seems to have had little reason for his choice but made bold statements. He thought Robin was born in *c.* 1225, was the grandson of Stephen's rebel baron Geoffrey de Mandeville and died in 1247 at 'Kirkley's' nunnery. For some of his points he followed Ritson but the comment on De Mandeville has no known precursor or evidence.[86]

Lately, the discovery of medieval Robinhood surnames has persuaded several historians that Robin Hood, whether real or fictional, must originate in the thirteenth century. Holt and Crook are among these but it still depends on how much stress or what explanation you put upon the surname Robinhood. We know there were quite a few Robert Hoods so it is not so surprising that there were some, given the medieval manner of making surnames, that took the surname Robinhood to denote simply the parental name.[87] And why did William, son of Robert Smith (or Le Fevre), in 1262 call himself William Robehod? Crook thought it must be a joke but other possible thoughts arise.[88]

THE FOURTEENTH CENTURY

We remember that the *Gest* said the king was called Edward and that he was comely. Edward I was tall and imposing, nick-named 'Longshanks'. Rather more historians have thought Edward II might fit the description best, being good looking even if considered to be homosexual. One contemporary comment that compares to the 'comely king' in the *Gest* is Lawrence Minot's reference to Edward III in 1339 as 'oure cumly king'.[89] In other words, any of the three Edwards could fit the bill and be the monarch concerned. Some have even thought that the comely Edward might be Edward IV through an updating of the legend to his period by the poet! However, we consider it best to limit the most likely period to the age of the first three Edwards — that is, between 1272 with the accession of Edward I and 1377 when Edward III died.

Joseph Hunter was an early historian to face up to this question of period.[90] In general the reference to the 'comely king' and the name of Edward in the *Gest* has encouraged historians to favour a fourteenth-century background for any real Robin Hood. Hunter plumped for Edward II because it is known that he visited the north in 1323, and went to Lancashire, Yorkshire, Holderness and Nottingham. He was in Nottingham for two weeks in November. It was Hunter who pointed out the payments to one Robyn Hode as a valet or porter in the king's chamber.

This Robin Hood is mentioned in the chamber accounts between April and July of 1324. There are also several Robins, a 'Grete Hobbe' and a Simon Hood.[91]

Probably the majority opinion among historians has been in support of a fourteenth-century background. Keen, Ohlgren and Maddicott are among those modern historians who have plumped for the first half or middle of the fourteenth century.[92] Keen based an argument on the contents of the *Gest* with its language of bastard feudalism, retainers, liveries and fees — though this might show the period of the poem rather than the hero. Maddicott wrote that it was likely that Robin's 'origins lay not more than a generation or two before the first reference to him in 1377' and that there is 'strong evidence for an early 14th-century origin'.[93] Several historians have followed Hunter's idea and plumped for the reign of Edward II, including J. W. Walker and P. V. Harris.[94] Bellamy seems to suggest that there were two Robin Hoods, one in the thirteenth century and another in the fourteenth century who found fame in the *Gest*.[95] With Robin Hood one begins to feel that almost anything is possible, but this double suggestion seems to go beyond reasonable probability. The truth is that both Hood and Robinhood were common names in the later Middle Ages, too common on the brief historical records to allow certainty over any one mention that we have to date.

Conclusions

The main and obvious conclusion on the evidence for a real Robin Hood is that there is very little evidence. What we have are clues, indications, possibilities, but never (so far) anything conclusive. We have some pointers towards Robin's geographical location, probably northern and probably in the Yorkshire/ Nottingham region. We have some pointers to his period of existence, if there was one, most probably in either the thirteenth or the fourteenth century.

We know that Robin Hood or other forms which could be represented in that way, such as Robert Hude or Hobbehod, was a common enough name, especially in northern regions. Robin Hoods have appeared in historical records, at court, in shires and as fugitives or criminals — but no single one of them can be with certainty said to be *the* Robin Hood.

One important and safe conclusion is that there is a distinct lack of significant evidence. Why is there no evidence for the existence of such a famous figure in literature? There seem to be two main possible answers. The first is that he never did exist — he was an invention, a fictional figure from the very beginning. Yet in many minds, including mine, the second possibility of a real existence cannot be dismissed, even though not yet discovered. The second main reason for the lack of evidence is that he was not a man of great social standing. Had he really been an earl then he would surely have appeared in chronicles in his own day. Hereward the Wake, Fulk fitz Warren and Eustace the Monk were all either of high social standing or holders of important posts.

We conclude, therefore, that we are searching for a man of lesser social rank and no great political importance. Such men might often fail to appear in medieval records and those that did would rarely appear in any detailed manner. Dobson has argued that 'it is no longer profitable to search for a late thirteenth- or fourteenth-century forest outlaw whose real name was Robin Hood'.[96] Well, it may not prove profitable, but the hope of finding something remains as compelling as it ever was. I have spent the last several years searching in vain but I shall go on searching and so I am sure will others. There may well be an item of evidence that has so far avoided discovery. Let us at least go on searching. Dr Luxford's discovery of the comment by the Annotator has not solved the problem but it does show that new evidence is still always possible.

Endnotes

[1] J. C. Holt, 'The Origins and Audience of the Ballads of Robin Hood, pp. 236-57 in Hilton, p. 257, from *Past and Present,* 1960.

[2] Holt, p. 7.

[3] Knight, *Mythic,* p. 206

[4] Dobson & Taylor, p. 11,

[5] Knight, *Complete,* p. 13

[6] See Crook, 'Sheriff', p. 59 for a list of the Robinhood names.

[7] Knight, *Complete,* p. 32.

[8] Keen, p. 176

[9] Wyntoun, ed. Laing, ii, p. 263.

[10] Bower, *Selections,* pp. xii-xiii.

[11] Bower, *Selections,* introduction.

[12] D. E. R. Watt in Bower, *Selections,* p. 186.

[13] Bower, *Selections,* p. 290.

[14] Bower, *Selections,* p. 186.

[15] Bower, *Selections,* p. 195.

[16] Bower, ed. D. E. R. Watt.

[17] Knight, *Complete,* p. 34.

[18] Knight, *Complete,* p. 34.

[19] Bower, ed. Watt, v, pp. 355-7.

[20] Knight, *Complete,* p. 35.

[21] Knight, *Complete,* p. 35.

[22] Bower, ed. Watt, v, p.354.

[23] Bower, ed. Watt, v, p. 355.

[24] Bower, ed. Watt, v, p. 357.

[25] Knight, *Complete,* p. 37.

[26] Keen, p. 177.

[27] Major, *Historia*; translation Major ed. Constable.

[28] Knight, *Complete,* p. 37.

[29] Luxford article. The original note is given on p. 72: 'Circa h[ec] temp[or]a vulg[us] opinat[ur] que[n]da[m] exlegatu[m] dict[um] Robyn hode cu[m] suis co[m]plicib[us] assiduis latrocinijs apud shirwode & alibi regios fideles Anglie infestasse'.

[30] Knight, *Complete,* p. 39.

[31] Knight, *Complete,* p. 40.

[32] Knight, *Complete,* p. 40.

[33] Keen, p. 179, for example.

[34] Dobson & Taylor, App. II, pp. 286-87.

[35] Knight, *Complete,* p. 17; Holt, p. 44; Bodleian Library, Dodsworth Manuscript 160, f. 64b; Hunter, p.69.

[36] Knight, *Complete,* p. 17.

[37] Dobson & Taylor, pp. 187-90, Knight, *Complete,* p. 91.

[38] Knight, *Complete,* p. 91.

[39] Knight, *Mythic,* p. 85; the version in Keen, p. 179 from the papers of the antiquary Gale reads: 'Hear undernead dis laitl stean/Laiz Robert earl of Huntingtun/Near arcir ver az hie sa geud/An pipl kauld im robin heud/Sick utlawz az hi an iz men/Vil England nivr si agen.'

[40] Knight, *Mythic, p. 86; fig. 7.*

[41] Knight, *Mythic,* p. 84; p. 88, fig. 9.

[42] Keen, p. 180.

[43] Knight, *Mythic,* p. 86; Keen, P. 180 - `spurious'..

[44] Knight, *Mythic,* p. 88; Keen, p. 181.

[45] Keen, p. 181.

[46] Knight, *Mythic,* p. 87, fig. 8.

[47] Bellamy, p. 3.

[48] Knight, *Complete,* p. 18.

[49] Knight, *Mythic,* p. 85.

[50] Knight, *Mythic,* p. 86.

[51] Holt, p. 42.

[52] Knight, *Complete,* p. 25; Crook.

[53] Dobson in Hahn, pp. 73-4.

[54] Dobson in Hahn, p. 75.

[55] Dobson in Hahn, p. 74, from the research of Henry Summerson.

[56] Dobson & Taylor, p. 12.

[57] David Crook, 'Some Further Evidence Concerning the Dating of the Origins of the Legend of Robin Hood, pp. 257-61, in Knight, *Anthology,* pp. 258,261 (first in *HER,* 99, 1984).

[58] E.g. Crook in Knight, *Anthology,* p. 257.

[59] Crook, 'Sheriff', p. 59.

[60] Dobson & Taylor, p. 3.

[61] Knight, *Complete,* p. 27; Holt, p. 54; Knight, *Mythic,* p. 194.

[62] Pipe Roll 1241-42, p. 41. A William Hood appears on p. 98.

[63] Owen, p. xxix; Knight, *Complete,* p. 24; Hilton, p. 254; Bellamy, p. 136.

[64] Dobson & Taylor, p. 16.

[65] Dobson in Hahn, p. 75.

[66] E.g. Douglas Gray, 'The Robin Hood Poems', pp. 3-37, in Knight, *Anthology*, p. 31.

[67] Crook, 'Sheriff', p. 60.

[68] Keen, p. 190 and n.

[69] Holt, p. 54.

[70] Crook, 'Sheriff', pp. 60-66.

[71] Crook, 'Sheriff', p. 66.

[72] Gorski, p. 106

[73] Knight, *Complete*, p. 23; Bellamy, p. 117: 'Poar cas quil ne poait pluis travailler'.

[74] Keen, p. 184.

[75] Bellamy, p. 117.

[76] Bellamy, p. 114-5.

[77] Holt, p. 50.

[78] Dobson & Taylor, pp. 12-4 summarises the recorded Hoods.

[79] J. C. Holt in Hilton, p. 241.

[80] Holt, p. 58.

[81] Wright, *Political Songs,* p. 49: 'Competenter per Robert, robbur designatur'.

[82] Cal. Pat. Rolls, 1416-22, pp. 84,141; and 1429-36, p. 10.

[83] Holt, p. 150; Rotuli Parl., v, 16; Knight, *Complete*, p. 25.

[84] Holt, p. 148; Dobson & Taylor, p. 4.

[85] R. H. Hilton, 'The Origins of Robin Hood'. Pp. 197-210, in Knight, *Anthology*, p. 200l; Powicke, p. 529.

[86] Gutch, pp. iii, 8.

[87] Crook, p. 59.

[88] Crook, p. 59.

[89] Pollard, p. 200, noted first by Ohlgren.

[90] Joseph Hunter, 'Robin Hood', pp. 187-95, in Knight, *Anthology*.

[91] Hunter in Knight, pp. 193-4.

[92] Maddicott, p. 277; Keen, p. 140.

[93] Maddicott, pp. 278,280.

[94] J. C. Holt, 'The Origins and Audience of the Ballads of Robin Hood', pp. 211-32 in Knight, *Anthology*, p. 229; Bellamy, p. 42.

[95] Bellamy, p. 136-7.

[96] Dobson in Hahn, p. 77.

9

Who Was Robin Hood?

Robin the Myth

We must now admit that if there was a real Robin Hood we have not found him. We are not convinced by those who claim to have found him that their evidence is good enough. Given this, it is understandable that some commentators have preferred to conclude that there never was a real Robin Hood, that he was a myth, an invention. Some argue that he was formed from very ancient ideas about wood spirits or similar pagan concepts. Unless a real Robin is finally identified this view cannot be dismissed.

If there was a Real Robin, where do we Look?

I have failed to find the real Robin despite a personal search over several years and despite examining the searches of many others who have worked over many more years. Some have claimed to have found the real Robin Hood but we have not been convinced that any one of them is right. Among the various candidates it may be hides the real Robin but the historical evidence as it now stands is not sufficient to reach the conclusion that he has been found. It may be that one of the preferred candidates really is Robin, and we retain that possibility, but so far the evidence is not good enough to prove it. At the same time we should not dismiss the candidates without good cause until we have reason to identify conclusively the real Robin.

Normally in history books one avoids use of the first person singular but this investigation needs to admit one's own view. At this point I wish to make a personal statement. I am inclined to think that there was a real Robin Hood. I shall lay out the reasons for my feeling, which, of course, inspired me to search for him. I have not found him but I think it more likely that he existed than that he did not. The evidence is not conclusive but it is not non-existent either — so let us look at what we do know. The evidence that we have examined gives us several points on which to base a search, for example, in time and place.

Now

We may not have found Robin but we feel that we have some idea of what to look for. We have clues as to his character, his life, his area of activity and the period in which he lived. Having shaped our conclusions into some sort of picture we can then compare and contrast it with the common popular modern view of Robin.

Let us review our earlier summary of how Robin is seen by the modern world. The anticipated answers to our ten questions would be as follows.

1. In what period is it thought Robin Hood lived? The common answer would be under the Plantagenets during the reigns of Richard the Lionheart and John, 1189-1216.
2. Given the many films about Robin that take him on crusade, it may be generally thought that Robin went on the Third Crusade with King Richard.
3. Many popular works, even today, provide an anachronistic picture of the Plantagenet world. Robin is presented as a man of Saxon England fighting against the ruling and unpleasant Normans.
4. Robin's chief enemies are the Normans in general and their ruler King John (though not good King Richard) and the representative of local Norman power, the sheriff of Nottingham.
5. Robin is seen as favouring the church but it is not a major factor in modern accounts in which it is played down. The main clerical element is the association of Robin with the jolly but not terribly religious Friar Tuck.
6. The members of the outlaw band, in most views, would include Friar Tuck, Little John, Will Scarlet and Much the Miller's son.
7. Practically all modern versions have a love interest and Maid Marian is always Robin's choice.
8. Robin's activities are pretty well always seen to take place in Sherwood Forest and the town of Nottingham.
9. It is broadly accepted that Robin was a good fellow who was not a typical violent criminal but rather sought to right social wrongs by taking from the rich, not for his own benefit but to give to the poor.
10. Nearly always now Robin is presented as really a noble, the earl of Huntingdon, cheated out of his true inheritance but generally in the end recovering it.

And then

Let us then draw together our view after looking at the early evidence. Let us try and answer the same ten questions with what we should accept as the best we can get from the earliest evidence.

1. THE PERIOD

Firstly then, in recent times most people have believed that Robin Hood lived in Plantagenet times under Richard the Lionheart and John. This is not impossible. We do not know for certain when Robin Hood lived. Some critics have attempted to answer this by dating the literature and even then have come to different answers — mainly the thirteenth or fourteenth century. This is unsatisfactory since no one knows when the literature began and what might have been lost. Many heroes inspired literature written long after their deaths. The clues in the literature about the period of the stories can also be confusing. The first mention of Robin Hood literature is in 1377 in *Piers Plowman* so at least we can say Robin must have lived (assuming he lived at all but let us assume that for now) before 1377.

One trouble with evidence from literature is that it might well reflect the period in which it is being written more than the period it is about. Given that, the best clue in the works is the reference to a king by name, the 'comely' king called Edward who appears in the poems as 'Edwarde, our comly kynge' in the *Gest*. Before 1377, this must be one of the first three Edwards — Edward I, Longshanks, (1272-1307); Edward II (1317-1327) who was deposed in 1327 and probably died shortly afterwards; and Edward III (1327-77) who took England into the Hundred Years War. It might be possible to refer to any of these three as comely. So far no one has satisfactorily and conclusively decided which of the three to prefer — except to their own satisfaction. In the *Gest* we do find Robin leaving the royal court to return north. We are told that he stayed for twenty-two years and did not choose to return to court. The impression is that the same Edward ruled through that time. That being the case we could possibly remove Edward II from our list of possible monarchs since he was the only one of the three to rule for less than twenty-two years. However, in general we can place Robin in the period between 1272 and 1377 which, after all, is only a single century.

2. THE CRUSADES

The second question we began by asking was what connection is presently seen between Robin Hood and the Crusades. Commonly Robin is presented as going on the Third Crusade with Richard the Lionheart. From the early works there is no evidence for this at all. The Plantagenet period does not seem the most likely one for Robin and in the poems there is absolutely no reference to our hero going on Crusade.

3. SAXON AND NORMAN

The third common view is that Robin fought on behalf of the Saxons against the Norman rulers of England. This is sheer invention from an eighteenth- and especially nineteenth-century view of the past. Robin became established in the Plantagenet period and writers like Walter Scott saw that world as divided between the suppressed and defeated Saxons and the triumphant and cruel Norman conquerors and rulers. They ignored the fact that Robin's very name, from Robert, was itself a French and Norman name and not Saxon. They also simplified the situation in England in the later twelfth century. Since we should choose to put Robin in the thirteenth or fourteenth century, this view is even more anachronistic. The early poems give no grounds for Robin viewing himself and his men as downtrodden Saxons fighting against the Normans.

4. ROBIN HOOD'S ENEMIES

The fourth point concerns Robin's enemies. Nowadays the main enemies are seen as the sheriff of Nottingham and Prince John who became King John. Quite often Guy of Gisborne, in various forms, is also presented as an enemy. John never appears in the early works either as prince or king and given that we are in the time of a King Edward, John along with Richard should be dismissed from the scene. The other two figures (the sheriff and Guy) do indeed appear in the early works and for the first time the modern view does reflect something of the early evidence though rarely quite in the form that it then appeared. The sheriff does operate for the king against Robin but in the early works he is not always the violent enemy. He is more put upon than active. In the *Gest* it is Robin who violently kills the sheriff, cutting off his head. The sheriff comes to a similar end in *Guy of Gisborne* when it is Little John who shoots and kills him with an arrow. In the *Potter* Robin tricks him by getting round his wife after acting as a potter in Nottingham. He is tricked again to go into the forest and then robbed. Robin has flirted with the sheriff's wife and she and, if more hesitantly, her husband end with a degree of respect for him. Even these few sentences show the problem of accepting literature as historical evidence — the sheriff could not have been both beheaded by Robin and killed by an arrow from John. He is not in the literature given much character so it might just be possible to suggest we have more than one sheriff — sheriffs were not appointed for life — but it rather points to the inventions of literature on the Robin Hood legend.

Guy of Gisborne in modern presentation is usually shown as a noble, close to Prince John and hostile to Robin. The poem about him makes it clear that he is named after where he is from — 'Guye of good Gysborne'. In the early works he seems to be a bounty hunter (not for Prince John) who seeks out Robin and is killed by him. In the poem about him he is often referred to as 'Sir Guy' but his social position remains in doubt even in the poem. When Robin pretends to be Guy, the poem seems to suggest that he should be rewarded with a knight's fee as if he is *not* a knight. In the poem, Guy, rather oddly, wears a horse hide including 'Topp, and tayle, and mayne'. Robin kills him, beheads him and disfigures the face. Guy is certainly not an ever present enemy. He appears in the one poem and is soon despatched and in a very violent manner with his face disfigured.

5. ATTITUDE TO THE CHURCH

We next asked about Robin's attitude to the church. This is virtually ignored in modern versions of his activities. The only connection that comes to mind is the relationship with Friar Tuck, but Tuck is rarely seen in much of a religious context apart from his costume and his haircut. His conduct is hardly that of a God-fearing friar. In the poems, Robin is presented as a good Christian despite being an outlaw. One feels that there is an attempt to present him in acceptable fashion to the readers of the day. Thus Robin is especially dedicated to the Virgin Mary. He also is shown worshipping in church when his enemies break in during Mass to try and capture him. The enemies are, therefore, at fault rather than Robin, who refuses to leave in the middle of the service. In the *Gest*, when Robin gives his reasons to the king for leaving court it is mentioned that he had built a chapel in Barnsdale dedicated to Mary Magdalene. Robin does rob churchmen, notably the abbot of St Mary's but this is presented as money wrongly taken by the church which Robin uses to good Christian purpose to aid the poor knight or the poor in general. Through these stories the poems do criticise certain aspects of the church including wandering friars and grasping abbots. The poems are never anti-Christian, only against individual clerics who do not follow a truly Christian life. Robin is presented as a better Christian than these hypocritical clerics. Then we have the version of Robin's death. Again, an ecclesiastic is shown in critical manner. In this case it is Robin's relative, the prioress of Kirklees. In *Robin Hood's Death* she is called the daughter of Robin Hood's aunt. She has an affair with Sir Roger, otherwise Red Roger, and helps to murder Robin by bleeding him to death. So once again we have a hypocritical and positively cruel church person and Robin suffering without deserving it.

6. THE OUTLAW BAND

Then we asked the names of the regular members of Robin's band. It soon becomes clear that the named members have been considerably expanded in number over the years. Very few actually appear in the earliest works. In the *Gest* we find the three most regular outlaws. First is Little John who is described as a good yeoman, and 'good Scarlok', otherwise Will Scarlet. Elsewhere in the poem he is called Willyam Scarloke which makes it quite clear that he is a precursor of our Will Scarlet. The third is 'Much, the myller's son'. A fourth member of the band is named but in a rather confusing manner. John pretends to the sheriff that he is called 'Reynold Grenelef' (Reynaud Grenelefe). Later in the poem, however, there does appear along with Little John a separate Reynold. This may result from the manner of construction of the *Gest* which probably linked together several separate stories — it is not the only instance of a confusion of this kind in the long poem. At any rate we can say that Reynold Greenleaf was the fourth member named in that poem — though he has generally disappeared in modern versions. The poem does actually give us a fifth band member and that is the sheriff's cook.

John comes to respect the cook and persuades him to join the band but we are not given his name. No later character in the band fits with this sheriff's cook.

The *Gest* also tells us the size of the whole band at 'seven score of wyght yemen' — 140 yeomen. It says that they wore not green but outfits in scarlet and striped cloth. Later the king does pretend to join them and at that point asks Robin for cloth of Lincoln green which is used to clothe the royal group. This seems to be another case of failure to co-ordinate the parts in the whole. The band is often referred to as merry men or in similar terms. Sometimes this has the modern meaning as in 'my mery yonge men' but sometimes it has rather the meaning of mesnie (his following) as, for example, 'my meyne' or Robin 'And al his fayre mene'.

Another figure named in the poem is Gilbert of the White Hand (Gylberte Wyth the white hande). He is an excellent archer but it is not clear if he is one of the outlaw band or an independent man who enters the archery competition. On the whole it seems more likely that Gilbert was not one of Robin's men. Only John and Will stay with Robin when he lives for a time in the king's court.

In the handful of other poems we have accepted as early we find very few members of the band named. In *Robin Hood and the Monk* we find Little John and Much the miller's son. Much is a local to the forest region as, when travelling with John, he passes his uncle's house. In *Robin Hood and the Potter* the only member of the band named is Little John. In *Robin Hood's Death* Little John takes a major part and the only other member of the band named is 'Will Scarlett'. In *Robin Hood and Guy of Gisborne* the same two outlaws are the only ones to be named — that is, Little John and 'Scarlett'.

There is one other early source, a medieval one, and that is the play about Robin and the sheriff. It is very brief and does not even name the speakers of the text though these can reasonably be guessed. Probably two outlaws speak and it is surmised that these might be Little John and Will Scarlet.[1] The play does, however, name one member of the band who does not appear in any of the earliest poems. This is none other than Friar Tuck (ffrere Tuke) who is now an ever-present in Robin's company. In the play the outlaw band is also clearly called a mesnie (Robin Hode and his menye').

7. ROBIN'S LOVE

There is no doubt about the answer in modern times about the name of Robin Hood's love. It is Maid Marian. Nor does it take long to answer who was his love in the early works. There was no one. The nearest one comes to any love interest in the early works is in the story of the potter. Robin flirts a little with the sheriff's wife but even here it is more in one's imagination than overtly stated in the poem. In the earliest poems, or in the earliest play, there is no Maid Marian. Her probable earliest entry was through the play-games, perhaps from the Marion who appeared in French works. Once she had entered the Robin Hood story, in the sixteenth century, she became a fixture. As the play stories expanded, the love interest became a vital component. The same factor plays in modern visual works when hardly any light plot can do without some love interest. Marian frequently becomes a major factor in plot invention — of noble birth, a place at court with the king and the sheriff, and so on.

8. The Location in which Robin Operated

We investigated this matter in chapter seven. Modern views place Robin in Sherwood Forest with urban events taking place in Nottingham. Historians have tended to note that this ignores early evidence about Robin's place in Yorkshire and especially in Barnsdale. This is true and Barnsdale does feature importantly in the early works. Robin claims to have built his chapel to Mary Magdalene there in the *Gest,* and in *Guy of Gisborne* he calls himself 'Robin Hood of Barnesdale' as if he were born there or lived there. Most recent historians have tended to prefer this location over Sherwood, a common explanation being that the Nottingham and Sherwood thread was added into the original Yorkshire placing.

Our own investigation in a previous chapter suggests that the early evidence gives no real preference between the two locations. We feel that recent historians have tended to emphasise Barnsdale because it had previously been ignored, which is fair enough. On the other hand should we then play down or even exclude Nottingham and Sherwood? My own answer is a clear 'no' on the present evidence. We must retain both locations. Robin may have acted in Yorkshire; he may have acted in Sherwood and Nottingham. The early works give almost equal emphasis to both locations. Must it be one or the other? It would be quite possible for an outlaw to move from one place to another and real outlaws often did. Nor are the two locations that far apart, moving from one to the other would have been quite natural. It would be quite possible for him to operate in one area and then be forced to move on to the other — Sherwood might offer better shelter than Barnsdale. Actual outlaws did tend to be forced into movement for their own safety. We have not managed satisfactorily to pin down the original Robin so we cannot pin down with any certainty his real location. The fact is we can give no clear answer to this question about his location since the evidence is inconclusive. What we can say is that it would be a mistake at present to exclude either location.

9. Rich and Poor

The modern version of Robin Hood is unequivocal on the attitude of Robin to rich and poor. He robbed from the rich in order to give to the poor. It is the basis of his character. He is not a typical vicious criminal and highwayman who murdered and robbed his victims for the sake of it. He stole from the rich only to aid the poor. He killed only from self defence against cruel enemies. The early poems do give some foundation for such a view. The story of the poor knight is one of the main plots in the *Gest.* Robin encounters the knight and finding he is poor does not rob him. Instead he gives him money to pay off his debt. When the knight comes to repay the debt with interest Robin refuses. He has in the meantime robbed churchmen but only in order to pay off the knight's creditor, the grasping abbot of St Mary's York. Nevertheless, Robin Hood in the early works acts more like a criminal in many ways than he would in modern versions. He shoots the sheriff of Nottingham with his bow in the *Gest* and then cuts off his head. The sheriff in that poem is not presented so much as a villain as the representative of authority. Robin steals from churchmen if they are rich, especially if they pretend to have less on them than they really have. The motto here seems to be they deserve to be robbed if they tell lies, yet in no age would that be a fair reason to validate robbery. In *Guy of Gisborne* Robin fights and kills Guy. This may seem fair enough since Guy is seeking bounty for the capture of Robin, and they do have a fair fight. Nevertheless Robin's following actions are pretty violent. He cuts off Guy's head and disfigures his face so that Robin can pretend he is Guy and the head is that of Robin Hood.

All in all, we must say that the modern view of Robin is a much softened one in comparison to the early poems. He has become less violent and more public spirited. In the poems it is true that he helps the knight but the early works do not suggest that as his only motive for robbery. Churchmen may be presented as lacking spiritual character, but that hardly justifies robbing them. In the poems Robin is closer to a real outlaw than he is in modern films and TV. He is a violent robber and murderer — though he does have his good points. He does help the poor knight, but in those earliest works there is no other poor man who benefits, and the knight after all is from the upper classes and owns lands and a castle — hardly the poorest of the poor in that period. One also suspects that the very poems themselves may have ameliorated the character of the real Robin Hood. They are surely some time after the real person existed and already are beginning to transform him with a more romantic eye. He is already less nasty than any actual criminal or outlaw was likely to be. Through time that process has continued to alter Robin's character.

10. ROBIN HOOD'S PLACE IN SOCIETY

Our final question related to Robin's position in medieval society. Today he is pretty well always viewed as a member of the nobility who has been unfairly disinherited and forced into outlawry. In the early medieval works Robin is never a noble. His social position is not given great emphasis. As an outlaw he is outside normal social levels. Some of the outlaws are from an ordinary background. Much, for example, is the son of a miller. Little John in the *Gest* persuades the sheriff's cook to join the band. The outlaws are frequently referred to as yeomen, including Robin himself. In the *Gest*, Little John is 'a good yeoman'. In that poem at times he fills the role of the serving man to a knight and takes on a similar role in the service of the sheriff. In the *Gest* the whole seven score of the outlaw band are called 'wyght yemen'. Robin himself is seen as a yeoman though he is the leader of the outlaw band and they wear his livery of either Lincoln green or scarlet and striped cloth. In the early works this is not because Robin is noble or high class but because he is the recognised leader and master and organises his band in imitation of a mesnie. It is not made clear how he was able to build a chapel in Barnsdale but that does suggest he is seen as more than an ordinary yeoman. In *Robin Hood and the Monk* it is interesting that John sees Robin more as an equal though he finally recognises him as deserving to be the leader. The incident in mind here is when Robin wants John to carry his bow and John retorts along the lines of 'carry it yourself'. It is also noteworthy that the outlaw band is seen as a band of archers or bowmen. It is true that nobles often knew how to shoot a bow but they would never be seen as a troop of archers. Archer troops were taken from the peasant or at best yeoman class not from the nobility. It seems clear enough that Robin and his men in the early poems are seen as being of middling to lower class, as yeomen and bowmen. As we have seen in an earlier chapter, it is only when Tudor and Stuart writers take up the story, well after the period of Robin's existence, that Robin is ennobled — a promotion that has survived ever since.

There is finally one question we did not ask at first as it would have seemed superfluous, but now becomes worth a mention. That is, what was Robin Hood called? We ask this because if there was a real Robin Hood, he needs to be identified from historical records and, as we have seen, even in the poems his name is not always spelled the same. Firstly, Robin was a common popular form of name for one christened Robert, as indeed can happen nowadays. I, for instance, am always called Jim though I was christened James and it is the form James that appears in all the official records. So, then, we look for a Robert Hood rather than a Robin. Secondly, we need to keep an eye open for the variant spellings common in the Middle Ages. What we write as Hood could be spelled in a whole range of ways, such as Hod, Hode, Hude, Hwd and so on. Then too, as we have seen, Robinhood was a fairly common surname too. It is not impossible that our man was really surnamed Robinhood — say John Robinhood, which would probably only mean that his father or an ancestor had been a Robert Hood. The point is in general that we need to keep a fairly open mind when looking for evidence in medieval records.

The Real Robin Hood: Conclusions

So what are our main conclusions? Who was Robin Hood? We have concluded that the presentation of Robin Hood in the modern era is seriously different from the Robin Hood of the earliest literature about him. But have we found the real Robin Hood? The answer has to be 'no' — though perhaps we have got a little closer to him. Assuming that Robin lived at all, let us try to narrow the bounds of our search for the real man. There are certainly some clues for any investigation.

These are now my conclusions rather than those of other people, whether historians or literary critics. This is, of course, not properly the task of an historian. But the fact is that trying to study Robin Hood is far from being entirely a matter of historical research. The only real evidence is literary and not historical, except that the literature needs to be placed in its time. Many have searched but none have found any definite evidence of the original hero — or none that convinces everyone. It is a bit like the search for Jack the Ripper. The important early evidence has disappeared. From what is left it is impossible to find the man. He will only be found if new evidence is forthcoming. This does not prevent people from choosing a candidate — some possible, others highly unlikely. I prefer to wait on further evidence and not decide on evidence that is not good enough. All that is left is conjecture, but at least we admit that it is conjecture and are not trying to make fact out of something less. It is at least conjecture based on the only evidence that we have to date.

ROBIN HOOD AND THE MEDIA

Starting from the present time we have moved back through the ages and thus have noted the additions and changes to the Robin Hood story through the years. The early Robin was an outlaw operating in Barnsdale, Sherwood and Nottingham. He had no lover. He lived under a King Edward. He has altered through the ages largely due to being adapted to suit different popular media. Robin probably began in literature in brief ballads, popular songs or recitations that were passed on in memory. The very first surviving reference, as we know, came from the comment in *Piers Plowman* in 1377. In that poem Sloth, as a lazy priest, is condemned because he admits he does know perfectly his 'Paternoster as the priest it singeth' but does know 'rhymes' of Robin Hood.[2] In other words, he is suggesting that he has committed to memory rhymes of Robin Hood better than those demanded of his religion. This clearly seems to mean that the Robin Hood rhymes were brief poems or songs that could be learned by heart.

We know how long this process can continue since relatively modern collections have come upon various individuals who had memorised old ballads clearly passed on over many generations. His story was so popular that it was caught up by courtly poets, as in the *Gest,* and for local entertainment, as in the play fragment.

In Tudor and Stuart times many works about Robin Hood were printed and the printed media dictated the nature of these works. Some poems or songs had to be shortened to fit on to a single page for broadsides. At the same time Robin's story had to be enlarged for use in the newly popular public theatres. These venues required longer and more sophisticated plays. This is when he was made into a noble and given Marian as a lover. The next major media move was the development of the novel. Again Robin became a popular subject taken up by such as Sir Walter Scott. Again, for that medium he had to be developed further, given more interior thoughts, made into a more three-dimensional person. Until this time Robin's period had remained something of a matter of conjecture and had varied. Some earlier works had used the Plantagenet period with King Richard and his brother John but this now became a basic feature. The final major change has come with the modern media of cinema and TV. For these, close-up visual media action was demanded and Robin became a handsome hero, an athletic figure, as with Douglas Fairbanks and Errol Flynn. In most recent times the repeated use of Robin as a hero has meant further invention with new characters and new plots. Mostly these have taken us not nearer to but further from the original Robin of medieval literature.

These then are our final conclusions about the original Robin Hood. Firstly, it seems probable that Robin Hood lived in the later thirteenth or earlier fourteenth century. We must still allow the possibility that he was a little earlier but 1377 and the mention in *Piers Plowman* gives us a definite final date. Robin was probably a man of the ordinary people, probably from the middling rank of yeomen. It remains possible that he came from a higher social group. The leaders of real outlaw bands of the period were certainly sometimes of middling or knightly class. Such a social position helped men to be respected as leaders and to attract a following. We leave the possibility of higher rank open. However, in the early works he is never presented as anything higher than a yeoman. It seems also quite probable that the reason we cannot find the real Robin in the records is that he was not socially important enough to merit the attention of chroniclers. My own feeling is that he was probably middling in origin and probably a yeoman.

As an outlaw he must have broken the law and failed to clear himself in court. One did not choose to be an outlaw; one was made an outlaw by judicial decision. There were recognised rules about what led to outlawry. The usual reason was that one had broken some law, possibly relating to the forest, and when called to answer for it in court had failed to attend. Robin probably turned first to highway robbery. It may even be that that was his original crime. We know nothing of his early existence, whether or not he was respectable, why he was outlawed — though in later literature various reasons were invented. It is likely that this highway robbery occurred in or around Barnsdale in Yorkshire.

If we believe 'Guy of Gisborne', a price was put on Robin's head. Many outlaws made use of forest and woodland regions to escape the clutches of the law and catching them was far from easy in the fourteenth century. There was often sympathy for them amongst poorer folk. Outlaws at this time could be politically and militarily useful and were at times employed by lords for their own reasons, sometimes obtaining a royal pardon as a result. Robin may well have moved on to Sherwood from Yorkshire and then, being near to Nottingham, have become involved there. If we accept the stories, Robin finally won his pardon from King Edward but eventually chose to abandon the court and return to his home country in the north.

The real Robin must have been a criminal who pursued a criminal and violent career. He operated in Yorkshire, Sherwood and Nottingham. He became leader of an outlaw band of men skilled as archers. He became useful to the authorities in the end but could not get used to courtly life. That is my picture of the real Robin Hood but it is in my imagination only — based on the early poems. As an historian I should not be so loose with the evidence. The fact is there is little evidence. We have examined the early poems and the one early play text but they are all literary and there is no guarantee of their historical accuracy. Indeed, it is clear that they contain much fictional material.

We need some sort of picture in order to continue the search and hence there is some point in giving play to one's imagination. Let us summarise our conclusions. Robin lived at some time between 1250 and 1350 during the reigns of the first three Edwards. He was outlawed and pursued a criminal career. He operated first in Yorkshire and then in Sherwood and Nottingham — probably with survival as his main aim. So far as we know he had nothing to do with the crusades, had no love called Marian, was not an enemy of Prince John or friend of King Richard, and was not especially caring about the poor. One day, let us hope, the search for the real Robin Hood may have a successful conclusion. If not we can still be consoled with the great tales that have survived of the most famous outlaw in English history, Robin Hood.

Endnotes

[1] Dobson & Taylor, p. 206.
[2] Piers Plowman ed. Kane, B Version, p. 331, ll.394-95. 'I kan nozt parfitly my Paternoster as Þe preest it singeÞ , But I kan rymes of Robyn hood'.

Bibliography for Robin Hood

Primary Sources

Anderson, Alan Orr, ed., *Early Sources of Scottish History A D 500 to 1286*, 2 vols., Stamford, 1990

Anderson, Alan Orr, ed., *Scottish Annals from English Chronicles, A.D. 500 to 1286*, Stamford, 1991

Anglo-Saxon Chronicle, The, ed. Dorothy Whitelock, London, 1961

Anonimalle Chronicle 1333 to 1381, The, ed. V.H. Galbraith, Manchester, reprint 1970

Aubrey, John, *Brief Lives*, ed. Richard Barber, London, 1975

Barbour, John, *The Bruce*, ed. and trans. A. A. M. Duncan, 2nd edn., Edinburgh, 1999

Benson, Larry D., *The Riverside Chaucer*, 3rd edn., Oxford, 1988

Blind Harry's Wallace, ed. William Hamilton of Gilbertfield 1722, introduction by Elspeth King, Edinburgh, 1998

Bower, Walter, *Scotichronicon*, General ed. D. E. R. Watt, ed. Simon Taylor, D. E. R. Watt with Brian Scott, 9 vols., St Andrews, 1989-93; in particular vol. 5, 1990

Bower, Walter, *A History Book for Scots, Selections from Scotichronicon*, ed. D. E. R. Watt, Edinburgh, 1998

Brown, Chris, *Robert the Bruce, a Life Chronicled*, Stroud, 2004

Chaucer, Geoffrey, *The Complete Works*, ed. W.W. Skeat, 8 vols., Oxford, 1894

Child, F. J., ed., *The English and Scottish Popular Ballads*, 5 vols., 1882-98

Chronicle of Melrose Abbey, The, A Stratigraphic Edition, eds. Dauvit Broun & Julian Harrison, vol. i, Woodbridge, 2007

Collins, J. Churton, ed., *The Plays and Poems of Robert Greene*, Oxford, 1905, 2 vols.

Conlon, Denis Joseph ed., *Li Romans de Witasse le Moine*, Chapel Hill North Carolina, 1972

Davis, Norman, ed., *Paston Letters and Papers of the 15th Century*, 2 vols., Oxford, 1971, 1976

Dobson, R. B. and J. Taylor, *Rymes of Robyn Hood, an Introduction to the English Outlaw*, London, 1976

Davis, Norman, *Paston Letters and Papers of the Fifteenth Century*, 2 vols., Oxford, 1971, 1976

Dunbar, William, *The Poems of William Dunbar*, ed. Priscilla Bawcutt, 2 vols., Glasgow, 1998

English Historical Documents, vol.iii, 1189-1327, ed. Harry Rothwell, London, 1975

English Historical Documents, vol. iv, 1327-1485, ed. A.R. Myers, London, 1969

Fordun, John of, *Chronicle of the Scottish Nation*, ed. William F. Skene, trans. Felix J. H. Skene, vol. 4, *Historians of Scotland*, Edinburgh, 1872, reprinted Llanerch, Lampeter, 2 vols., 1993

Fordun, John of, *Scottichronicon*, ed. T. Hearne, Oxford, 1722

Gesta Fulconis Filii Warini, pp. 275-415 in *Radulphi Chronicon Anglicanum*, ed. Joseph Stevenson, RS no. 66, London, 1875

Gray, Sir Thomas, *The Scalachronica, the Reigns of Edward I, Edward II and Edward III*, trans. Sir Herbert Maxwell, 1907, reprint Felinfach, 2000

Great Roll of the Pipe for the 20th Year of the Reign of Henry III, 1241-42, ed. H.L. Cannon, Oxford, 1918

Greene, Robert, *Groats-worth of Witte and The Repentance of Robert Greene 1592*, Bodley Head Quartos, VI, London, 1923

Greene, Robert, Mermaid Series, ed. Thomas H. Dickinson, London

Greg, W.E., *Ben Jonson's Sad Shepherd with Waldron's Continuation,* Louvain

Gutch, J.M., ed., *A Lytell Geste of Robin Hode, with other ancient and modern ballads and songs relating to this celebrated yeoman,* 2 vols., London, 1847

Hales, John W. and Frederick J. Furnivall, eds., *Bishop Percy's Folio Manuscript,* 3 vols., London, 1867-68

Hallam, Elizabeth, ed., *Chronicles of the Age of Chivalry,* London, 1987

Harrison, G.B., *The Elizabethan Journals,* 3 vols. in one, revised edn., London, 1938

Harvey, Gabriel, *Foure Letters and Certeine Sonnets, especially touching Robert Greene and other parties by him abused,* 1592, Bodley Head Quartos, ed. G.B. Harrison, London, 1922

Henslowe's Diary, ed. R.A. Foakes & R.T. Rickert, Cambridge, 1961

Knight, Stephen, ed., *The Forresters Manuscript (British Library Additional MS 71158),* Cambridge, 1998

Lanercost, The Chronicle of, 1272-1346, trans. Sir Herbert Maxwell, 1913, reprinted 2 vols., Llanerch, Cribyn, 2001

Langland, William, *The Vision of William concerning Piers the Plowman,* ed. W. W. Skeat, EETS, London, 1869

Langland, William, *Piers Plowman: the B Version,* ed. G. Kane & E. Talbot Donaldson, London, 1975

Langland, William, *Piers Plowman: the C Version,* ed. George Russell and George Kane, London, 1997

Langtoft, Pierre de, *The Chronicle of,* ed. Thomas Wright, 2 vols., RS, London, 1866, 1868

Lee, Maurice, Jr., *Dudley Carleton to John Chamberlain, 1603-1624, Jacobean Letters,* New Brunswick, 1972

Maior, John, *Historia Majoris Britanniae,* Edinburgh, 1740

Maior (Major), John, *A History of Greater Britain, 1521,* ed. A. Constable, Scottish History Society, x, Edinburgh, 1892

Melrose, The Chronicle of, (A Medieval Chronicle of Scotland), trans. Joseph Stevenson, reprinted Llanerch, Lampeter, 1991

Michel, F., ed., *Roman d'Eustache li Moine,* London, 1834

Minutes and Accounts of the Corporation of Stratford-upon-Avon and other Records 1553-1620, transcribed Richard Savage, notes and introduction Edgar Innes Fripp, Dugdale Society, 4 vols., 1921-9; vol v, ed. Levi Fox, 1990.

Munday, Anthony, *The Death of Robert, Earle of Huntington, otherwise called Robin Hood of merrie Sherwodde,* London, 1601, reprint Oxford, 1967

Munday, Anthony, *The Downfall of Robert, Earle of Huntington, afterward called Robin Hood of merrie Sherwodde,* London, 1601, reprint Oxford, 1965

Percy, Thomas, *Reliques of Ancient English Poetry,* 2 vols., London, 1906 (first published 1765)

Peterborough Chronicle, 1070-1154, The, ed. Cecily Clark, 2nd edn., Oxford, 1970

Reform and Revolution 1258-1267, excerpts from the RS, Oxford, 1963

Rishanger, William, *Chronica et Annales,* ed. Henry Thomas Riley, RS, London, 1865

Rishanger, William of, *The Chronicle of William de Rishanger, of the Barons' Wars, The Miracles of Simon de Montfort,* ed. James Orchard Halliwell, Camden Soc., xv, London, 1840

Ritson, Joseph, *Robin Hood: a Collection of all the ancient Poems, Songs and Ballads, 1795,* 4th edn., 1846

Roper, Michael & Christopher Kitching, eds., *Feet of Fines for the County of York from 1314 to 1326,* Woodbridge, 2006

Sargent, Helen Child, & George Lyman Kittredge, *English and Scottish Popular Ballads edited from the Collection of Francis James Child,* London, 1906

Sir Gawain and the Green Knight, trans. Simon Armitage, London, 2007

Stubbs, William, *Chronicles of the Reigns of Edward I and Edward II,* RS no. 76, 2 vols., London, 1882,1883

Walter of Guisborough, *Chronicle,* ed. Harry Rothwell, Camden series lxxxix, London, 1957

Wiles, David, *The Early Plays of Robin Hood,* Cambridge, 1981

Wright, Thomas, *Political Poems and Songs Relating to English History from the Accession of Edward III to that of Richard III,* 2 vols., London, 1859, 1861

Wright, Thomas, ed. and trans., *The Political Songs of England, from the Reign of John to that of Edward II,* Camden Soc., London, 1839, reprinted Hildesheim, 1968

Wright, Thomas, *Thomas Wright's Political Songs of England from the Reign of John to that of Edward II,* ed., Peter Coss, Cambridge, 1996

Wyntoun, Andrew de, *The Original Chronicle*, ed. F. J. Amours, 1907
Wyntoun, Androw of, *The Orygynale Cronykil of Scotland*, ed. David Laing, 3 vols., Edinburgh, 1872-79

Reworkings of Robin Hood Tales

McSpadden, J. W., and Charles Wilson, *Robin Hood and His Merry Outlaws*, London, 1921
Pyle, Howard, *The Adventures of Robin Hood*, 1983 edition, London
Scott, Sir Walter, *Ivanhoe, a Romance*, London (Everyman).
Tennyson, Alfred Lord, *The Foresters, Robin Hood and Maid Marian*, London, 1892

Secondary Sources

Alexander, Michael, *Medievalism, the Middle Ages in Modern England*, London, 2007
Beamish, Tufton, *Battle Royal*, London, 1965
Bellamy, John, *Crime and Public Order in England in the Later Middle Ages*, London, 1973
Bellamy, John, *Robin Hood, an historical enquiry*, London, 1985
Bémont, Charles, Simon de Montfort, Earl of Leicester, 1208-1265, new edn., trans. E.F. Jacob, Oxford, 1930
Bevington, David, *Tudor Drama and Politics*, Harvard, 1968
Birrell, Jean, 'Forest Law and the Peasantry in the Later 13th Century', *13th-Century England*, ii, 1987 (published 1988), pp. 149-63
Bradbrook, M.C., *The Rise of the Common Player, A Study of Actor and Society in Shakespeare's England*, London, 1962
Bradbury, Jim, *The Medieval Archer*, Woodbridge, 1985
Byrne, M. St Clare, *Elizabethan Life in Town and Country*, 7th edn. revised, London, 1954
Carruthers, Mary J., & Elizabeth D. Kirk, *Acts of Interpretation, the Text in its Contexts, 700-1600, Essays on Medieval & Renaissance Literature in Honor of E. Talbot Donaldson*, Norman, Oklahoma, 1982
Chambers, E.K., *English Literature at the Close of the Middle Ages*, Oxford, 2nd impression, 1947
Cheesman, Tom, & Sigurd Rieuwerts, *Ballads into Books, the Legacies of Francis James Child*, 2nd revised edn., Bern, 1999
Chute, Marchette, *Ben Jonson of Westminster*, New York, 1953
Chute, Marchette, *Shakespeare of London*, New York, 1949
Cottle, Basil, *The Triumph of English, 1350-1400*, London, 1969
Crook, David, 'The Sheriff of Nottingham and Robin Hood: the Genesis of the Legend', *13th-Century England*, ii, 1987, (published 1988), pp. 59-68.
Crupi, Charles W., *Robert Greene*, Boston Massachusetts, 1986
Dixon-Kennedy, Mike, *The Robin Hood Handbook, the Outlaw in History, Myth and Legend*, Stroud, 2006
Du Boulay, F. R. H., *The England of Piers Plowman*, Cambridge, 1991
Dunlop, Fiona S., *The Late Medieval Interlude, the Drama of Youth and Aristocratic Masculinity*, Woodbridge, 2007
Fowler, David C., *A Literary History of the Popular Ballad*, Durham N. C., 1968
Frankis, John, 'The Social Context of Vernacular Writing in 13th-century England: the Evidence of the Manuscripts', pp. 175-84, *13 Century England*, i, 1985 (1986)
Gerritsen, Willem P. and Anthony G. van Melle, eds., *A Dictionary of Medieval Heroes*, trans. Tanis Guest, Woodbridge, 1998
Gorski, Richard, *The 14th-Century Sheriff, English Local Administration in the Late Middle Ages*, Woodbridge, 2003
Gransden, Antonia, *Historical Writing in England*, 2 vols., London, 1974, 1982
Grove, Valerie, *A Voyage Round John Mortimer*, London, 2007
Hahn, Thomas, ed., *Robin Hood in Popular Culture*, Cambridge, 2000
Halliday, F. E., *Shakespeare, a pictorial biography*, London, 1956

Hamilton, Donna B., *Anthony Munday and the Catholics, 1560-1633*, Aldershot, 2005

Harris, P. Valentine, *The Truth About Robin Hood*, London

Hill, Christopher, *Libert Against the Law*, Harmondworth, 1996

Hill, Tracey, *Anthony Munday and Civic Culture, Theatre, history and power in early modern London, 1580-1633*, Manchester, 2004

Hilton, R. H., ed., *Peasants, Knights and Heretics*, Cambridge, 1976

Hotson, Leslie, *Shakespeare's Wooden O*, London, 1959

Hunter, Joseph, *South Yorkshire*, 2 vols., reprint, Wakefield, 1974

Keen, Maurice, *The Outlaws of Medieval Legend*, London, 2nd edn., 1977

Kendall, Alan, *Robert Dudley, Earl of Leicester*, London, 1986

Knight, Stephen, *Robin Hood, A Complete Study of the English Outlaw*, Oxford, 1994

Knight, Stephen, *Robin Hood, a Mythic Biography*, Ithaca, 2003

Knight, Stephen, ed., *Robin Hood: An Anthology of Scholarship and Criticism*, Cambridge, 1999

Knowles, Clive H., 'Provision for the Families of the Montfortians Disinherited after the Battle of Evesham', pp. 124-27, *13 Century England*, i, 1985 (1986)

Labarge, Margaret Wade, *Simon de Montfort*, London, 1962

Luxford, Julian M., 'An English Chronicle entry on Robin Hood', JMH, 35, 2009, pp. 70-76

MacCaffrey, Wallace T., *Queen Elizabeth and the Making of Policy, 1572-1588*, Princeton, 1981

MacCaffrey, Wallace T., *The Shaping of the Elizabethan Regime, Elizabethan Politics, 1558-72*, Princeton, 1968

Maddicott, J. R., 'Edward I & the Lessons of Baronial Reform, 1258-80', pp. 1-30, *13th Century England*, i, 1985 (1986)

Maddicott, J. R., *Simon de Montfort*, Cambridge, 1994

Maddicott, J. R., 'The birth and setting of the ballads of Robin Hood', EHR, xciii, 1978, pp.276-99

Mapstone, Sally & Juliette Wood, eds., *The Rose and the Thistle, Essays on the Culture of Late Medieval and Renaissance Scotland*, East Linton, 1998

Marvin, William Perry, *Hunting Law and Ritual in Medieval English Literature*, Cambridge, 2006

McDonald, R. Andrew, *Outlaws of Medieval Scotland*, East Linton, 2003

Midmer, Roy, *English Medieval Monasteries*, London, 1979

Miller, Edward, 'Rulers of 13th-century Towns: the Cases of York & Newcastle upon Tyne', pp. 128-41, *13th Century England*, i, 1985 (1986)

Moore, Margaret F., *The Lands of the Scottish Kings in England*, London, 1915, reprint New Jersey, 1973

Morey, Adrian, *The Catholic Subjects of Elizabeth I*, London, 1978

Morris, Marc, *A Great and Terrible King, Edward I and the Forging of Britain*, London, 2008

Nelson, M. A., 'The Robin Hood Tradition in the English Renaissance', *Salzburg Studies in English Literature, Elizabethan Studies*, 14, 1973.

Ohlgren, Thomas H., ed., *Medieval Outlaws, Ten Tales in Modern English*, Stroud, 1998

Ohlgren, Thomas H., *Robin Hood: The Early Poems, 1465-1560, Texts, Contexts, and Ideology*, Cranbury New Jersey, 2007

Ormrod, W. M., ed., *England in the Fourteenth Century*, Proceedings of the 1985 Harlaxton Symposium, Woodbridge, 1986

Pollard, A. J., *Imagining Robin Hood*, London, 2004

Powicke, F. M., *King Henry III and the Lord Edward, the Community of the Realm in the 13th Century*, Oxford, 1947, 1966 reprint

Prestwich, Michael, *Edward I*, London, 1988

Robinson, Ian, 'Doing a Bentley on Langland', *Cambridge Quarterly*, xxvii, pp. 235-49

Rodgers, Edith Cooperrider, *Discussion of Holidays in the Later Middle Ages*, New York, 1940

Rosental, Joel T., *Telling Tales, Sources and Narration*, Pennsylvania, 2003

Rutherford-Moore, Richard, *The Legend of Robin Hood*, Chieveley, 1998

Scott, Ronald McNair, *Robert the Bruce, King of Scots*, Edinburgh, 1982

Simons, John, ed., *From Medieval to Medievalism*, Basingstoke, 1992

Somerset, Anne, *Elizabeth I*, London, 1991

Thomis, Malcolm I., *Old Nottingham*, Newton Abbot, 1968

Thompson, Flora, *Lark Rise to Candleford*, Folio edn., London, 2009

Waldman, Milton, *Elizabeth and Leicester*, London, 1944

Westwood, Jennifer & Jacqueline Simpson, *The Lore of the Land*, London, 2005

White, Gilbert, *The Natural History and Antiquities of Selborne*, Folio edition, London, 1997

Wickham, Glynne, *Early English Stages, 1330-1660*, 4 vols., new edn., 1981-2
Wickham, Glynne, *The Medieval Theatre*, 3rd edn., London, 1987
Wiles, David, *The Early Plays of Robin Hood*, Cambridge, 1981
Wood, Michael, *In Search of Shakespeare*, London, 2003
Wright, T., 'On the popular cycle of the Robin Hood ballads', I, pp. 164-211 in *Essays on subjects connected with the literature, popular superstitions, and history of England in the Middle Ages*, 2 vols., London, 1846
Young, Alan, *Robert the Bruce's Rivals: the Comyns, 1212-1314*, East Linton, 1997
Young, Charles R., *The Royal Forests of Medieval England*, Philadelphia, 1979

Visual Sources

FILMS

Robin Hood and His Merry Men, Clarendon, 1909
Robin Hood – Outlawed, British and Colonial, 1912
In the Days of Robin Hood, Kinemacolour, 1912
Robin Hood, Eclair, 1913
Robin Hood, Thanhouser, 1913
Robin Hood, 1922, United Artists, dir. Alan Dwan, star Douglas Fairbanks Sr.
The Adventures of Robin Hood, 1938, Warner Brothers, dir. William Keighley & Michael Curtiz, star Errol Flynn
The Bandit of Sherwood Forest, 1946, Columbia, dir. George Sherman and Henry Levin, star Cornel Wilde
The Prince of Thieves, 1948, Columbia, dir. Howard Bretherton
Rogues of Sherwood Forest, 1950, Columbia, dir. Gordon Douglas, star John Derek
The Story of Robin Hood and his Merrie Men, 1952, Disney, dir. Ken Annakin, star Richard Todd
Men of Sherwood Forest, 1954, Hammer, dir. Val Guest, star Don Taylor
Son of Robin Hood, 1958, 20th Century Fox, dir. George Sherman, star June Laverick
Sword of Sherwood Forest, 1961, Hammer, dir. Terence Fisher, star Richard Greene
A Challenge for Robin Hood, 1967, 20th Century Fox/Hammer, dir. Penington Richards, star Barrie Ingham
Robin and Marian, 1976, Columbia, dir. Richard Lester, star Sean Connery
Robin Hood, 1991, 20th Century Fox, dir. John Irvin, star Patrick Bergin
Robin Hood – Prince of Thieves, 1991, Morgan Creek, dir. Kevin Reynolds, star Kevin Costner
The Zany Adventures of Robin Hood, 1984, Austin, star George Segal
Robin Hood – Men in Tights, 1993, Columbia, dir. Mel Brooks, star Cary Elwes

TELEVISION

The Adventures of Robin Hood, Sapphire Films for Associated Television, 1955-58, star Richard Greene
Robin of Sherwood, 1984-86, Goldcrest for HTV, stars Michael Praed, Jason Connery
Maid Marian and Her Merry Men, BBC TV, 1988-89, star Kate Lonergan
Robin Hood, 2006, star Jonas Armstrong

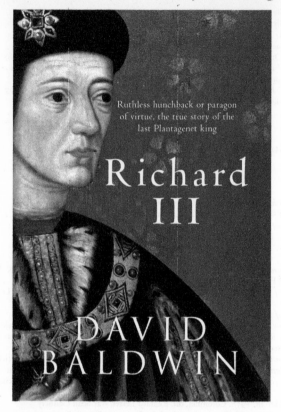

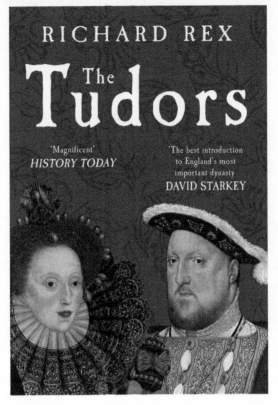

Index